The Women's Book of Positive Quotations

THE *W*OMEN'S BOOK OF

POSITIVE

QUOTATIONS

Compiled and Arranged
by Leslie Ann Gibson

Fairview Press
Minneapolis

Published by Fairview Press, 2450 Riverside Avenue, Minneapolis, Minnesota 55454.

Fairview Press is a division of Fairview Health Services, a nonprofit, community-focused health system affiliated with the University of Minnesota, providing a complete range of services, from the prevention of illness and injury to care for the most complex medical conditions.

Library of Congress Cataloging-in-Publication Data
The Women's book of positive quotations / compiled and arranged by Leslie Ann Gibson.
     p. cm.
ISBN 1-57749-123-8 (trade pbk : alk. paper)
1. Success—Quotations, maxims, etc. 2. Conduct of life—Quotations, maxims, etc. 3. Women—Quotations, maxims, etc. 4. Women—Quotations.
I. Gibson, Leslie Ann, 1956-
PN6084.S78 W58 2002
082'.082—dc21   2002011814

First printing: October 2002

Printed in Canada.

05 04 03 02   7 6 5 4 3 2 1

Cover: Laurie Ingram Design

For a free current catalog of Fairview Press titles, please call toll-free 1-800-544-8207. Or visit our Web site at www.fairviewpress.org.

For June and Verna

Contents

TWO: Developing Positive Habits

THREE: Achieving Your Goals

Overcoming Worries

Accepting Uncertainty as a Part of Life

Finding and Showing Courage

Adjusting to Change

ntroduction

THE PAST CENTURY HAS BEEN A BOON FOR THE PUBLICATION OF women's writing. Perhaps nowhere is this more evident than in the number of volumes of women's quotations that have been published in recent decades. Where once quotation books were filled predominantly or even exclusively with the words of men, today one can scan the shelves of any bookstore and find any number of books dedicated solely to the insights and wisdom of female writers.

Why, then, do we need another collection of women's quotations? Traditionally, compilations of quotations have been organized alphabetically by author or keyword. As a writer, I like to use quotations to illustrate themes or principles, such as the value of self-confidence or the importance of hard work. Unfortunately, in traditional compilations, finding just the right phrase to illustrate such themes can be very difficult.

There are, of course, many quotation books arranged thematically—books on leadership or personal relationships, for example—some of which have become popular gift books. I've received and given a few of them myself. But I've found that most of the ones I've received have ended up sitting unused on my bookshelf. These compilations simply lack the comprehensiveness to be useful as primary reference books.

It is my hope that this book will bridge the gap between the more comprehensive, traditionally arranged quotation books and the smaller, thematically focused volumes. I have found over the years that my need for the pithy quote stems from a desire to assuage, motivate, or inspire the reader—to help the reader see my point, accept my way of thinking. Whether I'm e-mailing a friend struggling with relationship issues or searching for the perfect nugget to illustrate a corporate report or slide presentation, I find myself always searching for uplifting or reassuring words. My goal in compiling this book was to produce something that would satisfy all these needs in a single volume: a comprehensive collection of positive and motivational quotations, arranged thematically and written by, for, or about women.

In organizing the book by theme, I found that the same quotation could be used to make several different points. For example, a quotation about "Showing Appreciation" fits as easily under the category of "Embracing Your True Friends," since we embrace our friends by showing our appreciation for their friendship. Consequently, some quotations appear more than once in the book. This is, I think, a positive thing, for the reader is much less likely to miss a piece of wisdom because of some organizational misjudgment on my part.

This compilation was years in the making. During the time I was putting it together, I experienced some of the hardships many people go through in their lives—changes in employment status, family illness, etc. Inevitably, whenever these hardships occurred, the book proved a dependable resource for the solace and encouragement I needed at that time. So, although I hope *The Women's Book of Positive Quotations* will be a useful reference work for speakers and writers, I hope, too, that it will be a source of inspiration for many readers. Apt quotations have a way of reaching out to us when we need them most—from guidance for starting the day on the right foot to comfort for a nagging problem before retiring to bed. Such are the gifts of the thousands of writers, philosophers, artists, and leaders whose insights are reproduced here. May their words encourage and inspire women for generations to come.

ONE

Finding Fulfillment

$\mathcal{W}$elcoming Joy into Your Life

Joy and Love Go Hand in Hand

Love, by its very nature, is unworldly, and it is for this reason rather than its rarity that it is not only apolitical but anti-political, perhaps the most powerful of all anti-political human forces.

~ HANNAH ARENDT

When love is out of your life, you're through in a way. Because while it is there it's like a motor that's going, you have such vitality to do things, big things, because love is goosing you all the time.

~ FANNY BRICE

When you come right down to it, the secret of having it all is loving it all.

~ DR. JOYCE BROTHERS

Where there is great love, there are always wishes.

~ WILLA CATHER

The cure for all ills and wrongs, the cares, the sorrows and the crimes of humanity, all lie in the one word 'love.' It is the divine vitality that everywhere produces and restores life.

~ LYDIA MARIA CHILD

I love, and the world is mine!

~ FLORENCE EARLE COATES

Love is a force more formidable than any other. It is invisible—it cannot be seen or measured, yet it is powerful enough to transform you in a moment, and offer you more joy than any material possession could.

~ BARBARA DE ANGELIS

Love is the only effective counter to death.

~ MAUREEN DUFFY

From the moment we walk out the door until we come back home our sensibilities are so assaulted by the world that we have to soak up as much love as we can get, simply to arm ourselves.

~ PATTY DUKE

'Tis what I love determines how I love.

~ GEORGE ELIOT

I was in love with the whole world and all that lived in its rainy arms.

~ LOUISE ERDRICH

Anyone can be passionate, but it takes real lovers to be silly.

~ ROSE FRANKEN

A heart that loves is always young.

~ GREEK PROVERB

The truth is that there is only one terminal dignity—love. And the story of a love is not important—what is important is that one is capable of love. It is perhaps the only glimpse we are permitted of eternity.

~ HELEN HAYES

Love is like pi—natural, irrational, and very important.
∼ LISA HOFFMAN

Joy is a net of love by which you can catch souls.
∼ MOTHER TERESA

Love is a fruit in season at all times, and within reach of every hand.
∼ MOTHER TERESA

Love is the vocation that includes all others.
∼ THÉRÈSE OF LISIEUX

Love is a universe of its own, comprising all time and space.
∼ THÉRÈSE OF LISIEUX

My heart is like a singing bird.
∼ CHRISTINA GEORGINA TOSSETTI

Love is the same as like except you feel sexier.
∼ JUDITH VIORST

Joy and Love Improve All Aspects of Life

Love is a great beautifier.
∼ LOUISA MAY ALCOTT

Love is the only thing we can carry with us when we go, and it makes the end so easy.
∼ LOUISA MAY ALCOTT

She was one of those happily created beings who please without effort, make friends everywhere, and take life so gracefully and easily that less fortunate souls are tempted to believe that such are born under a lucky star.
∼ LOUISA MAY ALCOTT

He who conquers endures.

~ ANON.

Laughter is the best medicine.

~ ANON.

The general rule is that people who enjoy life also enjoy marriage.

~ PHYLLIS BATTELLE

I went back to being an amateur, in the sense of somebody who loves what she is doing. If a professional loses the love of work, routine sets in, and that's the death of work and life.

~ ADA BETHUNE

There is no cosmetic for beauty like happiness.

~ LADY MARGUERITE BLESSINGTON

Where there is laughter there is always more health than sickness.

~ PHYLLIS BOTTOME

Whether you are talking about education, career, or service, you are talking about life. And life must really have joy. It's supposed to be fun.

~ BARBARA BUSH

Be happy. It's one way of being wise.

~ COLETTE

Joy is the feeling of grinning on the inside.

~ DR. MELBA COLGROVE

If you aren't good at loving yourself, you will have a difficult time loving anyone, since you'll resent the time and energy you give another person that you aren't even giving to yourself.

~ BARBARA DE ANGELIS

Loving, like prayer, is a power as well as a process. It's curative. It is creative.

~ ZONA GALE

Love is the great miracle cure. Loving ourselves works miracles in
our lives.

~ LOUISE L. HAY

Humor is an antidote to isolation.

~ ELIZABETH JANEWAY

Laughter is by definition healthy.

~ DORIS LESSING

Age does not protect you from love but love to some extent protects
you from age.

~ JEANNE MOREAU

She knew what all smart women knew: Laughter made you live
better and longer.

~ GAIL PARENT

Humor brings insight and tolerance.

~ AGNES REPPLIER

Laughter can be more satisfying than honor; more precious than
money; more heart-cleansing than prayer.

~ HARRIET ROCHLIN

Taking joy in life is a woman's best cosmetic.

~ ROSALIND RUSSELL

Laughter is ever young, whereas tragedy, except the very highest of
all, quickly becomes haggard.

~ MARGARET SACKVILLE

A chuckle a day may not keep the doctor away, but it sure does
make those times in life's waiting room a little more bearable.

~ ANNE WILSON SCHAEF

To love deeply in one direction makes us more loving in all others.

~ ANNE-SOPHIE SWETCHINE

One of the quickest ways to become exhausted is by suppressing your feelings.

~ SUE PATTON THOELE

A good laugh makes any interview, or any conversation, so much better.

~ BARBARA WALTERS

Joy Means Broadening Our Horizons

I don't want to get to the end of my life and find that I lived just the length of it. I want to have lived the width of it as well.

~ DIANE ACKERMAN

We learn the inner secret of happiness when we learn to direct our inner drives, our interest, and our attention to something besides ourselves.

~ ETHEL PERCY ANDRUS

That is happiness: to be dissolved into something completely great.

~ WILLA CATHER

A garden isn't meant to be useful. It's for joy.

~ RUMER GODDEN

There is always something left to love. And if you ain't learned that, you ain't learned nothing.

~ LORRAINE HANSBURY

Joy is the holy fire that keeps our purpose warm and our intelligence aglow.

~ HELEN KELLER

The genius of happiness is still so rare, is indeed on the whole the rarest genius. To possess it means to approach life with the humility of a beggar, but to treat it with the proud generosity of a prince; to bring to its totality the deep understanding of a great poet and to each of its moments the abandonment and ingenuousness of a child.

~ ELLEN KEY

The world is grand, awfully big and astonishingly beautiful, frequently thrilling.

　～ DOROTHY KILGALLEN

Happiness must be cultivated. It is like character. It is not a thing to be safely let alone for a moment, or it will run to weeds.

　～ ELIZABETH STUART PHELPS

My happiness is not the means to any end. It is the end. It is its own goal. It is its own purpose.

　～ AYN RAND

The more the heart is sated with joy, the more it becomes insatiable.

　～ GABRIELLE ROY

To love is to receive a glimpse of heaven.

　～ KAREN SUNDE

We Have Everything We Need to Be Happy

Paradise is exactly like where you are right now … only much, much better.

　～ LAURIE ANDERSON

To dream of the person you would like to be is to waste the person you are.

　～ ANON.

Time is compressed like the fist I close on my knee … I hold inside it the clues and solutions and the power for what I must do now.

　～ MARGARET ATWOOD

The major job was getting people to understand that they had something within their power that they could use.

　～ ELLA BAKER

Each moment in time we have it all, even when we think we don't.
~ MELODY BEATTIE

We have as much time as we need.
~ MELODY BEATTIE

Success is getting what you want; happiness is wanting what you get.
~ INGRID BERGMAN

To seek after beauty as an end, is a wild goose chase, a will-o'-the-wisp, because it is to misunderstand the very nature of beauty, which is the normal condition of a thing being as it should be.
~ ADA BETHUNE

Happiness consists not in having much, but in being content with little.
~ LADY MARGUERITE BLESSINGTON

We must not wish anything other than what happens from moment to moment, all the while, however, exercising ourselves in goodness.
~ SAINT CATHERINE OF GENOA

Eden is that old-fashioned house we dwell in every day without suspecting our abode until we drive away.
~ EMILY DICKINSON

Where thou art, that is home.
~ EMILY DICKINSON

To live is so startling it leaves little time for anything else.
~ EMILY DICKINSON

Here I am, where I ought to be.
~ LOUISE ERDRICH

Whatever is—is best.
~ ELLA WHEELER WILCOX

The Time to Be Happy Is Now

The most important thing in our lives is what we are doing now.
～ ANON.

Here's to the past. Thank God it's past!
～ ANON.

When I am anxious it is because I am living in the future. When I am depressed it is because I am living in the past.
～ ANON.

Then is then. Now is now. We must grow to learn the difference.
～ ANON.

The future belongs to those who live intensely in the present.
～ ANON.

If you have one eye on yesterday and one eye on tomorrow, you're going to be cockeyed today.
～ ANON.

Today was once the future from which you expected so much in the past.
～ ANON.

Everybody lives for something better to come.
～ ANON.

For years I wanted to be older, and now I am.
～ MARGARET ATWOOD

You have to do what you love to do, not get stuck in that comfort zone of a regular job. Life is not a dress rehearsal. This is it.
～ LUCINDA BASSET

Our faith in the present dies out long before our faith in the future.
～ RUTH BENEDICT

The idea came to me that I was, am, and will be, but perhaps will not become. This did not scare me. There was for me in being an intensity I did not feel in becoming.

~ NINA BERBEROVA

Forget the past and live the present hour.

~ SARAH KNOWLES BOLTON

Be glad today. Tomorrow may bring tears.
Be brave today. The darkest night will pass.
And golden rays will usher in the dawn.

~ SARAH KNOWLES BOLTON

Only when your consciousness is totally focused on the moment you are in can you receive whatever gift, lesson, or delight that moment has to offer.

~ BARBARA DE ANGELIS

The years seem to rush by now, and I think of death as a fast approaching end of a journey—double and treble reason for loving as well as working while it is day.

~ GEORGE ELIOT

When shall we live if not now?

~ M.F.K. FISHER

Losing the future is the best thing that ever happened to me.

~ MARILYN FRENCH

Looking repeatedly into the past, you do not necessarily become fascinated with your own life, but rather with the phenomenon of memory.

~ PATRICIA HAMPL

Life has got to be lived—that's all that there is to it.

~ ELEANOR ROOSEVELT

In great moments life seems neither right nor wrong, but something greater: it seems inevitable.

~ MARGARET SHERWOOD

The future is made of the same stuff as the present.

~ SIMONE WEIL

We Can Summon Joy Even in Times of Hardship

Hope is the last thing to abandon the unhappy.

~ ANON.

The sweetest joy, the wildest woe is love.

~ PEARL BAILEY

I like living. I have sometimes been wildly, despairingly, acutely miserable, racked with sorrow, but through it all I still know quite certainly that just to be alive is a grand thing.

~ AGATHA CHRISTIE

Hope costs nothing.

~ COLETTE

But here's what I've learned in this war, in this country, in this city: to love the miracle of having been born.

~ ORIANA FALLACI

Think of all the beauty that's still left in and around you and be happy!

~ ANNE FRANK

Love is like a beautiful flower which I may not touch, but whose fragrance makes the garden a place of delight just the same.

~ HELEN KELLER

The truth is, laughter always sounds more perfect than weeping. Laughter flows in a violent riff and is effortlessly melodic. Weeping is often fought, choked, half strangled, or surrendered to with humiliation.

~ ANNE RICE

If We're Positive, Joy Will Find Us

Always let them think of you as singing and dancing.
~ ANITA BROOKNER

Build a little fence of trust
Around today;
Fill the space with loving work,
And therein stay.
~ MARY FRANCES BUTTS

If someone said, "Write a sentence about your life," I'd write, "I want to go outside and play."
~ JENNA ELFMAN

Stop worrying about the potholes in the road and celebrate the journey!
~ BARBARA HOFFMAN

I love myself when I am laughing.
~ ZORA NEALE HURSTON

Exude happiness and you will feel it back a thousand times.
~ JOAN LUNDEN

The right to happiness is fundamental.
~ ANNA PAVLOVA

Happiness is that state of consciousness which proceeds from the achievement of one's values.
~ AYN RAND

To be kind to all, to like many and love a few, to be needed and wanted by those we love, is certainly the nearest we can come to happiness.
~ MARY ROBERTS RINEHART

Why is it that people who cannot show feeling presume that that is a strength and not a weakness?
~ MAY SARTON

It is only by expressing all that is inside that purer and purer streams come.

⌢ BRENDA UELAND

We Shouldn't Rely on External Things for Happiness

I don't sit around thinking that I'd like to have another husband; only another man would make me think that way.

⌢ LAUREN BACALL

Happiness is a conscious choice, not an automatic response.

⌢ MILDRED BARTHEL

Seek not outside yourself, heaven is within.

⌢ MARY LOU COOK

Our concern must be to live while we're alive ... to release our inner selves from the spiritual death that comes with living behind a facade designed to conform to external definitions of who and what we are.

⌢ ELISABETH KUBLER-ROSS

If We Are Open to Joy, It Will Reveal Itself

People see God every day, they just don't recognize Him.

⌢ PEARL BAILEY

It is always the simple that produces the marvelous.

⌢ AMELIA BARR

We hear voices in solitude, we never hear in the hurry and turmoil of life; we receive counsels and comforts we get under no other condition.

⌢ AMELIA BARR

Everything holds its breath except spring. She bursts through as strong as ever.

~ B.M. BOWER

Celebrate the happiness that friends are always giving, make every day a holiday and celebrate just living!

~ AMANDA BRADLEY

Growth itself contains the germ of happiness.

~ PEARL S. BUCK

We are new every day.

~ IRENE CLAREMONT CASTILLEGO

What a wonderful life I've had! I only wish I had realized it sooner.

~ COLETTE

Everything has its wonders, even darkness and silence, and I learn, whatever state I may be in, therein to be content.

~ HELEN KELLER

Happiness is something that comes into our lives through doors we don't even remember leaving open.

~ ROSE WILDER LANE

Today a new sun rises for me; everything lives, everything is animated, everything seems to speak to me of my passion, everything invites me to cherish it.

~ ANNE LENCLOS

Stretch out your hand and take the world's wide gift of Joy and Beauty.

~ CORINNE ROOSEVELT ROBINSON

Happiness lies in the consciousness we have of it.

~ GEORGE SAND

They seemed to come suddenly upon happiness as if they had surprised a butterfly in the winter woods.

~ EDITH WHARTON

Make the Most of Every Moment

You are younger today than you ever will be again. Make use of it for the sake of tomorrow.

~ ANON.

Sometimes I would rather have people take away years of my life than take away a moment.

~ PEARL BAILEY

The bliss e'en of a moment still is bliss.

~ JOANNA BAILLIE

I have always felt that the moment when first you wake up in the morning is the most wonderful of the twenty-four hours. No matter how weary or dreary you may feel, you possess the certainty that … absolutely anything may happen. And the fact that it practically always doesn't, matters not one jot. The possibility is always there.

~ MONICA BALDWIN

Every age can be enchanting, provided you live within it.

~ BRIGITTE BARDOT

The trouble is not that we are never happy—it is that happiness is so episodical.

~ RUTH BENEDICT

We have only this moment, sparkling like a star in our hand … and melting like a snowflake. Let us use it before it is too late.

~ MARIE BEYON RAY

Light tomorrow with today.

~ ELIZABETH BARRETT BROWNING

Truth has no beginning.

~ MARY BAKER EDDY

Youth troubles over eternity, age grasps at a day and is satisfied to have even the day.

~ DAME MARY GILMORE

She who laughs not in the morning, laughs not at noon.

~ GREEK PROVERB

To live exhilaratingly in and for the moment is deadly serious work, fun of the most exhausting sort.

~ BARBARA GRIZZUTI HARRISON

We sail, at sunrise, daily, "outward bound."

~ HELEN HUNT JACKSON

Day's sweetest moments are at dawn.

~ ELLA WHEELER WILCOX

Enjoy the Wonderful Things in Life

A private railroad car is not an acquired taste. One takes to it immediately.

~ ELEANOR R. BELMONT

Sweets are good for the nerves.

~ MARGARETE BIEBER

Little deeds of kindness, little words of love,
Help to make earth happy like the heaven up above.

~ JULIA A. FLETCHER CARNEY

All the great blessings of my life are present in my thoughts today.

~ PHOEBE CARY

Life is about enjoying yourself and having a good time.

~ CHER

Fat gives things flavor.

～ JULIA CHILD

Life is to be lived.

～ KATHARINE HEPBURN

Put a little fun into your life. Try dancing.

～ KATHRYN MURRAY

My child looked at me and I looked back at him in the delivery room, and I realized that out of a sea of infinite possibilities it had come down to this: a specific person, born on the hottest day of the year, conceived on a Christmas Eve, made by his father and me miraculously from scratch.

～ ANNA QUINDLEN

And when our baby stirs and struggles to be born it compels humility: what we began is now its own.

～ ANNE RIDLER

Is life worth living?
Aye, with the best of us,
Heights of us, depths of us—
Life is the test of us!

～ CORINNE ROOSEVELT ROBINSON

Holding hands is a very intimate thing to do, she found herself whispering. Even to hold a child's hand. It's very touching.

～ CYNTHIA PROPPER SETON

*B*eing Realistic

Understand What You Can and Can't Control

Who we are never changes. Who we think we are does.
~ MARY S. ALMANAC

Resistance causes pain and lethargy. It is when we practice acceptance that new possibilities appear.
~ ANON.

I think knowing what you cannot do is more important than knowing what you can.
~ LUCILLE BALL

In the face of an obstacle which is impossible to overcome, stubbornness is stupid.
~ SIMONE DE BEAUVOIR

You can't assume the responsibility for everything you do—or don't do.
~ SIMONE DE BEAUVOIR

You never conquer a mountain. You stand on the summit a few moments; then the wind blows your footprints away.

~ ARLENE BLUM

If I could I would always work in silence and obscurity, and let my efforts be known by their results.

~ EMILY BRONTË

I like trees because they seem more resigned to the way they have to live than other things do.

~ WILLA CATHER

Happiness is not a horse—you cannot harness it.

~ CHINESE PROVERB

Human beings aren't orchids; we must draw something from the soil we grow in.

~ SARA JEANNETTE DUNCAN

If you can keep your head when all about are losing theirs, it's just possible you haven't grasped the situation.

~ JEAN KERR

I know that I haven't powers enough to divide myself into one who earns and one who creates.

~ TILLIE OLSEN

Each of us does, in effect, strike a series of deals or compromises between the wants and longings of the inner self, and an outer environment that offers certain possibilities and sets certain limitations.

~ MAGGIE SCARF

Don't spend time beating on a wall, hoping to transform it into a door.

~ DR. LAURA SCHLESSINGER

Wisdom never kicks at the iron walls it can't bring down.

~ OLIVE SCHREINER

It is impossible to control creation.

~ EVELYN SCOTT

Better bend than break.

~ SCOTTISH PROVERB

Give and take makes good friends.

~ SCOTTISH PROVERB

Acceptance is not submission; it is acknowledgement of the facts of a situation. Then deciding what you're going to do about it.

~ KATHLEEN CASEY THEISEN

Most of us have trouble juggling. The woman who says she doesn't is someone whom I admire but have never met.

~ BARBARA WALTERS

A lion doesn't fear a fly.

~ YIDDISH PROVERB

We Should Try Not to Always See Ourselves as "East of Eden"

Why not seize the pleasure at once? How often is happiness destroyed by preparation, foolish preparation?

~ JANE AUSTEN

The dream is real, my friends. The failure to realize it is the only reality.

~ TONI CADE BAMBARA

The true exercise of freedom is—cannily and wisely and with grace—to move inside what space confines—and not seek to know what lies beyond and cannot be touched or tasted.

~ A.S. BYATT

Truth is simply whatever you can bring yourself to believe.

~ ALICE CHILDRESS

Most of our platitudes notwithstanding, self-deception remains the most difficult deception. The tricks that worked on others count for nothing in that very well-lit back alley where one keeps assignations with oneself: no winning smiles will do here, no prettily drawn list of good intentions.

~ JOAN DIDION

Death and taxes and childbirth! There's never any convenient time for any of them!

~ MARGARET MITCHELL

Let us accept truth, even when it surprises us and alters our views.

~ GEORGE SAND

To have ideals is not the same as to have impracticable ideals.

~ L. SUSAN STEBBING

Only a weak mind sees ultimate answers.

~ AGNES THORNTON

There has never been an age that did not applaud the past and lament the present.

~ LILLIAN EICHLER WATSON

We Shouldn't Bite Off More Than We Can Chew

Think of the going out before you enter.

~ ARABIC PROVERB

A pint can't hold a quart—if it holds a pint it is doing all that can be expected of it.

~ MARGARET DELAND

Truth has rough flavors if we bite it through.

~ GEORGE ELIOT

What had seemed easy in imagination was rather hard in reality.
~ L.M. MONTGOMERY

You can't move so fast that you try to change [a situation] faster than people can accept it. That doesn't mean you do nothing, but it means that you do the things that need to be done according to priority.
~ ELEANOR ROOSEVELT

Things Are Not Always What They Seem

Pioneers may be picturesque figures, but they are often rather lonely ones.
~ NANCY ASTOR

There is less in this than meets the eye.
~ TALLULAH BANKHEAD

I have been very happy, very rich, very beautiful, much adulated, very famous and very unhappy.
~ BRIGITTE BARDOT

Fame always brings loneliness. Success is as ice cold and lonely as the North Pole.
~ VICKI BAUM

People who don't have it think beauty is a blessing, but actually it sets you apart.
~ CANDICE BERGEN

Mountains appear more lofty the nearer they are approached, but great men resemble them not in this particular.
~ LADY MARGUERITE BLESSINGTON

I feel successful when the writing goes well. This lasts five minutes. Once, when I was on the bestseller list, I also felt successful. That lasted three minutes.
~ JACQUELINE BRISKIN

Not all speed is movement.
~ TONI CADE

Even I don't wake up looking like Cindy Crawford.
~ CINDY CRAWFORD

Success is counted sweetest
By those who ne'er succeed.
~ EMILY DICKINSON

Nothing is so good as it seems beforehand.
~ GEORGE ELIOT

All change is not growth, as all movement is not forward.
~ ELLEN GLASGOW

The truth isn't always beauty, but the hunger for it is.
~ NADINE GORDIMER

I slept, and dreamed that life was Beauty;
I woke, and found that life was Duty.
~ ELLEN STURGIS HOOPER

I can count the number of dates I've had on one hand. I wish that
guys would approach me, but they don't.
~ LATOYA JACKSON

Oh, I wish that God had not given me what I prayed for! It was not
so good as I thought.
~ JOHANNA SPYRI

If I had known what it would be like to have it all, I might have
been willing to settle for less.
~ LILY TOMLIN

A sobering thought: what if, right at this very moment, I am living
up to my full potential?
~ JANE WAGNER

[Being a parent] is tough. If you just want a wonderful little creature to love, you can get a puppy.

~ BARBARA WALTERS

So much perfection argues rottenness somewhere.

~ BEATRICE POTTER WEBB

Fear is worse than the ordeal itself.

~ YIDDISH PROVERB

Don't Take Things Too Seriously

By the time I'd grown up, I naturally supposed that I'd grown up.

~ EVE BABITZ

We would worry less about what others think of us if we realized how seldom they do.

~ ETHEL BARRETT

To say that my grief will be eternal would be ridiculous—nothing is eternal.

~ MARIE BASHKIRTSEFF

Virtue, like a dowerless beauty, has more admirers than followers.

~ LADY MARGUERITE BLESSINGTON

We don't strain at a gnat and swallow a camel, nor swim in an ocean and drown in a puddle.

~ TAYLOR CALDWELL

You always feel when you look it straight in the eye that you could have put more into it, could have let yourself go and dug harder.

~ EMILY CARR

Truth, however bitter, can be accepted, and woven into a design for living.

~ AGATHA CHRISTIE

When we start deceiving ourselves into thinking not that we want something or need something, not that it is a pragmatic necessity for us to have it, but that it is a moral imperative that we have it. Then is when we join the fashionable madmen, and then is when the thin whine of hysteria is heard in the land, and then is when we are in bad trouble.

~ JOAN DIDION

If, every day, I dare to remember that I am here on loan, that this house, this hillside, these minutes are all leased to me, not given, I will never despair.

~ ERICA JONG

Competition is easier to accept if you realize it is not an act of oppression or abrasion.... I've worked with my best friends in direct competition.

~ DIANE SAWYER

Any concern too small to be turned into a prayer is too small to be made into a burden.

~ CORRIE TEN BOOM

To wish to act like angels while we are still in this world is nothing but folly.

~ TERESA OF AVILA

Have Faith, and Truth Will Prevail

There is nothing new except what has been forgotten.

~ MARIE ANTOINETTE

For the facts that make up the world need the non-factual as a vantage point from which to be perceived.

~ INGEBORG BACHMANN

Doubt is a necessity of the mind, faith of the heart.

~ COMTESSE DIANE

For those who live neither with religious consolations about death nor with a sense of death (or of anything else) as natural, death is the obscene mystery, the ultimate affront, the thing that cannot be controlled. It can only be denied.

~ SUSAN SONTAG

Much sheer effort goes into avoiding the truth; left to itself, it sweeps in like the tide.

~ FAY WELDON

I've learned only that you never say never.

~ MARINA VON NEUMANN WHITMAN

What will be, will be.

~ YIDDISH PROVERB

Set Realistic Goals

Some people are still unaware that reality contains unparalleled beauties. The fantastic and unexpected, the ever-changing and renewing is nowhere so exemplified as in real life itself.

~ BERENICE ABBOTT

Who ever is adequate? We all create situations which others can't live up to, then break our hearts at them because they don't.

~ ELIZABETH BOWEN

Life is so constructed that the event does not, cannot, will not match the expectations.

~ CHARLOTTE BRONTË

Don't fool yourself that you are going to have it all. You are not. Psychologically, having it all is not even a valid concept. The marvelous thing about human beings is that we are perpetually reaching for the stars. The more we have, the more we want. And for this reason, we never have it all.

~ DR. JOYCE BROTHERS

Innovation! One cannot be forever innovating. I want to create classics.

~ COCO CHANEL

There is no such thing as expecting too much.

~ SUSAN CHEEVER

Your goal should be out of reach but not out of sight.

~ ANITA DEFRANTZ

It is unfair to hold people responsible for our illusions of them.

~ COMTESSE DIANE

A fool or idiot is one who expects things to happen that never can happen.

~ GEORGE ELIOT

The striking point about our model family is not simply the compete-compete, consume-consume style of life it urges us to follow. The striking point, in the face of all the propaganda, is how few Americans actually live this way.

~ LOUISE KAPP HOWE

The ultimate umpire of all things in life is—fact.

~ AGNES C. LAUT

Without imagination, nothing is dangerous.

~ GEORGETTE LEBLANC

Almost anything carried to its logical extreme becomes depressing, if not carcinogenic.

~ URSULA K. LE GUIN

People do think that if they avoid the truth, it might change to something better before they have to hear it.

~ MARSHA NORMAN

To expect too much is to have a sentimental view of life, and this is a softness that ends in bitterness.

~ FLANNERY O'CONNOR

You can no more win a war than you can win an earthquake.

~ JEANNETTE RANKIN

Perfectionism is self-abuse of the highest order.

~ ANNE WILSON SCHAEF

Perfection anywhere is very rare.

~ YIDDISH PROVERB

$\mathcal{B}$anishing Negative Thoughts

Don't Dwell on the Past

How we remember, what we remember, and why we remember form the most personal map of our individuality.
~ CHRISTINA BALDWIN

The past is finished. There is nothing to be gained by going over it. Whatever it gave us in the experiences it brought us was something we had to know.
~ REBECCA BEARD

Don't ruin the present with the ruined past.
~ ELLEN GILCHRIST

It will be a great thing for the human soul when it finally stops worshipping backwards.
~ CHARLOTTE P. GILMAN

Let the past drift away with the water.
~ JAPANESE PROVERB

They say you should not suffer through the past. You should be able to wear it like a loose garment, take it off and let it drop.

~ EVA JESSYE

Having harvested all the knowledge and wisdom we can from our mistakes and failures, we should put them behind us and go ahead.

~ EDITH JOHNSON

Very frequently, feminine activity also expresses itself in what is largely a retrospectively oriented pondering over what we ought to have done differently in life, and how we ought to have done it; or, as if under compulsion, we make up strings of causal connections. We like to call this thinking; though, on the contrary, it is a form of mental activity that is strangely pointless and unproductive, a form that really leads only to self-torture.

~ EMMA JUNG

Nobody gets to live life backward. Look ahead, that is where your future lies.

~ ANN LANDERS

Were it not better to forget
Than to remember and regret?

~ LETITIA LANDON

Ah tell me not that memory
Sheds gladness o'er the past;
What is recalled by faded flowers
Save that they did not last?

~ LETITIA LANDON

Anyone who limits her vision to memories of yesterday is already dead.

~ LILLIE LANGTRY

Whatever with the past is gone, the best is always yet to come.

~ LUCY LARCOM

The past cannot be changed. The future is yet in your power.

~ MARY PICKFORD

Pain is no longer pain when it is past.

~ MARGARET J. PRESTON

I have very strong feelings about how you lead your life. You always look ahead, you never look back.

~ ANN RICHARDS

Should-haves solve nothing. It's the next thing to happen that needs thinking about.

~ ALEXANDRA RIPLEY

The tasks are done and the tears are shed.
Yesterday's errors let yesterday cover;
Yesterday's wounds, which smarted and bled,
Are healed with the healing that night has shed.

~ SARAH CHAUNCEY WOOLSEY (SUSAN COOLIDGE)

Apologize, Forgive, and Forget

Forgetting is the cost of living cheerfully.

~ ZOË AKINS

Resentments are burdens we don't need to carry.

~ ANON.

Those who can't forget are worse off than those who can't remember.

~ ANON.

One of the secrets of a long and fruitful life is to forgive everybody everything every night before you go to bed.

~ ANON.

Forgiveness is the key to action and freedom.

~ HANNAH ARENDT

Life appears to me too short to be spent in nursing animosity or registering wrong.

~ CHARLOTTE BRONTË

Anger repressed can poison a relationship as surely as the cruelest words.

~ DR. JOYCE BROTHERS

I know now that patriotism is not enough; I must have no hatred and bitterness toward anyone.

~ EDITH CAVELL

Stretch out your hand! Let no human soul wait for a benediction.

~ MARIE CORELLI

May I forget what ought to be forgotten; and recall, unfailing, all that ought to be recalled, each kindly thing, forgetting what might sting.

~ MATY CAROLINE DAVIES

Anger as soon as fed is dead, 'tis starving makes it fat.

~ EMILY DICKINSON

Once a woman has forgiven a man, she must not reheat his sins for breakfast.

~ MARLENE DIETRICH

As long as you don't forgive, who and whatever it is will occupy a rent-free space in your mind.

~ ISABELLE HOLLAND

Courage and clemency are equal virtues.

~ MARY DELARIVIÈRE MANLEY

One may have been a fool, but there's no foolishness like being bitter.

~ KATHLEEN NORRIS

Forgiveness is all-powerful. Forgiveness heals all ills.

~ CATHERINE PONDER

The forgiving state of mind is a magnetic power for attracting good.
~ CATHERINE PORTER

Better a red face than a black heart.
~ PORTUGESE PROVERB

Better by far you should forget and smile, than you should remember and be sad.
~ CHRISTINA GEORGINA ROSETTI

Who understands much, forgives much.
~ MADAME DE STAËL

The heart has always the pardoning power.
~ ANNE-SOPHIE SWETCHINE

Forgiveness is an act of the will, and the will can function regardless of the temperature of the heart.
~ CORRIE TEN BOOM

Laugh It Off

Keep your sense of humor. There's enough stress in the rest of your life to let bad shots ruin a game you're supposed to enjoy.
~ AMY ALCOTT

A person of gladness rarely falls into madness.
~ ANON.

You don't get ulcers from what you eat. You get them from what's eating you.
~ VICKI BAUM

There is no sin nor wrong that gives a man such a foretaste of hell in this life as anger and impatience.
~ SAINT CATHERINE OF SIENA

Tears mess up your makeup.

~ JULIA CHILD

One loses many laughs by not laughing at oneself.

~ SARA JEANNETTE DUNCAN

To jealousy, nothing is more frightful than laughter.

~ FRANÇOISE SAGAN

Groan and forget it.

~ JESSAMYN WEST

Laugh and the world laughs with you;
Weep and you weep alone;
For the sad old earth must borrow its mirth,
But has trouble enough of its own.

~ ELLA WHEELER WILCOX

Keep Your Spirits Up

The optimism of a healthy mind is indefatigable.

~ MARGERY ALLINGHAM

Pain is inevitable. Suffering is optional.

~ ANON.

Wrinkles should only indicate where smiles have been.

~ ETHEL BARRYMORE

Some knowledge and some song and some beauty must be kept for those days before the world again plunges into darkness.

~ MARION ZIMMER BRADLEY

Tears are sometimes an inappropriate response to death. When a life has been lived completely honestly, completely successfully, or just completely, the correct response to death's perfect punctuation mark is a smile.

~ JULIE BURCHILL

A sneer is like a flame; it may occasionally be curative because it cauterizes, but it leaves a bitter scar.

~ MARGARET DELAND

High above hate I dwell,
O storms! Farewell.

~ LOUISE IMOGEN GUINEY

Hate is like acid. It can damage the vessel in which it is stored as well as destroy the object on which it is poured.

~ ANN LANDERS

Suffering is not a prerequisite for happiness.

~ JUDY TATELBAUM

Anger is the thorn in the heart.

~ YIDDISH PROVERB

Don't Succumb to Hate and Anger

Anger is only one letter short of danger.

~ ANON.

Some people are molded by their admirations, others by their hostilities.

~ ELIZABETH BOWEN

Anger and worry are the enemies of clear thought.

~ MADELEINE BRENT

I tell you, there is no such thing as creative hate!

~ WILLA CATHER

Reject hatred without hating.

~ MARY BAKER EDDY

Hatred is like fire—it makes even light rubbish deadly.

~ GEORGE ELIOT

Revenge may not be a particularly high consciousness-oriented activity.
⌒ CARRIE FISHER

The whole human race loses by every act of personal vengeance.
⌒ RAE FOLEY

You cannot shake hands with a clenched fist.
⌒ INDIRA GANDHI

Thinking evil is much the same as doing it.
⌒ GREEK PROVERB

Anger can be an expensive luxury.
⌒ ITALIAN PROVERB

My mother used to say, "He who angers you conquers you."
⌒ ELIZABETH KENNY

Hatred is a death wish for the hated, not a life wish for anything else.
⌒ AUDRE LORDE

Hatred is a passion requiring one hundred times the energy of love.
Keep it for a cause, not an individual. Keep it for intolerance,
injustice, stupidity. For hatred is the strength of the sensitive. Its
power and its greatness depend on the selflessness of its use.
⌒ OLIVE MOORE

Hate is all a lie, there is no truth in hate.
⌒ KATHLEEN NORRIS

Hate is not a good counselor.
⌒ VICTORIA WOLFF

Don't Criticize or Complain

A dog that barks all the time gets little attention.
⌒ ARGENTINE PROVERB

Never say anything on the phone that you wouldn't want your mother to hear at your trial.

~ SYDNEY BIDDLE BARROWS

You find yourself refreshed by the presence of cheerful people. Why not make an honest effort to confer that pleasure on others? Half the battle is gained if you never allow yourself to say anything gloomy.

~ LYDIA MARIA CHILD

A critic is someone who never actually goes to the battle, yet who afterwards comes out shooting the wounded.

~ TYNE DALY

The weak are the most treacherous of us all. They come to the strong and drain them. They are bottomless. They are insatiable. They are always parched and always bitter. They are everyone's concern and like vampires they suck our life's blood.

~ BETTE DAVIS

Grumbling is the death of love.

~ MARLENE DIETRICH

An ass may bray a good while before he shakes the stars down.

~ GEORGE ELIOT

Play not with paradoxes. That caustic which you handle in order to scorch others may happen to sear your own fingers and make them dead to the quality of things.

~ GEORGE ELIOT

Discussing how old you are is the temple of boredom.

~ RUTH GORDON

We criticize and separate ourselves from the process. We've got to jump right in there with both feet.

~ DOLORES HUERTA

Wit is the salt of conversation, not the food, and few things in the world are more wearying than a sarcastic attitude towards life.

～ AGNES REPPLIER

You just can't complain about being alive. It's self-indulgent to be unhappy.

～ GENA ROWLAND

Talk happiness. The world is sad enough without your woe. No path is wholly rough.

～ ELLA WHEELER WILCOX

If any has a stone to throw
It is not I, ever or now.

～ ELINOR WYLIE

If We're Not Part of the Solution, We're Part of the Problem

It takes two flints to make a fire.

～ LOUISA MAY ALCOTT

You live with your thoughts—so be careful what they are.

～ EVA ARRINGTON

Cease to be a drudge, seek to be an artist.

～ MARY MCLEOD BETHUNE

True revolutions ... restore more than they destroy.

～ LOUISE BOGAN

There are seeds of self-destruction in all of us that will bear only unhappiness if allowed to grow.

～ DOROTHEA BRANDE

We have seen too much defeatism, too much pessimism, too much of
a negative approach.

~ MARGO JONES

This is the way of peace—overcome evil with good, and falsehood
with truth, and hatred with love.

~ PEACE PILGRIM

Peace with a cudgel in hand is war.

~ PORTUGESE PROVERB

The evil of the world is made possible by nothing but the sanction
you give it.

~ AYN RAND

If you make fun of bad persons you make yourself beneath them....
Be kind to bad and good, for you don't know your own heart.

~ SARAH WINNEMUCCA

A quarrel is like an itch; the more you scratch, the more it itches.

~ YIDDISH PROVERB

Attitude Is Everything

It was only a sunny smile,
But it scattered the night
And little it cost in the giving;
Like morning light,
And made the day worth living.

~ ANON.

When good cheer is lacking, our friends will be packing.

~ ANON.

He who forecasts all perils will never sail the sea.

~ ANON.

Failure is impossible.

~ SUSAN B. ANTHONY

If you think you can, you can. And if you think you can't, you're right.

~ MARY KAY ASH

Sweet sleep be with us, one and all!
And if upon its stillness fall
The visions of a busy brain,
We'll have our pleasure o'er again,
To warm the heart, to charm the sight,
Gay dreams to all! good night, good night.

~ JOANNA BAILLIE

I have always felt that the moment when first you wake up in the
morning is the most wonderful of the twenty-four hours. No matter
how weary or dreary you may feel, you possess the certainty that ...
absolutely anything may happen. And the fact that it practically
always doesn't, matters not one jot. The possibility is always there.

~ MONICA BALDWIN

Both abundance and lack exist simultaneously in our lives, as parallel
realities. It is always our conscious choice which secret garden we
will tend ... when we choose not to focus on what is missing from
our lives but are grateful for the abundance that's present—love,
health, family, friends, work, the joys of nature, and personal pursuits
that bring us pleasure—the wasteland of illusion falls away and we
experience heaven on earth.

~ SARAH BAN BREATHNACH

A good heart will help you to a bonny face, my lad ... and a bad
one will turn the bonniest into something worse than ugly.

~ EMILY BRONTË

A woman's hopes are woven of sunbeams; a shadow annihilates them.

~ GEORGE ELIOT

Keep your face to the sunshine and you cannot see the shadow.

~ HELEN KELLER

I am optimistic and confident in all that I do. I affirm only the best for myself and others. I am the creator of my life and my world. I meet daily challenges gracefully and with complete confidence. I fill my mind with positive, nurturing, and healing thoughts.

～ ALICE POTTER

We are not interested in the possibilities of defeat.

～ QUEEN VICTORIA

To think of losing is to lose already.

～ SYLVIA TOWNSEND WARNER

Overcome Fear, Doubt, Jealousy, and Mistrust

Hope is putting faith to work when doubting would be easier.

～ ANON.

Fear is the dark room in which negatives are developed.

～ ANON.

The trouble with most people is that they think with their hopes or fears or wishes rather than with their minds.

～ NANCY ASTOR

If you banish fear, nothing terribly bad can happen to you.

～ MARGARET BOURKE-WHITE

Jealousy is no more than feeling alone against smiling enemies.

～ ELIZABETH BOWEN

The key to change ... is to let go of fear.

～ ROSANNE CASH

Grief and constant anxiety kill nearly as many women as men die on the battlefield.

～ MARY BOKIN CHESNUT

Jealousy is never satisfied with anything short of omniscience that would detect the subtlest fold in the heart.

~ GEORGE ELIOT

What loneliness is more lonely than distrust?

~ GEORGE ELIOT

Concern should drive us into action, not into depression.

~ KAREN HORNEY

Jealousy is all the fun you think they had.

~ ERICA JONG

In the kingdom of hope, there is no winter.

~ RUSSIAN PROVERB

A lock keeps out only the honest.

~ YIDDISH PROVERB

Tasty is the fish on someone else's dish.

~ YIDDISH PROVERB

When We're Negative, We Only Hurt Ourselves

Something of vengeance I had tasted for the first time; as aromatic wine it seemed, on swallowing, warm and racy; its after-flavor, metallic and corroding, gave me a sensation as if I had been poisoned.

~ CHARLOTTE BRONTË

When a proud woman hears another praised, she feels herself injured.

~ ENGLISH PROVERB

To oppose something is to maintain it.

~ URSULA K. LE GUIN

Dwelling on the negative simply contributes to its power.

~ SHIRLEY MACLAINE

The enslaver is enslaved, the hater, harmed.

~ MARIANNE MOORE

By putting his hand around my neck, he slowly strangled himself.

~ MINAKO OHBA

The one who deals the mortal blow receives the mortal wound.

~ MAUDE PARKER

In hatred as in love, we grow like the thing we brood upon. What we loathe, we graft into our very soul.

~ MARY RENAULT

Resentment is weak and lowers your self-esteem.

~ BARBARA SHER

A greedy person and a pauper are practically one and the same.

~ SWISS PROVERB

Hate smolders and eventually destroys, not the hated but the hater.

~ DOROTHY THOMPSON

A weapon is an enemy even to its owner.

~ TURKISH PROVERB

It is almost impossible to throw dirt on someone without getting a little on yourself.

~ ABIGAIL VAN BUREN

Fire destroys that which feeds it.

~ SIMONE WEIL

You cannot hate other people without hating yourself.

~ OPRAH WINFREY

Rage and bitterness do not foster femininity. They harden the heart and make the body sick.

~ MARION WOODMAN

Focus on the Good in Yourself and Others

We may draw good out of evil; we must not do evil, that good may come.

~ MARIA WESTON CHAPMAN

Was it always my nature to take a bad time and block out the good times, until any success became an accident and failure seemed the only truth?

~ LILLIAN HELLMAN

We can sometimes love what we do not understand, but it is impossible completely to understand what we do not love.

~ ANNA JAMESON

I seldom think about my limitations, and they never make me sad. Perhaps there is just a touch of yearning at times; but it is vague, like a breeze among flowers.

~ HELEN KELLER

So once I shut down my privilege of disliking anyone I choose and holding myself aloof if I could manage it, greater understanding, growing compassion came to me.

~ CATHARINE MARSHALL

In rejecting secrecy I had also rejected the road to cynicism.

~ CATHARINE MARSHALL

My friend and I have built a wall
Between us thick and wide:
The stones of it are laid in scorn
And plastered high with pride.

~ ELIZABETH CUTTER MORROW

People are more than the worst thing they have ever done in their lives.

~ HELEN PREJEAN

He that despiseth his neighbor sinneth; but he that hath mercy on the poor, happy is he.

~ PROVERBS

I couldn't claim that I have never felt the urge to explore evil, but when you descend into hell you have to be very careful.

~ KATHLEEN RAINE

It is healthier to see the good points of others than to analyze our own bad ones.

~ FRANÇOISE SAGAN

Kindness causes us to learn, and to forget, many things.

~ ANNE-SOPHIE SWETCHINE

You can either give in to negative feelings or fight them, and I'm of the belief that you should fight them.

~ DR. RUTH WESTHEIMER

Love lights more fires than hate extinguishes,
And men grow better as the world grows old.

~ ELLA WHEELER WILCOX

Developing a cheerful disposition can permit an atmosphere wherein one's spirit can be nurtured and encouraged to blossom and bear fruit. Being pessimistic and negative about our experiences will not enhance the quality of our lives.

~ BARBARA W. WINDER

$\mathcal{A}$ppreciating What You Have

Celebrate Yourself

Next to God we are indebted
to women, first for life itself,
and then for making it
worth living.

~ MARY MCLEOD BETHUNE

From self alone expect applause.

~ MARIAN L. BURTON

I am not belittling the brave pioneer men but the sunbonnet as well
as the sombrero has helped to settle this glorious land of ours.

~ EDNA FERBER

The older women were Sunbeams and I guess we were Cherubs or
Lambs, but our mothers were Nightingales.

~ JANET FLANNER

Solitude is one thing and loneliness is another.

~ MAY SARTON

Fond as we are of our loved ones, there comes at times during their absence an unexplained peace.

~ ANN SHAW

Give Thanks to Your Higher Power

Be not hot in prayer and cold in praise.

~ ANON.

For the rest of my life I'm going to trust that God is always at work in all things, and give Him thanks long before my simplest prayers are answered.

~ NANCY PARKER BRUMMETT

The best remedy for those who are afraid, lonely, or unhappy is to go outside, somewhere where they can be quiet, alone with the heavens, nature, and God. Because only then does one feel that all is as it should be and that God wishes to see people happy, amidst the simple beauty of nature. As long as this exists, and it certainly always will, I know that then there will always be comfort for every sorrow, whatever the circumstances may be. And I firmly believe that nature brings solace in all troubles.

~ ANNE FRANK

Much earnest philosophical thought is born of the life which springs from close association with nature.

~ LAURA GILPIN

My debt to you, Beloved,
Is one I cannot pay
In any coin of any realm
On any reckoning day.

~ JESSIE RITTENHOUSE

Be Thankful for the Little Things

One day of pleasure is worth two of sorrow.
~ ANON.

If you can't be thankful for what you receive, be thankful for what you escape.
~ ANON.

Nothing will content him who is not content with a little.
~ GREEK PROVERB

A harbor, even if it is a little harbor, is a good thing.... It takes something from the world, and has something to give in return.
~ SARAH ORNE JEWETT

One can get just as much exultation in losing oneself in a little thing as in a big thing. It is nice to think how one can be recklessly lost in a daisy.
~ ANNE MORROW LINDBERGH

If I had my life to live over, I would start barefoot earlier in the spring and stay that way later in the fall. I would go to more dances. I would ride more merry-go-rounds. I would pick more daisies.
~ NADINE STAIR

I am because my little dog knows me.
~ GERTRUDE STEIN

I have come to understand that every day is something to cherish.
~ KERRI STRUG

Count Your Blessings—Things Could Be Worse

If you can't be thankful for what you receive, be thankful for what you escape.

~ ANON.

Even though we can't have all we want, we ought to be thankful we don't get all we deserve.

~ ANON.

A fool bolts pleasure, then complains of indigestion.

~ MINNA ANTRIM

Glee! The great storm is over!

~ EMILY DICKINSON

I wept because I had no shoes, until I saw someone who had no feet.

~ PERSIAN PROVERB

A woman has got to love a bad man once or twice in her life to be thankful for a good one.

~ MARJORIE KINNAN RAWLINGS

It is better to be looked over than overlooked.

~ MAE WEST

Joy is what happens to us when we allow ourselves to recognize how good things really are.

~ MARIANNE WILLIAMSON

Keep a grateful journal. Every night, list five things that you are grateful for. What it will begin to do is change your perspective of your day and your life.

~ OPRAH WINFREY

Gratitude Enriches Our Lives

Gratitude unlocks the fullness of life. It turns what we have into enough, and more. It turns denial into acceptance, chaos to order, confusion to clarity. It can turn a meal into a feast, a house into a home, a stranger into a friend. Gratitude makes sense of our past, brings peace for today, and creates a vision for tomorrow.

> ∿ MELODY BEATTIE

Blessed are those who can give without remembering and take without forgetting.

> ∿ ELIZABETH ASQUITH BIBESCO

Remember that not to be happy is not to be grateful.

> ∿ ELIZABETH CARTER

Gratitude weighs heavy on us only when we no longer feel it.

> ∿ COMTESSE DIANE

Ingratitude is a kind of weakness; the clever are never ungrateful.

> ∿ FRENCH PROVERB

Appreciation is yeast, lifting ordinary to extraordinary.

> ∿ MARY-ANN PETRO

Enjoy What You Have

Be first at the feast, and last at the fight.

> ∿ AMERICAN INDIAN PROVERB

She is not rich that possesses much, but she that is content with what she has.

> ∿ ANON.

A wise woman cares not for what she cannot have.

> ∿ ANON.

The best way for a person to have happiness is to count her blessings and not her cash.

~ ANON.

All your youth you want to have your greatness taken for granted; when you find it taken for granted, you are unnerved.

~ ELIZABETH BOWEN

Non-cooks think it's silly to invest two hours' work in two minutes' enjoyment; but if cooking is evanescent, so is the ballet.

~ JULIA CHILD

Eden is that old-fashioned house we dwell in every day without suspecting our abode until we drive away.

~ EMILY DICKINSON

We never know the worth of water until the well is dry.

~ ENGLISH PROVERB

To say something nice about themselves, this is the hardest thing in the world for people to do.

~ NANCY FRIDAY

Every dog has its day, but it's not every dog that knows when he's having it.

~ WINIFRED GORDON

After my mother's death, I began to see her as she had really been.... It was less like losing someone than discovering someone.

~ NANCY HALE

Jesus, please teach me to appreciate what I have, before time forces me to appreciate what I had.

~ SUSAN L. LENZKES

What you have become is the price you paid to get what you used to want.

~ MIGNON MCLAUGHLIN

For one mother, joy is the quiet pleasure found in gently rubbing shampoo into her young child's hair. For another woman it's taking a long walk alone, while for yet another it's reveling in a much-anticipated vacation.

~ EILEEN STUKANE

We must give ourselves more earnestly and intelligently and generously than we have to the happy duty of appreciation.

~ MARIANA GRISWOLD VAN RENSSELAER

It made me gladsome to be getting some education, it being like a big window opening.

~ MARY WEBB

Too much of a good thing can be wonderful.

~ MAE WEST

Cherish Your Memories

I believe the true function of age is memory. I'm recording as fast as I can.

~ RITA MAE BROWN

Some memories are realities, and are better than anything that can ever happen to one again.

~ WILLA CATHER

The past with its pleasures, its rewards, its foolishness, its punishments, is there for each of us forever, and it should be.

~ LILLIAN HELLMAN

Fortunate are the people whose roots are deep.

~ AGNES MEYER

I look back on my life like a good day's work; it was done and I am satisfied with it.

~ GRANDMA MOSES

As the dew to the blossom, the bud to the bee,
As the scent to the rose, are those memories to me.
~ AMELIA C. WELBY

Appreciate the Things That Really Matter

If you want an accounting of your worth, count your friends.
~ MERRY BROWNE

A hungry ass keeps her kicking end down.
~ IRISH PROVERB

Better a mouse in the pot than no stew at all.
~ ITALIAN PROVERB

I've had an exciting life; I married for love and got a little money
along with it.
~ ROSE KENNEDY

My gratitude for good writing is unbounded; I'm grateful for it the
way I'm grateful for the ocean.
~ ANNE LAMOTT

When something does not insist on being noticed, when we aren't
grabbed by the collar or struck on the skull by a presence or an event,
we take for granted the very things that most deserve our gratitude.
~ CYNTHIA OZICK

Enjoy the successes that you have, and don't be too hard on yourself
when you don't do well. Too many times we beat up on ourselves.
Just relax and enjoy it.
~ PATTY SHEEHAN

I make the most of all that comes and the least of all that goes.
~ SARA TEASDALE

I take it as a prime cause of the present confusion of society that it is too sickly and too doubtful to use pleasure as a test of value.

~ REBECCA WEST

Show Appreciation for Others

The nice thing about teamwork is that you always have others on your side.

~ MARGARET CARTY

No music is so pleasant to my ears as that word—*father.*

~ LYDIA MARIA CHILD

There are some people who leave impressions not so lasting as the imprint of an oar upon the water.

~ KATE CHOPIN

A cheer, then, for the noblest breast
That fears not danger's post;
And like the lifeboat, proves a friend,
When friends are wanted most.

~ ELIZA COOK

The idea of thanking staff should mean giving them something that they would never buy for themselves.

~ JAYNE CROOK

A mother's arms are more comforting than anyone else's.

~ DIANA, PRINCESS OF WALES

Things that are lovely
Can tear my heart in two—
Moonlight on still pools,
You.

~ DOROTHY DOW

No matter what accomplishments you make, somebody helped you.

We are told that people stay in love because of chemistry, or because they remain intrigued with each other, because of many kindnesses, because of luck.... But part of it has got to be forgiveness and gratefulness.

~ ELLEN GOODMAN

Much misconstruction and bitterness are spared to him who thinks naturally upon what he owes to others, rather than on what he ought to expect from them.

~ ELIZABETH DE MEULAN GUIZOT

Parents, however old they and we may grow to be, serve among other things to shield us from a sense of our doom. As long as they are around, we can avoid the fact of our mortality; we can still be innocent children.

~ JANE HOWARD

One can never pay in gratitude; one can only pay "in kind" somewhere else in life.

~ ANNE MORROW LINDBERGH

An easygoing husband is the one indispensable comfort of life.

~ OUIDA

Silent gratitude isn't much use to anyone.

~ GLADYS BROWYN STERN

My father got me strong and straight and slim
And I give thanks to him.
My mother bore me glad and sound and sweet,
I kiss her feet.

~ MARGUERITE WILKINSON

Savor the Moment

Traveling is like flirting with life. It's like saying, "I would stay and love you, but I have to go; this is my station."

~ LISA ST. AUBIN DE TERAN

Normal day, let me be aware of the treasure you are. Let me learn from you, love you, bless you before you depart. Let me not pass you by in quest of some rare and perfect tomorrow. Let me hold you while I may, for it may not always be so.

~ MARY JEAN IRION

If, every day, I dare to remember that I am here on loan, that this house, this hillside, these minutes are all leased to me, not given, I will never despair.

~ ERICA JONG

Life isn't a matter of milestones, but of moments.

~ ROSE KENNEDY

The loneliness you get by the sea is personal and alive. It doesn't subdue you and make you feel abject. It's stimulating loneliness.

~ ANNE MORROW LINDBERGH

Death and taxes and childbirth! There's never any convenient time for any of them!

~ MARGARET MITCHELL

We inhabit ourselves without valuing ourselves, unable to see that here, now, this very moment is sacred; but once it's gone—its value is incontestable.

~ JOYCE CAROL OATES

My expectations—which I extended whenever I came close to accomplishing my goals—made it impossible to ever feel satisfied with my successes.

~ ELLEN SUE STERN

There has never been an age that did not applaud the past and lament the present.

~ LILLIAN EICHLER WATSON

The future is made of the same stuff as the present.

~ SIMONE WEIL

$\mathcal{H}$elping Others

When We Help, We Show Compassion

Sympathy is the charm of human life.
  ⁓ GRACE AGUILAR

Kindness is the ability to love people more than they deserve.
  ⁓ ANON.

A little help is worth a great deal of pity.
  ⁓ ANON.

I see their souls, and I hold them in my hands, and because I love them they weigh nothing.
  ⁓ PEARL BAILEY

One's life has value so long as one attributes value to the life of others, by means of love, friendship, indignation, and compassion.
  ⁓ SIMONE DE BEAUVOIR

It is not until you become a mother that your judgment slowly turns to compassion and understanding.
  ⁓ ERMA BOMBECK

I'd like people to think of me as someone who cares about them.
~ DIANA, PRINCESS OF WALES

Tenderness is greater proof of love than the most passionate of vows.
~ MARLENE DIETRICH

One of the most valuable things we can do to heal one another is listen to each other's stories.
~ REBECCA FALLS

Kindness consists in loving people more than they deserve.
~ JACQUELINE SCHIFF

It's a rare thing, graciousness. The shape of it can be acquired, but not, I think, the substance.
~ GERTRUDE SCHWEITZER

There are times when sympathy is as necessary as the air we breathe.
~ ROSE PASTOR STOKES

Kindness causes us to learn, and to forget, many things.
~ ANNE-SOPHIE SWETCHINE

As a woman I have no country. My country is the whole world.
~ VIRGINIA WOOLF

Help, But Don't Intrude

Don't give advice unless you're asked.
~ AMY ALCOTT

Listen long enough and the person will generally come up with an adequate solution.
~ MARY KAY ASH

Never help a child with a task at which he feels he can succeed.
~ MARIA MONTESSORI

We want to create an atmosphere in which creation is possible.

~ MARIE RAMBERT

We Help When We Set a Good Example

If you can't be a good example, then you'll just have to be a horrible warning.

~ CATHERINE AIRD

Children have more need of models than of critics.

~ CAROLYN COATS

My playground was the theatre. I'd sit and watch my mother pretend for a living. As a young girl, that's pretty seductive.

~ GWYNETH PALTROW

We deceive ourselves when we fancy that only weakness needs support. Strength needs it far more.

~ ANNE-SOPHIE SWETCHINE

What you teach your own children is what you really believe in.

~ CATHY WARNER WEATHERFORD

Helping Is Selfless

In real love you want the other person's good.

~ MARGARET ANDERSON

It is only in the giving of oneself to others that we truly live.

~ ETHEL PERCY ANDRUS

You cannot always have happiness, but you can always give happiness.

~ ANON.

Spiritual love is a position of standing with one hand extended into the universe and one hand extended into the world, letting ourselves be a conduit for passing energy.

~ CHRISTINA BALDWIN

One cannot make oneself, but one can sometimes help a little in the making of somebody else.

~ DINAH MARIA MULOCK CRAIK

Never reach out your hand unless you're willing to extend an arm.

~ ELIZABETH FULLER

Giving presents is a talent; to know what a person wants, to know when and how to get it, to give it lovingly and well.

~ PAMELA GLENCONNER

Love is a choice—not simply, or necessarily, a rational choice, but rather a willingness to be present to others without pretense or guile.

~ CARTER HEYWARD

My happiness derives from knowing the people I love are happy.

~ HOLLY KETCHEL

I wish that every child could have growing space because I think children are a little like plants. If they grow too close together, they become thin and sickly and never obtain maximum growth. We need room to grow.

~ PEACE PILGRIM

You have not lived a perfect day ... unless you have done something for someone who will never be able to repay you.

~ RUTH SMELTZER

Helping Others Helps Us Grow

Such to me is the new image of aging; growth in self, and service for all mankind.

~ ETHEL PERCY ANDRUS

What I spent, is gone; what I kept, I lost;
but what I gave away will be mine forever.

~ ETHEL PERCY ANDRUS

In helping others, we shall help ourselves, for whatever good we give out completes the circle and comes back to us.

~ FLORA EDWARDS

We challenge one another to be funnier and smarter.... It's the way friends make love to one another.

~ ANNIE GOTTLIEB

There is nothing to make you like other human beings so much as doing things for them.

~ ZORA NEALE HURSTON

The comforter's head never aches.

~ ITALIAN PROVERB

The true way to soften one's troubles is to solace those of others.

~ FRANCOISE D'AUBIGNE DE MAINTENON

Happiness is a byproduct of an effort to make someone else happy.

~ GRETTA BROOKER PALMER

Giving opens the way for receiving.

~ FLORENCE SCOVEL SHINN

Fill the cup of happiness for others, and there will be enough overflowing to fill yours to the brim.

~ ROSE PASTOR STOKES

Nothing liberates our greatness like the desire to help, the desire to serve.

~ MARIANNE WILLIAMSON

Life Is about Caring for Others

In a great romance, each person plays a part the other really likes.

~ ELIZABETH ASHLEY

If I can stop one heart from breaking,
I shall not live in vain;
If I can ease one life the aching,
Or cool one pain,
Or help one fainting robin
Unto his nest again,
I shall not live in vain.

~ EMILY DICKINSON

Follow your interests, get the best available education and training, set your sights high, be persistent, be flexible, keep your options open, accept help when offered, and be prepared to help others.

~ MILDRED SPIEWAK DRESSELHAUS

The legacy I want to leave is a child-care system that says no kid is going to be left alone or left unsafe.

~ MARIAN WRIGHT EDELMAN

We've got to work to save our children and do it with full respect for the fact that if we do not, no one else is going to do it.

~ DOROTHY HEIGHT

A happy life is made up of little things—a gift sent, a letter written, a call made, a recommendation given, transportation provided, a cake made, a book lent, a check sent.

~ CAROL HOLMES

A favor to come is better than a hundred received.

⌒ ITALIAN PROVERB

Believe, when you are most unhappy, that there is something for you to do in the world. So long as you can sweeten another's pain, life is not in vain.

⌒ HELEN KELLER

No one has ever loved anyone the way everyone wants to be loved.

⌒ MIGNON MCLAUGHLIN

If I didn't start painting, I would have raised chickens.

⌒ GRANDMA MOSES

Oh! may each youthful bosom, catch the sacred fire.

⌒ ANN PLATO

When you cease to make a contribution, you begin to die.

⌒ ELEANOR ROOSEVELT

We bear the world and we make it.... There was never a great man who had not a great mother—it is hardly an exaggeration.

⌒ OLIVE SCHREINER

We want to create hope for the person.... We must give hope, always hope.

⌒ MOTHER TERESA

Miss no single opportunity of making some small sacrifice, here by a smiling look, there by a kindly word; always doing the smallest right and doing it all for love.

⌒ THÉRÈSE OF LISIEUX

After the verb "to Love," "to Help" is the most beautiful verb in the world.

⌒ BERTHA VON SUTTNER

We Help by Teaching

Instead of getting hard ourselves and trying to compete, women should try to give their best qualities to men—bring them softness, teach them how to cry.

~ JOAN BAEZ

If a child is too keep alive his inborn sense of wonder … he needs the companionship of at least one adult who can share it, rediscovering with him the joy, excitement, and mystery of the world we live in.

~ RACHEL CARSON

We ought to be doing all we can to make it possible for every child to fulfill his or her God-given potential.

~ HILLARY RODHAM CLINTON

You cannot create genius. All you can do is nurture it.

~ NINETTE DE VALOIS

Most convicted felons are just people who were not taken to museums or Broadway musicals as children.

~ LIBBY GELMAN-WAXNER

No one has yet realized the wealth of sympathy, the kindness and generosity hidden in the soul of a child. The effort of every true education should be to unlock that treasure.

~ EMMA GOLDMAN

I'm not an American hero. I'm a person who loves children.

~ CLARA MCBRIDE HALE

The greatest gift is the passion for reading. It is cheap, it consoles, it distracts, it excites, it gives you knowledge of the world and experience of a wide kind. It is a moral illumination.

~ ELIZABETH HARDWICK

Giving kids clothes and food is one thing, but it's much more important to teach them that other people besides themselves are important and that the best thing they can do with their lives is to use them in the service of other people.

~ DOLORES HUERTA

What its children become, that will the community become.

~ SUZANNE LAFOLLETTE

A child is fed with milk and praise.

~ MARY LAMB

Children are forced to live very rapidly in order to live at all. They are given only a few years in which to learn hundreds of thousands of things about life and the planet and themselves.

~ PHYLLIS MCGINLEY

Establishing lasting peace is the work of education; all politics can do is keep us out of war.

~ MARIA MONTESSORI

The greatness of the human personality begins at the hour of birth. From this almost mystic affirmation there comes what may seem a strange conclusion: that education must start from birth.

~ MARIA MONTESSORI

What we remember from childhood we remember forever— permanent ghosts, stamped, imprinted, eternally seen.

~ CYNTHIA OZICK

I don't believe civilization can do a lot more than educate a person's senses.

~ GRACE PALEY

I was a fantastic student until ten, and then my mind began to wander.

~ GRACE PALEY

If you feed a man a meal, you only feed him for a day—but if you teach a man to grow food, you feed him for a lifetime.

~ PEACE PILGRIM

A good education is that which prepares us for our future sphere of action and makes us contented with that situation in life in which God, in his infinite mercy, has seen fit to place us, to be perfectly resigned to our lot in life, whatever it may be.

~ ANN PLATO

A good education is another name for happiness.

~ ANN PLATO

To remove ignorance is an important branch of benevolence.

~ ANN PLATO

Teaching was the hardest work I had ever done, and it remains the hardest work I have done to date.

~ ANN RICHARDS

To me education is a leading out of what is already there in the pupil's soul.

~ MURIEL SPARK

To throw obstacles in the way of a complete education is like putting out the eyes.

~ ELIZABETH CADY STANTON

No other job in the world could possibly dispossess one so completely as this job of teaching. You could stand all day in a laundry, for instance, still in possession of your mind. But this teaching utterly obliterates you. It cuts right into your being: essentially, it takes over your spirit.

~ SYLVIA ASHTON WARNER

The truth is that I am enslaved ... in one vast love affair with seventy children.

~ SYLVIA ASHTON WARNER

When I teach people, I marry them.

~ SYLVIA ASHTON WARNER

It made me gladsome to be getting some education, it being like a big window opening.

~ MARY WEBB

Teaching is the royal road to learning.

~ JESSAMYN WEST

Teaching was the best way to learn.

~ EDNA GARDNER WHYTE

Teaching is the greatest act of optimism.

~ COLLEEN WILCOX

I think education is power. I think that being able to communicate with people is power. One of my main goals on the planet is to encourage people to empower themselves.

~ OPRAH WINFREY

Helping Creates Lasting Bonds

Sons branch out, but one woman leads to another.

~ MARGARET ATWOOD

It's really important that, as women, we tell our stories. That is what helps seed our imaginations.

~ ANN BANCROFT

Female friendships that work are relationships in which women help each other belong to themselves.

~ LOUISE BERNIKOW

Helping Our Families

You leave home to seek your fortune and, when you get it, you go home and share it with your family.

~ ANITA BAKER

My heart is happy, my mind is free.
I had a father who talked with me.

~ HILDE BIGELOW

It is not until you become a mother that your judgment slowly turns to compassion and understanding.

~ ERMA BOMBECK

If a child is too keep alive his inborn sense of wonder ... he needs the companionship of at least one adult who can share it, rediscovering with him the joy, excitement, and mystery of the world we live in.

~ RACHEL CARSON

Discipline is a symbol of caring to a child. He needs guidance. If there is love, there is no such thing as being too tough with a child.

~ BETTE DAVIS

A mother is not a person to lean on but a person to make leaning unnecessary.

~ DOROTHY CANFIELD FISHER

To nourish children and raise them against odds is in any time, any place, more valuable than to fix bolts in cars or design nuclear weapons.

~ MARILYN FRENCH

A wise parent humors the desire for independent action, so as to become the friend and advisor when his absolute rule shall cease.

~ ELIZABETH GASKELL

Parenting, at its best, comes as naturally as laughter. It is automatic, involuntary, unconditional love.

~ SALLY JAMES

I looked on child rearing not only as a work of love and duty but as a profession that was fully as interesting and challenging as any honorable profession in the world and one that demanded the best I could bring to it.

~ ROSE KENNEDY

Do not, on a rainy day, ask your child what he feels like doing, because I assure you that what he feels like doing, you won't feel like watching.

~ FRAN LEBOWITZ

Every child has a right to a good home.

~ ETTIE LEE

If you bungle raising your children, I don't think whatever else you do matters very much.

~ JACQUELINE KENNEDY ONASSIS

A busy mother makes slothful daughters.

~ PORTUGUESE PROVERB

There are four things a child needs: plenty of love, nourishing food, regular sleep, and lots of soap and water.

~ IVY BAKER PRIEST

Examine the personality of the mother, who is the medium through which the primitive infant transforms herself into a socialized human being.

~ BEATA RANK

When their children flourish, almost all mothers have a sense of well-being.

~ SARA RUDDICK

Don't forget that compared to a grownup person every baby is a genius. Think of the capacity to learn! The freshness, the temperament, the will of a baby a few months old!

~ MAY SARTON

No matter how old a mother is, she watches her middle-aged children for signs of improvement.

~ FLORIDA SCOTT-MAXWELL

Making a decision to have a child—it's momentous. It is to decide forever to have your heart go walking around outside your body.

~ ELIZABETH STONE

We worry about what a child will be tomorrow, yet we forget that he is someone today.

~ STACIA TAUSCHER

Let our children grow tall, and some taller than others if they have it in them to do so.

~ MARGARET THATCHER

We Help When We Liberate

As long as you keep a person down, some part of you has to be down there to hold him down, so it means you cannot soar as you otherwise might.

~ MARIAN ANDERSON

When you dig another out of their troubles, you find a place to bury your own.

~ ANON.

When God made up this world of ours,
He made it long and wide,
And meant that it should shelter all,
And none should be denied.

~ CARRIE JACOBS BOND

When anything gets freed, a zest goes round the world.

~ HORTENSE CALISHER

If we can't turn the world around we can at least bolster the victims.

~ LIZ CARPENTER

Let our girls feel that we expect something more of them than that they merely look pretty and appear well in society. Teach them that there is a race with special needs which they and only they can help; that the world needs and is already asking for their trained and efficient forces.

~ ANNA JULIA COOPER

I've always thought that people need to feel good about themselves and I see my role as offering support to them, to provide some light along the way.

~ DIANA, PRINCESS OF WALES

The finest inheritance you can give a child is to allow it to make its own way, completely on its own feet.

~ ISADORA DUNCAN

A child is a temporarily disabled and stunted version of a larger person, whom you will someday know. Your job is to help them overcome the disabilities associated with their size and inexperience so that they get on with being that larger person.

~ BARBARA EHRENREICH

We have to improve life, not just for those who have the most skills and those who know how to manipulate the system. But also for and with those who often have so much to give but never get the opportunity.

~ DOROTHY HEIGHT

The most notable fact that culture imprints on women is the sense of our limits. The most important thing one woman can do for another is to illuminate and expand her sense of actual possibilities.

~ ADRIENNE RICH

First, teach a person to develop to the point of his limitations and then—pfft!—break the limitations.

 ⁓ VIOLA SPOLIN

If you want a baby, have a new one. Don't baby the old one.

 ⁓ JESSAMYN WEST

Embracing Your True Friends

Our Friends Are Always There for Us

That's the risk you take if you change: that people you've been involved with won't like the new you. But other people who do will come along.

~ LISA ALTHER

The rich woman knows not who is her friend.

~ ANON.

Friendship has splendors that love knows not. It grows stronger when crossed, whereas obstacles kill love. Friendship resists time, which wearies and severs couples. It has heights unknown to love.

~ MARIAMA BÂ

True friends are those who really know you but love you anyway.

~ EDNA BUCHANAN

A friend is someone you can be alone with and have nothing to do and not be able to think of anything to say and be comfortable in the silence.

~ SHERYL CONDIE

Oh, the comfort, the inexpressible comfort of feeling safe with a person, having neither to weigh thoughts nor measure words, but pouring them all out, just as they are, chaff and grain together, certain that a faithful hand will take and sift them, keep what is worth keeping, and with a breath of kindness blow the rest away.
~ DINAH MARIA MULOCK CRAIK

It's the friends you can call up at 4:00 a.m. that matter.
~ MARLENE DIETRICH

Perhaps the most delightful friendships are those in which there is much agreement, much disputation, and yet more personal liking.
~ GEORGE ELIOT

The most beautiful discovery true friends make is that they can grow separately without growing apart.
~ ELIZABETH FOLEY

Trouble is a sieve through which we sift our acquaintances. Those too big to pass through are our friends.
~ ARLENE FRANCIS

In times of difficulty, friendship is on trial.
~ GREEK PROVERB

It is better in times of need to have a friend rather than money.
~ GREEK PROVERB

I have come to esteem history as a component of friendships. In my case at least friendships are not igneous but sedimentary.
~ JANE HOWARD

The growth of true friendship may be a lifelong affair.
~ SARAH ORNE JEWETT

Constant use had not worn ragged the fabric of their friendship.
~ DOROTHY PARKER

Even where the affections are not strongly moved by any superior excellence, the companions of our childhood always possess a certain power over our minds which hardly any later friend can obtain.

~ MARY SHELLEY

Friends and wine should be old.

~ SPANISH PROVERB

There's no friend like someone who has known you since you were five.

~ ANNE STEVENSON

Satan's friendship reaches to the prison door.

~ TURKISH PROVERB

Lots of people want to ride with you in the limo, but what you want is someone who will take the bus with you when the limo breaks down.

~ OPRAH WINFREY

I have lost friends, some by death ... others by sheer inability to cross the street.

~ VIRGINIA WOOLF

Friends Come in All Shapes and Sizes

Nature has been for me, for as long as I remember, a source of solace, inspiration, adventure, and delight; a home, a teacher, a companion.

~ LORRAINE ANDERSON

A friend is never known until a woman has a need.

~ ANON.

Love your friend with her faults.

~ ANON.

Writers seldom choose as friends those self-contained characters who are never in trouble, never unhappy or ill, never make mistakes, and always count their change when it is handed to them.

~ CATHERINE DRINKER BOWEN

However deep our devotion may be to parents or to children, it is our contemporaries alone with whom understanding is instinctive and entire.

~ VERA BRITTAIN

Yes'm, old friends is always best, 'less you can catch a new one that's fit to make an old one out of.

~ SARAH ORNE JEWETT

My friends have made the story of my life. In a thousand ways they have turned my limitations into beautiful privileges, and enabled me to walk serene and happy in the shadow cast by my deprivation.

~ HELEN KELLER

I am treating you as my friend, asking you to share my present minuses in the hope I can ask you to share my future plans.

~ KATHERINE MANSFIELD

I always feel that the great high privilege, relief, and comfort of friendship was that one had to explain nothing.

~ KATHERINE MANSFIELD

Friendship is mutual blackmail elevated to the level of love.

~ ROBIN MORGAN

I cannot concentrate all my friendship on any single one of my friends because no one is complete enough in himself.

~ ANAÏS NIN

We need old friends to help us grow old and new friends to help us stay young.

~ LETTY COTTIN POGREBIN

She who seeks a faultless friend remains friendless.

~ TURKISH PROVERB

Our Relationships Are What Matter Most

A true friend is the best possession.

       ~ ANON.

The company makes the feast.

       ~ ANON.

Four be the things I am wisest to know: idleness, sorrow, a friend and a foe.

       ~ ANON.

Pioneers may be picturesque figures, but they are often rather lonely ones.

       ~ NANCY ASTOR

Friends are the thermometer by which we may judge the temperature of our fortunes.

       ~ LADY MARGUERITE BLESSINGTON

And we find at the end of a perfect day,
The soul of a friend we've made.

       ~ CARRIE JACOBS BOND

Love is like the wild-rose briar;
Friendship is like the holly-tree.
The holly is dark when the rose briar blooms,
But which will bloom most constantly?

       ~ EMILY BRONTË

If you want an accounting of your worth, count your friends.

       ~ MERRY BROWNE

The great difference between voyages rests not in ships but in the people you meet on them.

       ~ AMELIA BURR

Only solitary men know the full joys of friendship. Others have their family; but to a solitary and an exile his friends are everything.

~ WILLA CATHER

My friends are my estate.

~ EMILY DICKINSON

My only sketch, profile, of heaven is a large blue sky, and larger than the biggest I have seen in June—and in it are my friends—every one of them.

~ EMILY DICKINSON

It is better in times of need to have a friend rather than money.

~ GREEK PROVERB

If I don't have friends, then I ain't nothing.

~ BILLIE HOLIDAY

It seems to me that trying to live without friends is like milking a bear to get cream for your morning coffee. It is a whole lot of trouble, and then not worth much after you get it.

~ ZORA NEALE HURSTON

If you have a good name, if you are right more often than you are wrong, if your children respect you, if your grandchildren are glad to see you, if your friends can count on you and you can count on them in time of trouble, if you can face your God and say "I have done my best," then you are a success.

~ ANN LANDERS

The richer your friends, the more they will cost you.

~ ELIZABETH MARBURY

Friendship is the bread of the heart.

~ MARY RUSSELL MITFORD

Today a man discovered gold and fame,
Another flew the stormy seas;
Another set an unarmed world aflame,
One found the germ of a disease.
But what high fates my path attend
for I—today—I found a friend.

～ HELEN BARKER PARKER

Though Love be deeper, Friendship is more wide.

～ CORINNE ROOSEVELT ROBINSON

Life without a friend is death without a witness.

～ SPANISH PROVERB

Loneliness is a terrible blindness.

～ CHRISTINA STEAD

Loneliness is the most terrible poverty.

～ MOTHER TERESA

Success ... depends on your ability to make and keep friends.

～ SOPHIE TUCKER

That is the best—to laugh with someone because you think the
same things are funny.

～ GLORIA VANDERBILT

Friendships Require Effort

To have a good friend is one of the highest delights of life; to be a
good friend is one of the noblest and most difficult undertakings.

～ ANON.

Friendship is a plant which must be often watered.

～ ANON.

You can make more friends in two months by becoming more interested in other people than you can in two years by trying to get people interested in you.

~ ANON.

The best rule of friendship is to keep your heart a little softer than your head.

~ ANON.

The easiest kind of relationship for me is with ten thousand people. The hardest is with one.

~ JOAN BAEZ

It takes a lot of courage to show your dreams to someone else.

~ ERMA BOMBECK

Intimacies between women often go backwards, beginning in revelations and ending in small talk.

~ ELIZABETH BOWEN

It is easier to forgive an enemy than it is a friend.

~ MADAME DOROTHEE DELUZY

To act the part of a true friend requires more conscientious feeling than to fill with credit and complacency any other station or capacity in social life.

~ SARAH ELLIS

Friends are lost by calling often and calling seldom.

~ FRENCH PROVERB

How desperately we wish to maintain our trust in those we love! In the face of everything, we try to find reasons to trust. Because losing faith is worse than falling out of love.

~ SONIA JOHNSON

Friendship is an art, and very few persons are born with a natural gift for it.

~ KATHLEEN NORRIS

We all need somebody to talk to. It would be good if we talked ...
not just pitter-patter, but real talk. We shouldn't be so afraid, because
most people really like this contact; that you show you are vulnerable
makes them free to be vulnerable.

~ LIV ULLMANN

Our Friends Help Us Grow

The best mirror is an old friend.

~ ANON.

A real friend helps us think our best thoughts, do our noblest deeds,
be our finest selves.

~ ANON.

O lovely Sisters! is it true
That they are all inspired by you,
And write by inward magic charm'd,
And high enthusiasm warm'd?

~ JOANNA BAILLIE

Female friendships that work are relationships in which women help
each other belong to themselves.

~ LOUISE BERNIKOW

I can trust my friends.... These people force me to examine myself,
encourage me to grow.

~ CHER

Tell me who you frequent, and I will tell you who you are.

~ FRENCH PROVERB

If I made it, it's half because I was game enough to take a lot of
punishment along the way and half because there were a lot of
people who cared enough to help me.

~ ALTHEA GIBSON

We challenge one another to be funnier and smarter.... It's the way friends make love to one another.

~ ANNIE GOTTLIEB

The support of one's personality is friends.

~ KATHERINE HATHAWAY

Each friend represents a world in us, a world possibly not born until they arrive, and it is only by this meeting that a new world is born.

~ ANAÏS NIN

In a friend you find a second self.

~ ISABELLE NORTO

My philosophy is: anyone or anything that gives you knowledge inspires you.

~ GABRIELLE REECE

The particular human chain we're a part of is central to our individual identity.

~ ELIZABETH STONE

No person is your friend who demands your silence, or denies your right to grow.

~ ALICE WALKER

A friend can tell you things you don't want to tell yourself.

~ FRANCES WARD WELLER

I suppose there is one friend in the life of each of us who seems not a separate person, however dear and beloved, but an expansion, an interpretation, of one's self.

~ EDITH WHARTON

We Must Not Take Our Friends for Granted

Friendship increases in visiting friends, but not in visiting them too often.
~ ANON.

A hedge between keeps friendships green.
~ ANON.

It isn't easy to be the person who sometimes has to try to preserve your happiness at the expense of your fun.
~ MARGARET CULKIN BANNING

The best time to make friends is before you need them.
~ ETHEL BARRYMORE

If we would build on a sure foundation in friendship, we must love friends for their sake rather than for our own.
~ CHARLOTTE BRONTË

It is easier to visit friends than to live with them.
~ CHINESE PROVERB

Treat your friends as you do your picture, and place them in their best light.
~ JENNIE JEROME CHURCHILL

The only way not to break a friendship is not to drop it.
~ JULIE HOLZ

Friendship is a furrow in the sand.
~ TONGAN PROVERB

None is so rich as to throw away a friend.
~ TURKISH PROVERB

We flatter those we scarcely know,
We please the fleeting guest,
And deal full many a thoughtless blow
To those who love us best.

~ ELLA WHEELER WILCOX

We Must Not Jeopardize Our Friendships

If we were all given by magic the power to read each other's
thoughts, I suppose the first effect would be to dissolve all friendships.

~ ANON.

When good cheer is lacking, our friends will be packing.

~ ANON.

Friends come and go, enemies linger.

~ ANON.

It is better not to say "lend." There is only giving.

~ PEARL S. BUCK

Friendship, which is of its nature a delicate thing, fastidious, slow of
growth, is easily checked, will hesitate, demur, recoil where love, good
old blustering love, bowls ahead and blunders through every obstacle.

~ COLETTE

True friendship is never serene.

~ MARIE DE RABUTIN-CHANTAL

The hearts that never lean must fall.

~ EMILY DICKINSON

Friends are lost by calling often and calling seldom.

~ FRENCH PROVERB

The days are too short even for love; how can there be enough time for quarreling?

~ MARGARET GATTY

They never raised a statue to a critic.

~ MARTHA GRAHAM

A friend is one who withholds judgment no matter how long you have his unanswered letter.

~ SOPHIE IRENE LOEB

It's important to our friends to believe that we are unreservedly frank with them, and important to our friendship that we are not.

~ MIGNON MCLAUGHLIN

My friend and I have built a wall
Between us thick and wide:
The stones of it are laid in scorn
And plastered high with pride.

~ ELIZABETH CUTTER MORROW

Hold a true friend with both your hands.

~ NIGERIAN PROVERB

You can keep your friends by not giving them away.

~ MARY PETTIBONE POOLE

There Is Nothing More Precious Than a Friend

One enemy is too many; a hundred friends too few.

~ ANON.

Have but few friends, though many acquaintances.

~ ANON.

Books and friends should be few but good.

~ ANON.

Between flattery and admiration there often flows a river of contempt.

~ MINNA ANTRIM

Friendship's a noble name, 'tis love refined.

~ SUSANNAH CENTLIVRE

One is taught by experience to put a premium on those few people who can appreciate you for what you are.

~ GAIL GODWIN

To those who know thee not, no words can paint! And those who know thee, know all words are faint!

~ HANNAH MOORE

A friend is like a poem.

~ PERSIAN PROVERB

You are my lover and I am your mistress and kingdoms and empires and governments have tottered and succumbed before now to that mighty combination.

~ VIOLET TREFUSIS

In meeting again after a separation, acquaintances ask after our outward life, friends after our inner life.

~ MARIE VON EBNER-ESCHENBACH

That's What Friends Are For

The nice thing about teamwork is that you always have others on your side.

~ MARGARET CARTY

Do not protect yourself by a fence, but rather by your friends.

~ CZECH PROVERB

In real friendship the judgment, the genius, the prudence of each party become the common property of both.

~ MARIA EDGEWORTH

A friend in need is a friend indeed.

~ SUSAN FERRIER

Women's propensity to share confidences is universal. We confirm our reality by sharing.

~ BARBARA GRIZZUTI HARRISON

There is nothing better than the encouragement of a good friend.

~ KATHERINE HATHAWAY

Love me, please, I love you; I can bear to be your friend. So ask of me anything.... I am not a tentative person. Whatever I do, I give up my whole self to it.

~ EDNA ST. VINCENT MILLAY

Women rely on friends.... That's where we draw sustenance and find safety. We can count on our women friends when we need a good laugh or a good cry.

~ COKIE ROBERTS

Those who conceal their grief find no remedy for it.

~ TURKISH PROVERB

It's the folks that depend on us for this and for the other that we most do miss.

~ MARY WEBB

Friendship ought to be a gratuitous joy, like the joys afforded by art.

~ SIMONE WEIL

The people you need to help you make your dream come true are everywhere, and within your reach.

~ MARCIA WIEDER

Friends Make Life Bearable

There is no physician like a true friend.
　　　　　∽ ANON.

The smartest thing I ever said was "Help me."
　　　　　∽ ANON.

Good company upon the road is the shortest cut.
　　　　　∽ ANON.

But I have certainty enough,
For I am sure of you.
　　　　　∽ AMELIA BURR

Best friend, my well-spring in the wilderness!
　　　　　∽ GEORGE ELIOT

Plant a seed of friendship; reap a bouquet of happiness.
　　　　　∽ LOIS L. KAUFMAN

Our happiness in this world depends on the affections we are able to inspire.
　　　　　∽ DUCHESS PRAZLIN

It is good to have friends, even in hell.
　　　　　∽ SPANISH PROVERB

No route is long with good company.
　　　　　∽ TURKISH PROVERB

Some people go to priests; others to poetry; I to my friends.
　　　　　∽ VIRGINIA WOOLF

Family Members Are Often Our Best Friends

My heart is happy, my mind is free.
I had a father who talked with me.

               ~ HILDE BIGELOW

The family. We are a strange little band of characters trudging
through life sharing diseases and toothpaste, coveting one another's
desserts, hiding shampoo, locking each other out of our rooms,
inflicting pain and kissing to heal it in the same instant, loving,
laughing, defending, and trying to figure out the common thread
that bound us all together.

               ~ ERMA BOMBECK

You hear a lot of dialogue on the death of the American family.
Families aren't dying. They're merging into big conglomerates.

               ~ ERMA BOMBECK

Kind words smooth all the "Paths o' Life"
And smiles make burdens light,
And uncomplainin' friends can make
A daytime out o' night.

               ~ CARRIE JACOBS BOND

If ever two were one, then surely we. If ever man were loved by
wife, then thee.

               ~ ANNE BRADSTREET

Friends are the family we choose for ourselves.

               ~ EDNA BUCHANAN

I think togetherness is a very important ingredient to family life. It's
a cliche and we use it too much but I think for a husband and wife,
the way to stay close is to do things together and share.

               ~ BARBARA BUSH

Jimmy and I were always partners.

               ~ ROSALYNN CARTER

He [Winston Churchill] has a future and I have a past, so we should be all right.

~ JENNIE JEROME CHURCHILL

Parents are friends that life gives us; friends are parents that the heart chooses.

~ COMTESSE DIANE

[My father] was generous with his affection, given to great, awkward, engulfing hugs, and I can remember so clearly the smell of his hugs, all starched shirt, tobacco, Old Spice, and Cutty Sark. Sometimes I think I've never been properly hugged since.

~ LINDA ELLERBEE

Both within the family and without, our sisters hold up our mirrors: our images of who we are and of who we can dare to become.

~ ELIZABETH FISHEL

Sisters define their rivalry in terms of competition for the gold cup of parental love. It is never perceived as a cup which runneth over, rather a finite vessel from which the more one sister drinks, the less is left over for the others.

~ ELIZABETH FISHEL

The desire to be and have a sister is a primitive and profound one that may have everything or nothing to do with the family a woman is born to. It is a desire to know and be known by someone who shares blood and body, history and dreams.

~ ELIZABETH FISHEL

Where there is lasting love, there is a family.

~ SHERE HITE

Call it a clan, call it a network, call it a tribe, call it a family: Whatever you call it, whoever you are, you need one.

~ JANE HOWARD

God gave us our relatives; thank God we can choose our friends.

~ ETHEL WATTS MUMFORD

Old as she was, she still missed her daddy sometimes.

~ GLORIA NAYLOR

A good marriage is at least 80 percent good luck in finding the right person at the right time. The rest is trust.

~ NANETTE NEWMAN

[Families] are made to make you forget yourself occasionally, so that the beautiful balance of life is not destroyed.

~ ANAÏS NIN

The family unit plays a critical role in our society and in the training of the generation to come.

~ SANDRA DAY O'CONNOR

Families will not be broken. Curse and expel them, send their children wandering, drown them in floods and fires, and old women will make songs of all these sorrows and sit in the porches and sing them on mild evenings.

~ MARILYNNE ROBINSON

The family is the building block for whatever solidarity there is in society.

~ JILL RUCKELSHAUS

Who ran to help me when I fell
And would some pretty story tell
Or kiss the place to make it well?
My mother.

~ JANE TAYLOR

Is solace anywhere more comforting than in the arms of sisters?

~ ALICE WALKER

All love that has not friendship for its base,
Is like a mansion built upon the sand.

~ ELLA WHEELER WILCOX

Caring for Your Soul

Love and Faith Are the Most Important Things

Without faith, nothing is possible. With it, nothing is impossible.
~ MARY MCLEOD BETHUNE

Happiness is a rare plant that seldom takes root on earth—few ever enjoyed it, except for a brief period; the search after it is rarely rewarded by the discovery, but there is an admirable substitute for it … a contented spirit.
~ LADY MARGUERITE BLESSINGTON

I can't see (or feel) the conflict between love and religion. To me, they're the same thing.
~ ELIZABETH BOWEN

I believe that a worthwhile life is defined by a kind of spiritual journey and a sense of obligation.
~ HILLARY RODHAM CLINTON

Spirit is the real and eternal; matter is the unreal and the temporal.
~ MARY BAKER EDDY

Truth is immortal; error is mortal.

~ MARY BAKER EDDY

Every law of matter or the body, supposed to govern man, is rendered null and void by the law of Life, God.

~ MARY BAKER EDDY

The first condition of human goodness is something to love; the second, something to revere.

~ GEORGE ELIOT

The truth is that there is only one terminal dignity—love, and the story of a love is not important—what is important is that one is capable of love. It is perhaps the only glimpse we are permitted of eternity.

~ HELEN HAYES

Whether we name divine presence synchronicity, serendipity, or graced moment matters little. What matters is the reality that our hearts have been understood. Nothing is as real as a healthy dose of magic which restores our spirits.

~ NANCY LONG

I need nothing but God, and to lose myself in the heart of God.

~ SAINT MARGARET MARY ALACOQUE

The soul can split the sky in two, and let the face of God shine through.

~ EDNA ST. VINCENT MILLAY

You're not free until you've been made captive by supreme belief.

~ MARIANNE MOORE

To love one that is great, is almost to be great one's self.

~ MADAME NECKAR

That's the thing about faith. If you don't have it you can't understand it. And if you do, no explanation is necessary.

~ MAJOR KIRA NERYS

Kill reverence and you've killed the hero in man.
 ⌢ AYN RAND

Spiritual life is like a moving sidewalk. Whether you go with it or
spend your whole life running against it, you're still going to be
taken along.
 ⌢ BERNADETTE ROBERTS

Faith is the subtle chain which binds us to the infinite.
 ⌢ ELIZABETH O. SMITH

Faith is nothing at all tangible.... It is simply believing God; and like
sight, it is nothing apart from its object. You might as well shut your
eyes and look inside, and see whether you have sight, as to look
inside to discover whether you have faith.
 ⌢ HANNAH WHITALL SMITH

Faith and doubt are both needed—not as antagonists but working
side by side—to take us around the unknown curve.
 ⌢ LILLIAN SMITH

Spirituality leaps where science cannot yet follow, because science
must always test and measure, and much of reality and human
experience is immeasurable.
 ⌢ STARHAWK

The best thing must be to flee from all to the All.
 ⌢ TERESA OF AVILA

Holy church—that mother who is also a queen because she is a
king's bride.
 ⌢ TERESA OF AVILA

I believe devoutly in the Word. The Word can save all, destroy all,
stop the inevitable, and express the inexpressible.
 ⌢ NINA VORONEL

Our Faith Will Carry Us Through

Prayer begins where human capacity ends.

~ MARIAN ANDERSON

Prayer changes things.

~ ANON.

Security is not the absence of danger, but the presence of God, no matter what the danger.

~ ANON.

I plunged into the job of creating something from nothing.... Though I hadn't a penny left, I considered cash money as the smallest part of my resources. I had faith in a living God, faith in myself, and a desire to serve.

~ MARY MCLEOD BETHUNE

A red-hot belief in eternal glory is probably the best antidote to human panic that there is.

~ PHYLLIS BOTTOME

I see not a step before me as I tread on another year;
But I've left the Past in God's keeping, the Future
His mercy shall clear;
And what looks dark in the distance may brighten as I draw near.

~ MARY GARDINER BRAINARD

I would rather walk with God in the dark than go alone in the light.

~ MARY GARDINER BRAINARD

Our body is not made of iron. Our strength is not that of stone. Live and hope in the Lord, and let your service be according to reason.

~ SAINT CLARE OF ASSISI

What allows us, as human beings, to psychologically survive life on earth, with all of its pain, drama, and challenges, is a sense of purpose and meaning.

~ BARBARA DE ANGELIS

Divine love always has met and always will meet every human need.

~ MARY BAKER EDDY

God is incorporeal, divine, supreme, infinite. Mind, Spirit, Soul, Principle, Life, Truth, Love.

~ MARY BAKER EDDY

Boys, this is only a game. But it's like life in that you will be dealt some bad hands. Take each hand, good or bad, and don't whine and complain, but play it out. If you're men enough to do that, God will help you and you will come out well.

~ IDA EISENHOWER

If I saw the gates of hell open and I stood on the brink of the abyss, I would not despair, I would not lose hope of mercy, because I would trust in You, my God.

~ GEMMA GALGANI

For the truly faithful, no miracle is necessary. For those who doubt, no miracle is sufficient.

~ NANCY GIBBS

My faith has wavered but has saved me.

~ HELEN HAYES

God tests His real friends more severely than the lukewarm ones.

~ KATHERINE HULME

There are no atheists on turbulent airplanes.

~ ERICA JONG

I believe in the immortality of the soul because I have within me immortal longings.

~ HELEN KELLER

A human being does not cease to exist at death. It is change, not destruction, which takes place.

~ FLORENCE NIGHTENGALE

If a door slams shut it means that God is pointing to an open door
further on down.

~ ANNA DELANEY PEALE

God will help you if you try, and you can if you think you can.

~ ANNA DELANEY PEALE

Impermanence is the law of the universe.

~ CARLENE HATCHER POLITE

You do build in darkness if you have faith. When the light returns,
you have made yourself a fortress which is impregnable to certain
kinds of trouble; you may even find yourself needed and sought by
others as a beacon in their dark.

~ OLGA ROSMANITH

Faith is an excitement and an enthusiasm, a state of intellectual
magnificence which we must not squander on our way through life.

~ GEORGE SAND

Out of the chill and the shadow,
Into the thrill and the shine;
Out of the dearth and the famine,
Into the fullness divine.

~ MARGARET ELIZABETH SANGSTER

The accidents of life separate us from our dearest friends, but let us
not despair. God is like a looking glass in which souls see each other.
The more we are united to Him by love, the nearer we are to those
who belong to Him.

~ ELIZABETH ANN SETON

Let nothing disturb thee,
Let nothing affright thee,
All things are passing,
God changeth never.

~ TERESA OF AVILA

It constantly happens that the Lord permits a soul to fall so that it may grow humbler.

～ TERESA OF AVILA

Life is to life in such a way that we are not afraid to die.

～ TERESA OF AVILA

Let nothing disturb you, nothing frighten you; all things are passing; God never changes.

～ TERESA OF AVILA

As to the aridity you are suffering from, it seems to me our Lord is treating you like someone He considers strong: He wants to test you and see if you love Him as much at times of aridity as when He sends you consolations. I think this is a very great favor for God to show you.

～ TERESA OF AVILA

Jesus makes the bitterest mouthful taste sweet.

～ THÉRÈSE OF LISIEUX

In the life of the spirit there is no ending that is not a beginning.

～ HENRIETTA ZOLDE

Faith Means Having Compassion and Respect

I knew without a glimmer of doubt that all things in the universe were connected by a living truth that would not relent its continuing search for wholeness until every form of life was united.

～ LYNN V. ANDREWS

By virtue of love is the lover transformed in the beloved and the beloved transformed in the lover.

～ SAINT ANGELA OF FOLIGNO

Spiritual love is a position of standing with one hand extended into the universe and one hand extended into the world, letting ourselves be a conduit for passing energy.

~ CHRISTINA BALDWIN

One's life has value so long as one attributes value to the life of others, by means of love, friendship, indignation and compassion.

~ SIMONE DE BEAUVOIR

Patience with others is Love, Patience with self is Hope, Patience with God is Faith.

~ ADEL BESTAVROS

God is universal; confined to no spot, defined by no dogma, appropriated by no sect.

~ MARY BAKER EDDY

To live and let live, without clamor for distinction or recognition; to wait on divine love; to write truth first on the tablet of one's own heart—this is the sanity and perfection of living, and my human ideal.

~ MARY BAKER EDDY

Who offends writes on sand; who is offended, on marble.

~ ITALIAN PROVERB

A person who believes ... that there is a whole of which one is a part, and that in being a part one is whole: such a person has no desire whatever, at any time, to play God. Only those who have denied their being yearn to play at it.

~ URSULA K. LE GUIN

Trying to do good to people without God's help is no easier than making the sun shine at midnight. You discover that you've got to abandon all your own preferences, your own bright ideas, and guide souls along the road our Lord has marked out for them. You mustn't coerce them into some path of your own choosing.

~ THÉRÈSE OF LISIEUX

Faith Is Selfless

We learn the inner secret of happiness when we learn to direct our inner drives, our interest, and our attention to something besides ourselves.

~ ETHEL PERCY ANDRUS

I never really look for anything. What God throws my way comes. I wake up in the morning and whichever way God turns my feet, I go.

~ PEARL BAILEY

In order to experience everyday spirituality, we need to remember that we are spiritual beings spending some time in a human body.

~ BARBARA DE ANGELIS

We must move from asking God to take care of the things that are breaking our hearts, to praying about the things that are breaking His heart.

~ MARGARET GIBB

No matter what accomplishments you make, somebody helped you.

~ ALTHEA GIBSON

Peace ... was contingent upon a certain disposition of the soul, a disposition to receive the gift that only detachment from self made possible.

~ ELIZABETH GOUDGE

You must never lose the awareness that in yourself you are nothing, you are only an instrument. An instrument is nothing until it is lifted.

~ KATHERINE HULME

It's very reassuring and spiritual to be connected with something larger than yourself and the inside of your own head.

~ JOAN OSBORNE

With all this wide and beautiful creation before me, the restless soul longs to enjoy its liberty and rest beyond its bound.

~ TERESA OF AVILA

God has not called me to be successful; he has called me to be faithful.

~ MOTHER TERESA

I do not pray for success. I ask for faithfulness.

~ MOTHER TERESA

The country in which I live is not my native country, that lies elsewhere, and it must always be the center of my longings.

~ THÉRÈSE OF LISIEUX

The great majority of men use their own short-sighted ideas as a yardstick for measuring the divine omnipotence.

~ THÉRÈSE OF LISIEUX

Faith is the centerpiece of a connected life. It allows us to live by the grace of invisible strands. It is a belief in a wisdom superior to our own. Faith becomes a teacher in the absence of fact.

~ TERRY TEMPEST WILLIAMS

Faith Requires Commitment

When the knees are not often bent, the feet do slide.

~ ANON.

He who cannot pray when the sun is shining will not know how to pray when the clouds come.

~ ANON.

I've been readen th Bible an a hunten God fer a long while—off an on—but it ain't so easy as picken up a nickel off the floor.

~ HARRIETTE ARNOW

The minds of people are so cluttered up with everyday living these days that they don't, or they won't, take time out for a little prayer— for mental cleansing, just as they take a bath for physical, outer cleansing. both are necessary.

~ JO ANN CARLSON

In prayer one must hold fast and never let go, because the one who gives up loses all. If it seems that no one is listening to you, then cry out even louder. If you are driven out of one door, go back in by the other.

~ JANE FRANCES DE CHANTAL

I pray hard, work hard, and leave the rest to God.

~ FLORENCE GRIFFITH JOYNER

It is for us to pray not for tasks equal to our powers, but for powers equal to our tasks, to go forward with a great desire forever beating at the door of our hearts as we travel towards our distant goal.

~ HELEN KELLER

Possessing faith is not convenient. You still have to live it.

~ FRANÇOISE MALLET-JORIS

Faith is to believe in something not yet proved and to underwrite it with our lives; it is the only way we can leave the future open.

~ LILLIAN SMITH

Faith is a curious thing, It must be renewed; it has its own spring.

~ GLADYS TABER

However much we do to avoid them, we shall never lack crosses in this life if we are in the ranks of the Crucified.

~ TERESA OF AVILA

It is only mercenaries who expect to be paid by the day.

~ TERESA OF AVILA

For so must it be, and help me do my part.

~ TIBETAN PROVERB

Answers Come through Prayer or Meditation

When we lose God, it is not God who is lost.

       ~ ANON.

For the believer, there is no question, for the nonbeliever, there is no answer.

       ~ ANON.

God tells us to burden him with whatever burdens us.

       ~ ANON.

When at night you cannot sleep, talk to the Shepherd and stop counting sheep.

       ~ ANON.

God's ear lies close to the believer's lip.

       ~ ANON.

A problem not worth praying about is not worth worrying about.

       ~ ANON.

Grant us peace, Almighty Father, so to pray as to deserve to be heard.

       ~ JANE AUSTEN

When life knocks you to your knees, and it will, why, get up! If it knocks you to your knees again, as it will, well, isn't that the best position from which to pray?

       ~ ETHEL BARRYMORE

There is no sinner in the world, however much at enmity with God, who cannot recover God's grace by recourse to Mary, and by asking her assistance.

       ~ SAINT BRIDGET OF SWEDEN

With God there is no need for long speeches.

       ~ JANE FRANCES DE CHANTAL

In prayer, more is accomplished by listening than by talking.

~ JANE FRANCES DE CHANTAL

By learning to contact, listen to, and act on our intuition, we can directly connect to the higher power of the universe and allow it to become our guiding force.

~ SHAKTI GAWAIN

Just pray for a tough hide and a tender heart.

~ RUTH GRAHAM

I know not by what methods rare,
But this I know: God answers prayer.
I know not if the blessing sought
Will come in the guise I thought.
I leave my prayer to Him alone
Whose will is wiser than my own.

~ ELIZA M. HICKOK

Women don't have halos built in.

~ LORRAINE HINE

Poverty, chastity, and obedience are extremely difficult. But there are always the graces if you will pray for them.

~ KATHERINE HULME

All who have walked with God have viewed prayer as the main business of their lives.

~ DELMA JACKSON

Prayer is more than meditation. In meditation the source of strength is one's self. When one prays he goes to a source of strength greater than his own.

~ MADAME CHIANG KAI-SHEK

Jesus, please teach me to appreciate what I have, before time forces me to appreciate what I had.

~ SUSAN L. LENZKES

There are four ways God answers prayer: No, not yet; No, I love you too much; Yes, I thought you'd never ask; Yes, and here's more.

~ ANNE LEWIS

Prayer is not eloquence, but earnestness; not the definition of helplessness, but the feeling of it; not figures of speech, but earnestness of soul.

~ HANNAH MOORE

There are three answers to prayer: yes, no, and wait a while. It must be recognized that no is an answer.

~ RUTH STAFFORD PEALE

And now, Lord, what wait I for?

~ PSALMS

Any concern too small to be turned into a prayer is too small to be made into a burden.

~ CORRIE TEN BOOM

Granting that we are always in the presence of God, yet it seems to me that those who pray are in His presence in a very different sense; for they, as it were, see that He is looking upon them, while others may go for days on end without even once recollecting that God sees them.

~ TERESA OF AVILA

Why is it when we talk to God we're said to be praying, but when God talks to us we're schizophrenic?

~ LILY TOMLIN

Devotion and Sincerity Are the Keys to Enlightenment

Do not pray by heart, but with the heart.

~ ANON.

Without the incense of heartfelt prayer, even the greatest of cathedrals is dead.

⌒ ANON.

Follow your own way of speaking to our Lord sincerely, lovingly, confidently, and simply, as your heart dictates.

⌒ JANE FRANCES DE CHANTAL

Logic is the key to an all-inclusive spiritual well-being.

⌒ MARLENE DIETRICH

There is only one way to end a self-pity cycle: stop comparing yourself to others, and simply follow Christ.

⌒ LINDA HARRY

Prayer opens our eyes that we may see ourselves and others as God sees us.

⌒ CLARA PALMER

Let him never cease from prayer who has once begun it, be his life ever so wicked, for prayer is the way to amend it, and without prayer such amendment will be much more difficult.

⌒ TERESA OF AVILA

Commitment to Ourselves Is Commitment to a Higher Power

What we are is God's gift to us. What we become is our gift to God.

⌒ ANON.

Earth, my Mother, whom I love.

⌒ MARGARET FAIRLESS BARBER

If you do not find peace in yourself, you will never find it anywhere else.

⌒ PAULA A. BENDRY

There is no object that we see; no action that we do; no good that we enjoy; no evil that we feel, or fear, but we may make some spiritual advantage of all: and he that makes such improvement is wise, as well as pious.

～ ANNE BRADSTREET

If we're not growing, we must feel guilty, because we are not fulfilling Christ's demand.

～ EVA BURROWS

Father! Blessed word.

～ MARIA S. CUMMINS

I always say my God will take care of me. If it's my time I'll go, and if it's not I won't. I feel that He really has a lot of important things for me to do. And He's going to make sure that I'm here to do them.

～ JOYCELYN ELDERS

As in heaven Your will is punctually performed, so may it be done on earth by all creatures, particularly in me and by me.

～ SAINT ELIZABETH OF HUNGARY

A woman consists of her faith. Whatever is her faith, even so is she.

～ HINDU PROVERB

Maybe the tragedy of the human race was that we had forgotten that we are each divine.

～ SHIRLEY MACLAINE

If I could know me, I could know the universe.

～ SHIRLEY MACLAINE

We are going to the moon, that is not very far. Man has so much farther to go within himself.

～ ANAÏS NIN

I believe that in our constant search for security we can never gain any peace of mind until we are secure in our own soul.

～ MARGARET CHASE SMITH

God prefers your health, and your obedience, to your penances.

~ TERESA OF AVILA

Let us remember that within us there is a palace of immense magnificence.

~ TERESA OF AVILA

Christ has no body on earth but yours, no hands but yours, no feet but yours. Yours are the eyes through which Christ's compassion for the world is to look out; yours are the feet with which He is to go about doing good; and yours are the hands with which He is to bless us now.

~ TERESA OF AVILA

We Find Divinity When We Are Open to It

So great was my joy in God that I took no heed of looking at the angels and the saints, because all their goodness and all their beauty was from Him and in Him.

~ SAINT ANGELA OF FOLIGNO

Our condition is most noble, being so beloved of the Most High God that He was willing to die for our sake—which He would not have done if man had not been a most noble creature and of great worth.

~ SAINT ANGELA OF FOLIGNO

Our perfection certainly consists in knowing God and ourselves.

~ SAINT ANGELA OF FOLIGNO

People see God every day, they just don't recognize Him.

~ PEARL BAILEY

In every out-thrust headland, in every curving beach, in every grain of sand, there is the story of the earth.

~ RACHEL CARSON

Hunting God is a great adventure.

~ MARIE DEFLORIS

To those leaning on the sustaining infinite, today is big with blessings.

~ MARY BAKER EDDY

Oh, if everyone knew how beautiful Jesus is, how amiable He is! They would all die from love.

~ GEMMA GALAGANI

We will discover the nature of our particular genius when we stop trying to conform to our own or to other people's models, learn to be ourselves, and allow our natural channel to open.

~ SHAKTI GAWAIN

Eventually I lost interest in trying to control my life, to make things happen in a way that I thought I wanted them to be. I began to practice surrendering to the universe and finding out what "it" wanted me to do.

~ SHAKTI GAWAIN

He loves, He hopes, He waits. Our Lord prefers to wait Himself for the sinner for years rather than keep us waiting an instant.

~ MARIA GORETTI

The Creator and Lord of all so loved the world, that He sent His Son for its salvation, the Prince and Savior of the faithful, who washed and dried our wounds, and from Him also came that most sweet medicine, from which all the good things of salvation flow.

~ HILDEGARD OF BINGEN

Sometimes I try my hand at turning out small profundities and uncertain short stories, but I always end up with just one single word: God.

~ ETTY HILLESUM

You have to believe in gods to see them.

~ HOPI INDIAN SAYING

I used to pray that God would do this or that; now I pray that God will make His will known to me.

～ MADAME CHIANG KAI-SHEK

The million little things that drop into your hands
The small opportunities each day brings
He leaves us free to use or abuse
And goes unchanging along His silent way.

～ HELEN KELLER

Faith is kind of like jumping out of an airplane at 10,000 feet. If God doesn't catch you, you splatter. But how do you know whether or not he is going to catch you unless you jump out?

～ ANN KIEMEL

I could be whatever I wanted to be if I trusted that music, that song, that vibration of God that was inside of me.

～ SHIRLEY MACLAINE

You cannot know what you cannot feel.

～ MARYA MANNES

Acceptance says, "True, this is my situation at the moment. I'll look unblinkingly at the reality of it. But I'll also open my hands to accept willingly whatever a loving Father sends me."

～ CATHARINE MARSHALL

He is more within us than we are ourselves.

～ ELIZABETH ANN SETON

The Father most tender, Father of all, my immense God—I His atom.

～ ELIZABETH ANN SETON

The Blessed Virgin used me like a broom, and then put me back in my place.

～ BERNADETTE SOUBIROUS

All our acts have sacramental possibilities.

～ FREYA STARK

Many a humble soul will be amazed to find that the seed it sowed in weakness, in the dust of daily life, has blossomed into immortal flowers under the eye of the Lord.

～ HARRIET BEECHER STOWE

All sorts of spiritual gifts come through privations, if they are accepted.

～ JANET ERSKINE STUART

I thank the goodness and the grace
Which on my birth have smiled,
And made me, in these Christian days,
A happy Christian child.

～ JANE TAYLOR

We know only that we are living in these bodies and have a vague idea, because we have heard it, and because our faith tells us so, that we possess souls. As to what good qualities there may be in our souls, or who dwells within them, or how precious they are, those are things which we seldom consider and so we trouble little about carefully preserving the soul's beauty.

～ TERESA OF AVILA

How is it, Lord, that we are cowards in everything save in opposing thee?

～ TERESA OF AVILA

From silly devotions and from sour-faced saints, good Lord, deliver us.

～ TERESA OF AVILA

The experience of God, or in any case the possibility of experiencing God, is innate.

～ ALICE WALKER

*D*iscovering Your Strengths

Do What You Love

The great thing to learn about life is, first, not to do what you don't want to do, and, second, to do what you do want to do.

~ MARGARET ANDERSON

What I do, I do very well, and what I don't do well, I don't do at all.

~ ANON.

[There] is a need to find and sing our own song, to stretch our limbs and shake them in a dance so wild that nothing can roost there, that stirs the yearning for solitary voyage.

~ BARBARA LAZEAR ASCHER

I know a lot of people think it's monotonous, down the black lines over and over, but it's not if you're enjoying what you're doing. I love to swim and I love to train.

~ TRACY CAULKINS

Find something you're passionate about and keep tremendously interested in it.

~ JULIA CHILD

We only do well the things we like doing.

~ COLETTE

There must be bands of enthusiasts for everything on earth—fanatics who shared a vocabulary, a batch of technical skills and equipment, and, perhaps, a vision of some single slice of the beauty and mystery of things, of their complexity, fascination, and unexpectedness.

~ ANNIE DILLARD

I want to do it because I want to do it.

~ AMELIA EARHART

Duty is an icy shadow. It will freeze you. It cannot fill the heart's sanctuary.

~ AUGUSTA EVANS

What I wanted was to be allowed to do the thing in the world that I did best—which I believed then and believe now is the greatest privilege there is. When I did that, success found me.

~ DEBBI FIELDS

Follow what you love! Don't deign to ask what "they" are looking for out there. Ask what you have inside. Follow not your interests, which change, but what you are and what you love, which will and should not change.

~ GEORGIE ANNE GEYER

The first duty of a human being is to assume the right relationship to society—more briefly, to find your real job, and do it.

~ CHARLOTTE P. GILMAN

We don't know who we are until we see what we can do.

~ MARTHA GRIMES

Dress to please yourself.... Forget you are what you wear.... Wear what you are.

~ ELIZABETH HAWKES

Don't do anything that someone else can do for you because there are only so many things that only you can do.

~ JINGER HEATH

If you always do what interests you, at least one person is pleased.

~ KATHARINE HEPBURN

The things that one most wants to do are the things that are probably most worth doing.

~ WINIFRED HOLTBY

What really matters is what you do with what you have.

~ SHIRLEY LORD

I have the feeling when I write poetry that I am doing what I am supposed to do. You don't think about whether you're going to get money or fame, you just do it.

~ DORIS LUND

In the first grade, I already knew the pattern of my life. I didn't know the living of it, but I knew the line.... From the first day in school until the day I graduated, everyone gave me one hundred plus in art. Well, where do you go in life? You go to the place where you got one hundred plus.

~ LOUISE NEVELSON

I am a writer because writing is the thing I do best.

~ FLANNERY O'CONNOR

I know that I haven't powers enough to divide myself into one who earns and one who creates.

~ TILLIE OLSEN

If we do not rise to the challenge of our unique capacity to shape our lives, to seek the kinds of growth that we find individually fulfilling, then we can have no security: we will live in a world of sham, in which our selves are determined by the will of others, in which we will be constantly buffeted and increasingly isolated by the changes round us.

～ NENA O'NEIL

For a long time the only time I felt beautiful—in the sense of being complete as a woman, as a human being, and even female—was when I was singing.

～ LEONTYNE PRICE

The source of continuing aliveness was to find your passion and pursue it, with whole heart and single mind.

～ GAIL SHEEHY

Do what you love, the money will follow.

～ MARSHA SINETAR

Any talent that we are born with eventually surfaces as a need.

～ MARSHA SINETAR

True inward quietness … is not vacancy, but stability—the steadfastness of a single purpose.

～ CAROLINE STEPHEN

The best career advice given to the young … is "Find out what you like doing best and get someone to pay you for doing it."

～ KATHARINE WHITEHORN

If you're skilled, your wallet will be filled.

～ YIDDISH PROVERB

Find the Genius Within

My unreality is chiefly this: I have never felt much like a human being. It's a splendid feeling.

~ MARGARET ANDERSON

The mind can store an estimated 100 trillion bits of information—compared with which a computer's mere billions are virtually amnesiac.

~ SHARON BEGLEY

The mind's cross-indexing puts the best librarian to shame.

~ SHARON BEGLEY

If school results were the key to power, girls would be running the world.

~ SARAH BOSELEY

An artist can show things that other people are terrified of expressing.

~ LOUISE BOURGEOIS

If I had influence with the good fairy who is supposed to preside over the christening of all children, I should ask that her gift to each child in the world be a sense of wonder so indestructible that it would last throughout life as an unfailing antidote against the boredom and disenchantments of later years, the sterile preoccupation with things that are artificial, the alienation from the sources of our strength.

~ RACHEL CARSON

Genius hath electric power
Which earth can never tame,
Bright suns may scorch and dark clouds lower,
Its flash is still the same.

~ LYDIA MARIA CHILD

You are unique, and if that is not fulfilled then something has been lost.

~ MARTHA GRAHAM

Next to genius is the power of feeling where true genius lies.
~ SARAH JOSEPHA HALE

The thing that makes you exceptional, if you are at all, is inevitably that which must also make you lonely.
~ LORRAINE HANSBURY

Genius is an infinite capacity for taking life by the scruff of the neck.
~ KATHARINE HEPBURN

Cherish forever what makes you unique, 'cuz you're really a yawn if it goes!
~ BETTE MIDLER

I didn't belong as a kid, and that always bothered me. If only I'd known that one day my differentness would be an asset, then my early life would have been much easier.
~ BETTE MIDLER

Every single one of us can do things that no one else can do—can love things that no one else can love. We are like violins. We can be used for doorstops, or we can make music.
~ BARBARA SHER

Since you are like no other being ever created since the beginning of time, you are incomparable.
~ BRENDA UELAND

Everybody is talented, original, and has something important to say.
~ BRENDA UELAND

Everyone is kneaded out of the same dough, but not baked in the same oven.
~ YIDDISH PROVERB

With Age and Experience Comes Strength

Such to me is the new image of aging; growth in self, and service for all mankind.

~ ETHEL PERCY ANDRUS

The older I get, the greater power I seem to have to help the world; I am like a snowball—the further I am rolled, the more I gain.

~ SUSAN B. ANTHONY

I'm not interested in age. People who tell me their age are silly. You're as old as you feel.

~ ELIZABETH ARDEN

It is sad to grow old, but nice to ripen.

~ BRIGITTE BARDOT

Maturity is coming to terms with that other part of yourself.

~ DR. RUTH TIFFANY BARNHOUSE

Character contributes to beauty. It fortifies a woman as her youth fades. A mode of conduct, a standard of courage, discipline, fortitude and integrity can do a great deal to make a woman beautiful.

~ JACQUELINE BISSET

I believe the true function of age is memory. I'm recording as fast as I can.

~ RITA MAE BROWN

A woman's always younger than a man of equal years.

~ ELIZABETH BARRETT BROWNING

It is often the case with finer natures, that when the fire of the spirit dies out with increasing age, the power of the intellect is unaltered or increased.

~ MARGARET GATTY

I'm like old wine. They don't bring me out very often, but I'm well preserved.

~ ROSE KENNEDY

The great thing about getting older is that you don't lose all the other ages you've been.

~ MADELEINE L'ENGLE

Perhaps middle age is, or should be, a period of shedding shells; the shell of ambition, the shell of material accumulations and possessions, the shell of the ego.

~ ANNE MORROW LINDBERGH

Age is totally unimportant. The years are really irrelevant. It's how you cope with them.

~ SHIRLEY LORD

There is a fountain of youth: it is your mind, your talents, the creativity you bring to your life and the lives of the people you love. When you learn to tap this source, you will truly have defeated age.

~ SOPHIA LOREN

I am much younger now than I was at twelve or anyway, less burdened.

~ FLANNERY O'CONNER

There are no old people nowadays; they are either "wonderful for their age" or dead.

~ MARY PETTIBONE POOLE

For inside all the weakness of old age, the spirit, God knows, is as mercurial as it ever was.

~ MAY SARTON

Age puzzles me. I thought it was a quiet time. My seventies were interesting and fairly serene, but my eighties are passionate. I grow more intense as I age.

~ FLORIDA SCOTT-MAXWELL

We who are old know that age is more than a disability. It is an intense and varied experience, almost beyond our capacity at times, but something to be carried high.

~ FLORIDA SCOTT-MAXWELL

Be on the alert to recognize your prime at whatever time of your life it may occur.

~ MURIEL SPARK

We are always the same age inside.

~ GERTRUDE STEIN

Women may be the one group that grows more radical with age.

~ GLORIA STEINEM

So much has been said and sung of beautiful young girls, why doesn't somebody wake up to the beauty of old women?

~ HARRIET BEECHER STOWE

Old age is that night of life, as night is the old age of day. Still night is full of magnificence and, for many, it is more brilliant than the day.

~ ANNE-SOPHIE SWETCHINE

In youth we learn; in age we understand.

~ MARIE VON EBNER-ESCHENBACH

Change excites me. I am fifty years old. It's when the mind catches up with the body.

~ RAQUEL WELCH

Don't buy the garbage that you're over the hill at fifty. This country makes such a big thing about age, particularly if you're a woman. What I think is relevant is your experience, what you have to offer. I hope people will recognize that and keep going.

~ MOLLY YARD

Believe in Yourself

Oh, yes. I'd do it all again; the spirit is willing yet; I feel the same desire to do the work but the flesh is weak. It's too bad that our bodies wear out while our interests are just as strong as ever.

~ SUSAN B. ANTHONY

I'm not funny. What I am is brave.

~ LUCILLE BALL

I'm a real pussycat—with an iron tail.

~ RONA BARRETT

Let women be provided with living strength of their own.

~ SIMONE DE BEAUVOIR

Whether there are innately female leadership styles … is not really the right question. It is more important to ask why there has been so little attention paid to women leaders over the years as well as why the styles of leading more often exhibited by women are particularly useful at this critical moment in history.

~ CHARLOTTE BUNCH

In politics, guts is all.

~ BARBARA CASTLE

Life is not easy for any of us. But what of that? We must have perseverance and above all confidence in ourselves. We must believe that we are gifted for something, and that this thing, at whatever cost, must be attained.

~ MARIE CURIE

Some leaders are born women.

~ GERALDINE FERRARO

I truly believe that women of my generation can bring a new cleansing element to American public life.

~ GEORGIE ANNE GEYER

Once, power was considered a masculine attribute. In fact, power has no sex.

～ KATHERINE GRAHAM

Your father used to say, "Never give away your work. People don't value what they don't have to pay for."

～ NANCY HALE

Every family is a "normal" family—no matter whether it has one parent, two, or no children at all.

～ SHERE HITE

I don't think being an athlete is unfeminine. I think of it as a kind of grace.

～ JACKIE JOYNER-KERSEE

Sometimes the strength of motherhood is greater than natural laws.

～ BARBARA KINGSOLVER

I define sexy as a real salt-of-the-earth woman who knows who she is, who feels strong and powerful.

～ ANDIE MACDOWELL

Women are the fulfilled sex. Through our children we are able to produce our own immortality, so we lack that divine restlessness which sends men charging off in pursuit of fortune or fame or an imagined Utopia.

～ PHYLLIS MCGINLEY

Women are not inherently passive or peaceful. We're not inherently anything but human.

～ ROBIN MORGAN

Never in the history of the big, round world has anything like us occurred.

～ KATHLEEN NORRIS

I can shoot as well as you.

～ ANNIE OAKLEY, TO HER HUSBAND

I've always been independent, and I don't see how it conflicts with femininity.

~ SYLVIA PORTER

I know how to do anything—I'm a mom.

~ ROSEANNE

Where there is woman, there is magic.

~ NTOZAKE SHANGE

You will be a failure until you impress the subconscious with the conviction you are a success. This is done by making an affirmation which "clicks."

~ FLORENCE SCOVEL SHINN

Each arc of color may be lovely to behold, but it is the full spectrum of our woman rainbow that glows with the brightest promise of better things to come.

~ MERLIN STONE

Why are we surprised when fig trees bear figs?

~ MARGARET TEAD

It may be the cock that crows, but it is the hen that lays the eggs.

~ MARGARET THATCHER

And ar'n't I a woman?

~ SOJOURNER TRUTH

There is nothing Madison Avenue can give us that will make us more beautiful women. We are beautiful because God created us that way.

~ MARIANNE WILLIAMSON

Women have always been the guardians of wisdom and humanity which makes them natural, but usually secret, rulers.

~ CHARLOTTE WOLFF

Express Your Convictions

A voice is a human gift; it should be cherished and used, to utter as fully human speech as possible. Powerlessness and silence go together.
~ MARGARET ATWOOD

A word after a word after a word is power.
~ MARGARET ATWOOD

A person who can write a long letter with ease, cannot write ill.
~ JANE AUSTEN

Journal writing is a voyage to the interior.
~ CHRISTINA BALDWIN

Our lives preserved. How it was; and how it will be. Passing it along in the relay. That is what I work to do: to produce stories that save our lives.
~ TONI CADE BAMBARA

To know how to say what others only know how to think is what makes men poets or sages; and to dare to say what others only dare to think makes men martyrs or reformers—or both.
~ ELIZABETH CHARLES

That which is nearest a woman's heart is the first to come out.
~ IRISH PROVERB

I write lustily and humorously. It isn't calculated; it's the way I think. I've invented a writing style that expresses who I am.
~ ERICA JONG

My voice is still the same, and this makes me beside myself with Joy! Oh, mon Dieu, when I think what I might be able to do with it!
~ JENNY LIND

For me, writing is the only thing that passes the three tests of metier: (1) when I'm doing it, I don't feel that I should be doing something else instead; (2) it produces a sense of accomplishment and, once in a while, pride; and (3) it's frightening.

~ GLORIA STEINEM

Overcome Fear

The truly fearless think of themselves as normal.

~ MARGARET ATWOOD

I may be compelled to face danger, but never fear it, and while our soldiers can stand and fight, I can stand and feed and nurse them.

~ CLARA BARTON

Everyone has a talent. What is rare is the courage to nurture it in solitude and to follow the talent to the dark places where it leads.

~ ERICA JONG

One of the marks of a gift is to have the courage of it.

~ KATHERINE ANNE PORTER

We're frightened of what makes us different.

~ ANNE RICE

Know Yourself

There's a period of life when we swallow a knowledge of ourselves and it becomes either good or sour inside.

~ PEARL BAILEY

You never find yourself until you face the truth.

~ PEARL BAILEY

No one can figure out your worth but you.

~ PEARL BAILEY

Femininity appears to be one of those pivotal qualities that is so important no one can define it.

~ CAROLINE BIRD

I shall be an autocrat, that's my trade; and the good Lord will forgive me, that's his.

~ CATHERINE THE GREAT

We are the same people as we were at three, six, ten or twenty years old. More noticeably so, perhaps, at six or seven, because we were not pretending so much then.

~ AGATHA CHRISTIE

What families have in common the world around is that they are the place where people learn who they are and how to be that way.

~ JEAN ILLSLEY CLARKE

I knew what my job was; it was to go out and meet the people and love them.

~ DIANA, PRINCESS OF WALES

People who concentrate on giving good service always get more personal satisfaction as well as better business. How can we get better service? One way is by trying to see ourselves as others do.

~ PATRICIA FRIPP

Until we see what we are, we cannot take steps to become what we should be.

~ CHARLOTTE P. GILMAN

I believe that dreams transport us through the underside of our days, and that if we wish to become acquainted with the dark side of what we are, the signposts are there, waiting for us to translate them.

~ GAIL GODWIN

I think self-awareness is probably the most important thing towards becoming a champion.

~ BILLIE JEAN KING

Long ago I understood that it wasn't merely my being a woman that was preventing my being welcomed into the world of what I long thought of as my peers. It was that I had succeeded in an undertaking few men have even attempted: I have become myself.

~ ALICE KOLLER

Only when one is connected to one's own core is one connected to others.... And, for me, the core, the inner spring, can best be refound through solitude.

~ ANNE MORROW LINDBERGH

An aim in life is the only fortune worth finding.

~ JACQUELINE KENNEDY ONASSIS

Real apprenticeship is ultimately always to the self.

~ CYNTHIA OZICK

Somehow we learn who we really are and then live with that decision.

~ ELEANOR ROOSEVELT

The delights of self-discovery are always available.

~ GAIL SHEEHY

There is a solitude which each and every one of us has always carried within. More inaccessible than the ice-cold mountains, more profound than the midnight sea: the solitude of self.

~ ELIZABETH CADY STANTON

Freedom is knowing who you really are.

~ LINDA THOMSON

I, woman, give birth: and this time to myself.

~ ALMA VILLANUEVA

There are two ways of spreading light: to be the candle or the mirror that reflects it.

~ EDITH WHARTON

It isn't until you come to a spiritual understanding of who you are—not necessarily a religious feeling, but deep down, the spirit within—that you can begin to take control.

~ OPRAH WINFREY

Each has his past shut in him like the leaves of a book shown to him by heart, and his friends can only read the title.

~ VIRGINIA WOOLF

If you do not tell the truth about yourself you cannot tell it about other people.

~ VIRGINIA WOOLF

Don't Focus on Your Shortcomings

Long tresses down to the floor can be beautiful, if you have that, but learn to love what you have.

~ ANITA BAKER

I am no longer what I was. I will remain what I have become.

~ COCO CHANEL

Everyone must row with the oars they have.

~ ENGLISH PROVERB

I always introduce myself as an encyclopedia of defects which I do not deny. Why should I? It took me a whole life to build myself as I am.

~ ORIANA FALLACI

To say something nice about themselves, this is the hardest thing in the world for people to do.

~ NANCY FRIDAY

After my screen test, the director clapped his hands gleefully and yelled, "She can't talk! She can't act! She's sensational!"

~ AVA GARDNER

The things we hate about ourselves aren't more real than the things we like about ourselves.

~ ELLEN GOODMAN

Whenever I dwell for any length of time on my own shortcomings, they gradually begin to seem mild, harmless, rather engaging little things, not at all like the staring defects in other people's characters.

~ MARGARET HALSEY

There is only one way to end a self-pity cycle: stop comparing yourself to others, and simply follow Christ.

~ LINDA HARRY

A woman of mystique is fully aware of her flaws and weaknesses, yet she is strong enough to admit them and not be embarrassed by them.

~ JEAN LUSH

Learning too soon our limitations, we never learn our powers.

~ MIGNON MCLAUGHLIN

Your thorns are the best part of you.

~ MARIANNE MOORE

The basic experience of everyone is the experience of human limitation.

~ FLANNERY O'CONNOR

We do not make beams from the hollow, decaying trunk of the fallen oak. We use the upsoaring tree in the full vigor of its sap.

~ SYLVIA PANKHURST

We must use what we have to invent what we desire.

~ ADRIENNE RICH

Oh, I'm so inadequate. And I love myself!

~ MEG RYAN

I am simple, complex, generous, selfish, unattractive, beautiful, lazy, and driven.

~ BARBARA STREISAND

If your head tells you one thing and your heart tells you another, before you do anything, you should first decide whether you have a better head or a better heart.

~ MARILYN VOS SAVANT

I did not lose myself all at once. I rubbed out my face over the years washing away my pain, the same way carvings on stone are worn down by water.

~ AMY TAN

Find Things to Be Proud Of

There may be ways in which we can work for change. We don't have to do dramatic things or devote our entire lives to it. We can lead normal lives but at the same time try hard not to be bystanders.

~ HELEN BAMBER

From the first, I made my learning, what little it was, useful every way I could.

~ MARY MCLEOD BETHUNE

Some people give time, some money, some their skills and connections, some literally give their life's blood ... but everyone has something to give.

~ BARBARA BUSH

I was once the typical daughter, then the easily recognizable wife, and then the quintessential mother. I seem always to have reminded people of someone in their family. Perhaps I am just the triumph of Plain Jane.

~ HELEN HAYES

Plain women know more about men than beautiful ones do.

~ KATHARINE HEPBURN

Though I have no productive worth, I have a certain value as an indestructible quantity.

~ ALICE JAMES

God wastes nothing.

~ JAN KARON

Believe, when you are most unhappy, that there is something for you to do in the world. So long as you can sweeten another's pain, life is not in vain.

~ HELEN KELLER

To be a housewife is ... a difficult, a wrenching, sometimes ungrateful job if it's looked on as only a job. Regarded as a profession, it is the noblest as it is the most ancient of the catalogue. Let none persuade us differently, or the world will be lost indeed.

~ PHYLLIS MCGINLEY

It's this no-nonsense side of women that is pleasant to deal with. They are the real sportsmen.

~ PHYLLIS MCGINLEY

Not being beautiful was the true blessing.... Not being beautiful forced me to develop my inner resources. The pretty girl has a handicap to overcome.

~ GOLDA MEIR

There is not one big cosmic meaning for all, there is only the meaning we each give to our life, an individual meaning, an individual plot, like an individual novel, a book for each person.

~ ANAÏS NIN

I see myself as Rhoda, not Mary Tyler Moore.

~ ROSIE O'DONNELL

We may fail of our happiness, strive we ever so bravely; but we are less likely to fail if we measure with judgment our chances and our capabilities.

~ AGNES REPPLIER

The surest sign of fitness is success.
~ OLIVE SCHREINER

I was not a classic mother. But my kids were never palmed off to boarding school. So, I didn't bake cookies. You can buy cookies, but you can't buy love.
~ RAQUEL WELCH

I am an ordinary person, but carried to extremes.
~ FAY WELDON

Seek to Improve and Grow

The deeper interior you have the more you have in your library.
~ JACQUELINE BISSET

Follow your interests, get the best available education and training, set your sights high, be persistent, be flexible, keep your options open, accept help when offered, and be prepared to help others.
~ MILDRED SPIEWAK DRESSELHAUS

It's all to do with the training: you can do a lot if you're properly trained.
~ QUEEN ELIZABETH

As it turns out, social scientists have established only one fact about single women's mental health: employment improves it.
~ SUSAN FALUDI

Saying "yes" to yourself means acknowledging what you have that's good and working on the things that aren't.
~ PATRICIA FRIPP

There is no good reason why we should not develop and change until the last day we live.
~ KAREN HORNEY

We can't take any credit for our talents. It's how we use them that counts.

~ MADELEINE L'ENGLE

As simple as it sounds, we all must try to be the best person we can: by making the best choices, by making the most of the talents we've been given.

~ MARY LOU RETTON

What is most beautiful in virile men is something feminine; what is most beautiful in feminine women is something masculine.

~ SUSAN SONTAG

You must love and care for yourself, because that's when the best comes out.

~ TINA TURNER

Contribute Something New

Be yourself. The world worships the original.

~ INGRID BERGMAN

Best be yourself, imperial, plain, and true!

~ ELIZABETH BARRETT BROWNING

In order to be irreplaceable one must always be different.

~ COCO CHANEL

We should try to bring to any power what we have as women. We will destroy it all if we try to imitate that absolutely unfeeling, driving ambition that we have seen coming at us across the desk.

~ COLLEEN DEWHURST

Change occurs when one becomes what she is, not when she tries to become what she is not.

~ RUTH P. FREEDMAN

It is the duty of youth to bring its fresh powers to bear on social progress. Each generation of young people should be to the world like a vast reserve force to a tired army. They should lift the world forward. That is what they are for.

~ CHARLOTTE P. GILMAN

I looked always outside of myself to see what I could make the world give me instead of looking within myself to see what was there.

~ BELLE LIVINGSTONE

The trouble with specialists is that they tend to think in grooves.

~ ELAINE MORGAN

Why can a man not act himself, be himself, and think for himself? It seems to me that naturalness alone is power; that a borrowed word is weaker than our own weakness, however small we may be.

~ MARIA MITCHELL

When one is pretending the entire body revolts.

~ ANAÏS NIN

When you affirm your own rightness in the universe, then you co-operate with others easily and automatically as part of your own nature. You, being yourself, help others be themselves.

~ JANE ROBERTS

So prodigal was I of youth,
Forgetting I was young;
I worshipped dead men for their strength,
Forgetting I was strong.

~ VITA SACKVILLE-WEST

It is not easy to be sure that being yourself is worth the trouble, but [we do know] it is our sacred duty.

~ FLORIDA SCOTT-MAXWELL

Why not be oneself? That is the whole secret of a successful appearance. If one is a greyhound, why try to look like a Pekingese?

~ DAME EDITH SITWELL

Nature never repeats herself, and the possibilities of one human soul will never be found in another.

~ ELIZABETH CADY STANTON

Style is something peculiar to one person; it expresses one personality and one only; it cannot be shared.

~ FREYA STARK

If you put a woman in a man's position, she will be more efficient, but no more kind.

~ FAY WELDON

Believing in Yourself

Don't Let Others Stand in Your Way

As you go along your road in life, you will, if you aim high enough,
also meet resistance ... but no matter how tough the opposition may
seem, have courage still—and persevere.
> ~ MADELEINE ALBRIGHT

The Wright brothers flew through the smoke screen of impossibility.
> ~ DOROTHEA BRANDE

When a just cause reaches its flood-tide, as ours has done...,
whatever stands in the way must fall before its overwhelming power.
> ~ CARRIE CHAPMAN CATT

We must remember that one determined person can make a
significant difference, and that a small group of determined people
can change the course of history.
> ~ SONIA JOHNSON

I am only one, but still I am one. I cannot do everything, but still I can do something. And because I cannot do everything I will not refuse to do the something that I can do.

~ HELEN KELLER

I was and I always shall be hampered by what I think other people will say.

~ VIOLETTE LEDUC

No one can make you feel inferior without your consent.

~ ELEANOR ROOSEVELT

Whatever you want in life, other people are going to want it too. Believe in yourself enough to accept the idea that you have an equal right to it.

~ DIANE SAWYER

Your real security is yourself. You know you can do it, and they can't ever take that away from you.

~ MAE WEST

I argue that we deserve the choice to do whatever we want with our faces and bodies without being punished by an ideology that is using attitudes, economic pressure, and even legal judgments regarding women's appearance to undermine us psychologically and politically.

~ NAOMI WOLF

Everything Begins with Self-Love

Who we are never changes. Who we think we are does.

~ MARY S. ALMANAC

To love others, we must first learn to love ourselves.

~ ANON.

You cannot belong to anyone else, until you belong to yourself.

～ PEARL BAILEY

Love yourself first and everything else falls into line. You really have to love yourself to get anything done in this world.

～ LUCILLE BALL

If you do not find peace in yourself, you will never find it anywhere else.

～ PAULA A. BENDRY

A strong, positive self-image is the best possible preparation for success.

～ DR. JOYCE BROTHERS

No matter what age you are, or what your circumstances might be, you are special, and you still have something unique to offer. Your life, because of who you are, has meaning.

～ BARBARA DE ANGELIS

To have that sense of one's intrinsic worth which constitutes self-respect is potentially to have everything.

～ JOAN DIDION

"Glamour" is assurance. It is a kind of knowing that you are all right in every way, mentally and physically and in appearance, and that, whatever the occasion or the situation, you are equal to it.

～ MARLENE DIETRICH

I've learned to take time for myself and to treat myself with a great deal of love and respect 'cause I like me.... I think I'm kind of cool.

～ WHOOPI GOLDBERG

You are all you will ever have for certain.

～ JUNE HAVOC

I've finally stopped running away from myself. Who else is there better to be?

～ GOLDIE HAWN

Life is to be lived. If you have to support yourself, you had bloody well better find some way that is going to be interesting., and you don't do that by sitting around wondering about yourself.

~ KATHARINE HEPBURN

The worst walls are never the ones you find in your way. The worst walls are the ones you put there—you build yourself. Those are the high ones, the thick ones, the ones with no doors in.

~ URSULA K. LE GUIN

To succeed is nothing—it's an accident. But to feel no doubts about oneself is something very different: it is character.

~ MARIE LENÉRU

I define sexy as a real salt-of-the-earth woman who knows who she is, who feels strong and powerful.

~ ANDIE MACDOWELL

I want to be remembered as the person who helped us restore faith in ourselves.

~ WILMA PEARL MANKILLER

Until you make peace with who you are, you'll never be content with what you have.

~ DORIS MORTMAN

Beauty to me is being comfortable in your own skin.

~ GWYNETH PALTROW

I am the only real truth I know.

~ JEAN RHYS

We must be steady enough in ourselves, to be open and to let the winds of life blow through us, to be our breath, our inspiration; to breathe with them, mobile and soft in the limberness of our bodies, in our agility, our ability, as it were, to dance, and yet to stand upright.

~ MARY CAROLINE RICHARDS

No man is defeated without until he has first been defeated within.

~ ELEANOR ROOSEVELT

Friendship with one's self is all important, because without it one cannot be friends with anyone else in the world.

~ ELEANOR ROOSEVELT

Love your self's self where it lives.

~ ANNE SEXTON

To make the choice for independent survival, the great man's wife has to become convinced of her own intrinsic worth.

~ JOANNA T. STEICHEN

Self-esteem isn't everything; it's just that there's nothing without it.

~ GLORIA STEINEM

Who is not good for himself is no good for others.

~ YIDDISH PROVERB

Overcome Your Fears

It's the moment you think you can't that you realize you can.

~ CELINE DION

From a shy, timid girl I had become a woman of resolute character, who could no longer be frightened by the struggle with troubles.

~ ANNA DOSTOEVSKY

I have never been nervous in all my life and I have no patience with people who are. If you know what you are going to do, you have no reason to be nervous. And I knew what I was going to do.

~ MARY GARDEN

Doubt indulged soon becomes doubt realized.

~ FRANCES RIDLEY HAVERGAL

You must do the thing you think you cannot do.

~ ELEANOR ROOSEVELT

Kill the snake of doubt in your soul, crush the worms of fear in your heart, and mountains will move out of your way.

~ KATE SEREDY

I think I look good out there. I'm strong, powerful, and artistic. But I have my doubts as much as anyone.

~ JILL TRENARY

If I ever felt inclined to be timid as I was going into a room full of people, I would say to myself, "You're the cleverest member of one of the cleverest families in the cleverest class of the cleverest nation.... Why should you be frightened?"

~ BEATRICE POTTER WEBB

Be Confident (But Not Arrogant)

Make yourself indispensable and you'll be moved up. Act as if you're indispensable and you'll be moved out.

~ ANON.

If you think you can, you can. And if you think you can't, you're right.

~ MARY KAY ASH

I've never had a humble opinion in my life. If you're going to have one, why bother to be humble about it?

~ JOAN BAEZ

Women who are confident of their abilities are more likely to succeed than those who lack confidence, even though the latter may be much more competent and talented and industrious.

~ DR. JOYCE BROTHERS

Life is not easy for any of us. But what of that? We must have perseverance and above all confidence in ourselves. We must believe that we are gifted for something, and that this thing, at whatever cost, must be attained.

~ MARIE CURIE

Might, could, would—they are contemptible auxiliaries.

~ GEORGE ELIOT

You've got to take the initiative and play your game ... confidence makes the difference.

~ CHRIS EVERT

Shyness is just egotism out of its depth.

~ PENELOPE KEITH

It's better to be a lion for a day than a sheep all your life.

~ ELIZABETH KENNY

I am optimistic and confident in all that I do. I affirm only the best for myself and others. I am the creator of my life and my world. I meet daily challenges gracefully and with complete confidence. I fill my mind with positive, nurturing, and healing thoughts.

~ ALICE POTTER

I felt a comedy ego beginning to grow, which gave me the courage to begin tentatively looking into myself for material.

~ JOAN RIVERS

My mother taught me very early to believe I could achieve any accomplishment I wanted to. The first was to walk without braces.

~ WILMA RUDOLPH

Let us remember that within us there is a palace of immense magnificence.

~ TERESA OF AVILA

If there be a faith that can move mountains, it is faith in one's own power.

~ MARIE VON EBNER-ESCHENBACH

When one must, one can.

~ YIDDISH PROVERB

You're as Young as You Feel

I refuse to admit that I am more than fifty-two, even if that does make my sons illegitimate.

~ NANCY ASTOR

I used to dread getting older because I thought I would not be able to do all the things I wanted to do, but now that I am older I find that I don't want to do them.

~ NANCY ASTOR

Another belief of mine: that everyone else my age is an adult, whereas I am merely in disguise.

~ MARGARET ATWOOD

I think your whole life shows in your face and you should be proud of that.

~ LAUREN BACALL

I am not a has-been. I'm a will-be.

~ LAUREN BACALL

I am immortal! I know it! I feel it!

~ MARGARET WITTER FULLER

Youth is not a time of life, it is a state of mind. You are as old as your doubt, your fear, your despair. The way to keep young is to keep your faith young. Keep your self-confidence young. Keep your hope young.

~ LUELLA F. PHEAN

Beauty is a radiance that originates from within and comes from inner security and strong character.

~ JANE SEYMOUR

Set Goals for Yourself and You'll Achieve Them

Each time I leaped I seemed to touch the sky and when I regained earth it seemed to be mine alone.

~ JOSEPHINE BAKER

There is a place in God's sun for the youth "farthest down" who has the vision, the determination, and the courage to reach it.

~ MARY MCLEOD BETHUNE

Nearly every glamorous, wealthy, successful career woman you might envy now started out as some kind of schlepp.

~ HELEN GURLEY BROWN

The fact that I was a girl never damaged my ambitions to be a pope or an emperor.

~ WILLA CATHER

Tell them that as soon as I can walk I'm going to fly!

~ BESSIE COLEMAN

He who demands little gets it.

~ ELLEN GLASGOW

I probably hold the distinction of being one movie star who, by all laws of logic, should never have made it. At each stage of my career, I lacked the experience.

~ AUDREY HEPBURN

If we want a free and peaceful world, if we want to make the deserts bloom and man grow to greater dignity as a human being—we can do it.

~ ELEANOR ROOSEVELT

You can change your beliefs so they empower your dreams and desires. Create a strong belief in yourself and what you want.
　　　　　　　∽ MARCIA WIEDER

Nothing is too difficult—you only need to know how.
　　　　　　　∽ YIDDISH PROVERB

Strength Comes from Mysterious Places

I used to tremble from nerves so badly that the only way I could hold my head steady was to lower my chin practically to my chest and look up at Bogie. That was the beginning of "The Look."
　　　　　　　∽ LAUREN BACALL

Whenever there is chaos, it creates wonderful thinking. I consider chaos a gift.
　　　　　　　∽ SEPTIMA POINSETTE CLARK

Everyone has inside of him a piece of good news. The good news is that you don't know how great you can be! How much you can love! What you can accomplish! And what your potential is!
　　　　　　　∽ ANNE FRANK

When all that hate energy was focused on me, it was transformed into a fantastic energy. It was supporting me. If you are centered and you can transform all this energy that comes in, it will help you. If you believe it is going to kill you, it will kill you.
　　　　　　　∽ YOKO ONO

If you think you're too small to have an impact, try going to bed with a mosquito.
　　　　　　　∽ ANITA RODDICK

Out of desperation, one finds.
　　　　　　　∽ YIDDISH PROVERB

Follow Your Heart

The first and worst of all frauds is to cheat one's self. All sin is easy after that.

~ PEARL BAILEY

A willing heart adds feather to the heel.

~ JOANNA BAILLIE

The brain is not, and cannot be, the sole or complete organ of thought and feeling.

~ ANTOINETTE BROWN BLACKWELL

Let the world know you as you are, not as you think you should be, because sooner or later, if you are posing, you will forget the pose, and then where are you?

~ FANNY BRICE

I am a woman who understands the necessity of an impulse whose goal or origin still lie beyond me.

~ OLGA BROUMAS

You really can change the world if you care enough.

~ MARIAN WRIGHT EDELMAN

If you're a champion, you have to have it in your heart.

~ CHRIS EVERT

Yes, I have doubted. I have wandered off the path, but I always return. It is intuitive, an intrinsic, built-in sense of direction. I seem always to find my way home.

~ HELEN HAYES

The world may take your reputation from you, but it cannot take your character.

~ EMMA DUNHAM KELLEY

We have to dare to be ourselves, however frightening or strange that self may prove to be.

~ MAY SARTON

Be Proud of What You Have

Long tresses down to the floor can be beautiful if you have that, but learn to love what you have.

~ ANITA BAKER

Nobody can be exactly like me. Sometimes even I have trouble doing it.

~ TALLULAH BANKHEAD

If you are going to think black, think positive about it. Don't think down on it, or think it is something in your way. And this way, when you really do want to stretch out and express how beautiful black is, everybody will hear you.

~ LEONTYNE PRICE

Who I am is the best I can be.

~ LEONTYNE PRICE

Oh, I'm so inadequate. And I love myself!

~ MEG RYAN

Believing in our hearts that who we are is enough is the key to a more satisfying and balanced life.

~ ELLEN SUE STERN

No matter how lonely you get or how many birth announcements you receive, the trick is not to get frightened. There's nothing wrong with being alone.

~ WENDY WASSERSTEIN

Women Have Unique Strengths

Whatever glory belongs to the race for a development unprecedented in history for the given length of time, a full share belongs to the womanhood of the race.

⌒ MARY MCLEOD BETHUNE

The sexes in each species of beings … are always true equivalents—equals but not identicals.

⌒ ANTOINETTE BROWN BLACKWELL

There is a potential heroine in every woman.

⌒ JEAN SHINODA BOLEN

Normal is not something to aspire to, it's something to get away from.

⌒ JODIE FOSTER

Never bend your head. Hold it high. Look the world straight in the eye.

⌒ HELEN KELLER

We are volcanoes. When we women offer our experience as our truth, as human truth, all the maps change. There are new mountains.

⌒ URSULA K. LE GUIN

I have brightness in my soul, which strains toward Heaven. I am like a bird!

⌒ JENNY LIND

A small group of thoughtful people could change the world. Indeed, it's the only thing that ever has.

⌒ MARGARET MEAD

For women there are, undoubtedly, great difficulties in the path, but so much the more to overcome. First no woman would say "I am but a woman!" But a woman! What more can you ask to be?

⌒ MARIA MITCHELL

Ability is sexless.

⌒ CHRISTABEL PANKHURST

Remember the dignity of your womanhood. Do not appeal, do not beg, do not grovel. Take courage, join hands, stand beside us, fight with us.

~ CHRISTABEL PANKHURST

I hear the singing of the lives of women. The clear mystery, the offering, the pride.

~ MURIEL RUKEYSER

We bear the world and we make it.... There was never a great man who had not a great mother—it is hardly an exaggeration.

~ OLIVE SCHREINER

I have met brave women who are exploring the outer edge of human possibility, with no history to guide them, and with a courage to make themselves vulnerable that I find moving beyond words.

~ GLORIA STEINEM

Remember, Ginger Rogers did everything Fred Astaire did, but she did it backwards and in high heels.

~ FAITH WHITTLESEY

Exercising Self-Restraint

Don't Meddle

A little kingdom I possess,
Where thoughts and feelings dwell;
And very hard the task I find
Of governing it well.
～ LOUISA MAY ALCOTT

Everybody's business is nobody's business, and nobody's business is
my business.
～ CLARA BARTON

I listen and give input only if somebody asks.
～ BARBARA BUSH

Too often in ironing out trouble someone gets scorched.
～ MARCELENE COX

Give neither counsel nor salt till you are asked for it.
～ ITALIAN PROVERB

When you borrow trouble you give your peace of mind as security.

～ MYRTLE REED

Don't be curious of matters that don't concern you; never speak of them, and don't ask about them.

～ TERESA OF AVILA

Don't Take Yourself Too Seriously

Conceit spoils the finest genius. There is not much danger that real talent or goodness will be overlooked long; even if it is, the consciousness of possessing and using it well should satisfy one.

～ LOUISA MAY ALCOTT

What makes humility so desirable is the marvelous thing it does to us; it creates in us a capacity for the closest possible intimacy with God.

～ MONICA BALDWIN

We would worry less about what others think of us if we realized how seldom they do.

～ ETHEL BARRETT

You grow up the day you have your first real laugh—at yourself.

～ ETHEL BARRYMORE

Blessed are those who can give without remembering and take without forgetting.

～ ELIZABETH ASQUITH BIBESCO

Big egos are big shields for lots of empty space.

～ DIANA BLACK

You never conquer a mountain. You stand on the summit a few moments; then the wind blows your footprints away.

～ ARLENE BLUM

Proud people breed sad sorrows for themselves.

~ EMILY BRONTË

Beware of over-great pleasure in being popular or even beloved.

~ MARGARET FULLER

Soften my hard self-opinionatedness, which time has hardened so exceedingly!

~ GERTRUDE THE GREAT

The nice thing about egotists is that they don't talk about other people.

~ LUCILLE S. HARPER

It is to please herself that the cat purrs.

~ IRISH PROVERB

Modesty is the beauty of women.

~ IRISH PROVERB

There is nothing so skillful in its own defense as imperious pride.

~ HELEN HUNT JACKSON

Wounded vanity knows when it is mortally hurt; and limps off the field, piteous, all disguises thrown away. But pride carries its banner to the last; and fast as it is driven from one field unfurls it in another.

~ HELEN HUNT JACKSON

Class is an aura of confidence that is being sure without being cocky. Class has nothing to do with money. Class never runs scared. It is self-discipline and self-knowledge. It's the surefootedness that comes with having proved you can meet life.

~ ANN LANDERS

In our society those who are in reality superior in intelligence can be accepted by their fellows only if they pretend they are not.

~ MARYA MANNES

It is far more impressive when others discover your good qualities without your help.

~ JUDITH MARTIN (MISS MANNERS)

Humility is like underwear, essential but indecent if it shows.

~ HELEN NIELSEN

The more important the title, the more self-important the person, the greater the amount of time spent on the Eastern shuttle, the more suspicious the man and the less vitality in the organization.

~ JANE O'REILLY

I'm glad I never feel important, it does complicate life.

~ ELEANOR ROOSEVELT

More people are ruined by victory, I imagine, than by defeat.

~ ELEANOR ROOSEVELT

Vanity is the quicksand of reason.

~ GEORGE SAND

I was somewhat drunk with what I had done. And I am always one to prefer being sober.

~ GERTRUDE STEIN

Our vanity is the constant enemy of our dignity.

~ ANNE-SOPHIE SWETCHINE

'Tis the ignorant who boast.

~ CARMEN SYLVA

Being powerful is like being a lady. If you have to tell people you are, you aren't.

~ MARGARET THATCHER

If arrogance is the heady wine of youth, then humility must be its eternal hangover.

~ HELEN VAN SLYKE

Conquer but never triumph.

~ MARIE VON EBNER-ESCHENBACH

Success can make you go one of two ways. It can make you a prima donna, or it can smooth the edges, take away the insecurities, let the nice things come out.

~ BARBARA WALTERS

Humility is attentive patience.

~ SIMONE WEIL

When you look to the heights, hold on to your hat.

~ YIDDISH PROVERB

An empty barrel makes a lot of noise.

~ YIDDISH PROVERB

Ask and you won't get lost.

~ YIDDISH PROVERB

The scholar knows what she lacks knowledge of.

~ YIDDISH PROVERB

If you can't bite, don't show your teeth.

~ YIDDISH PROVERB

Don't Overdo It

Friendship increases in visiting friends, but not in visiting them too often.

~ ANON.

A hedge between keeps friendships green.

~ ANON.

Here's a rule I recommend. Never practice two vices at once.

~ TALLULAH BANKHEAD

It goes without saying that you should never have more children than you have car windows.

~ ERMA BOMBECK

If you can't write your message in a sentence, you can't say it in an hour.

~ DIANNA BOOHER

Sweet words are like honey, a little may refresh, but too much gluts the stomach.

~ ANNE BRADSTREET

Striving for excellence motivates you; striving for perfection is demoralizing.

~ DR. HARRIET BRAIKER

Since everything is in our heads, we better not lose them.

~ COCO CHANEL

Do not remove a fly from your friend's forehead with a hatchet.

~ CHINESE PROVERB

A woman that's too soft and sweet is like tapioca pudding—fine for them as likes it.

~ OSA JOHNSON

No gain satisfies a greedy mind.

~ LATIN PROVERB

A little of what you fancy does you good.

~ MARIE LLOYD

Gammy used to say, "Too much scrubbing takes the life right out of things."

~ BETTY MACDONALD

Who is apt, on occasion, to assign a multitude of reasons when one will do? This is a sure sign of weakness in argument.

~ HARRIET MARTINEAU

The point of good writing is knowing when to stop.

~ L.M. MONTGOMERY

Superior people never make long visits.

~ MARIANNE MOORE

The longest absence is less perilous to love than the terrible trials of incessant proximity.

~ OUIDA

Never eat more than you can lift.

~ MISS PIGGY

I know too well the poison and the sting
Of things too sweet.

~ ADELAIDE PROCTOR

Would that there were an award for people who come to understand the concept of enough. Good enough. Successful enough. Thin enough. Rich enough. Socially responsible enough. When you have self-respect you have enough.

~ GAIL SHEEHY

Transformation also means looking for ways to stop pushing yourself so hard professionally or inviting so much stress.

~ GAIL SHEEHY

To wear your heart on your sleeve isn't a very good plan; you should wear it inside, where it functions best.

~ MARGARET THATCHER

For fast-acting relief try slowing down.

~ LILY TOMLIN

Don't Worry about Things You Can't Control

A wise woman cares not for what she cannot have.

~ ANON.

You always feel when you look it straight in the eye that you could have put more into it, could have let yourself go and dug harder.

~ EMILY CARR

To create is to boggle the mind and alter the mood. Once the urge has surged, it maintains its own momentum. We may go along for the ride, but when we attempt to steer the course, the momentum dies.

~ SUE ATCHLEY EBAUGH

If you can react the same way to winning and losing, that's a big accomplishment. That quality is important because it stays with you the rest of your life.

~ CHRIS EVERT

Much growth is stunted by too careful prodding,
Too eager tenderness.
The things we love we have to learn to leave alone.

~ NAOMI LONG MADGETT

Believe there is a great power silently working all things for good, behave yourself and never mind the rest.

~ BEATRIX POTTER

One by one the sands are flowing,
One by one the moments fall;
Some are coming, some are going;
Do not strive to grasp them all.

~ ADELAIDE PROCTOR

Don't Pass Judgment

With compassion, we see benevolently our own human condition and the condition of our fellow beings. We drop prejudice. We withhold judgment.
~ CHRISTINA BALDWIN

A major advantage of age is learning to accept people without passing judgment.
~ LIZ CARPENTER

A few observations and much reasoning lead to error; many observations and a little reasoning to truth.
~ ALEXIS CARREL

A critic is someone who never actually goes to the battle, yet who afterwards comes out shooting the wounded.
~ TYNE DALY

Sainthood is acceptable only in saints.
~ PAMELA HANSFORD JOHNSON

Youth condemns; maturity condones.
~ JOSEPHINE PRESTON PEABODY

Tact is the ability to describe others as they see themselves.
~ MARY PETTIBONE POOLE

Don't Hold Grudges

Forgiveness is the act of admitting we are like other people.
~ CHRISTINA BALDWIN

Grace fills empty spaces, but it can only enter where there is a void to receive it, and it is grace itself which makes this void.
~ SIMONE WEIL

Have Realistic Expectations

I long to see everything, to know everything, to learn everything!
~ MARIE BASHKIRTSEFF

And remember, expect nothing and life will be velvet.
~ LISA GARDINER

One cannot collect all the beautiful shells on the beach.
~ ANNE MORROW LINDBERGH

Don't try to teach a whole course in one lesson.
~ KATHRYN MURRAY

If we could learn how to balance rest against effort, calmness against strain, quiet against turmoil, we would assure ourselves of joy in living and psychological health for life.
~ JOSEPHINE RATHBONE

The whole point of getting things done is knowing what to leave undone.
~ LADY STELLA READING

What is destructive is impatience, haste, expecting too much too fast.
~ MAY SARTON

If it goes, it goes, don't force it.
~ YIDDISH PROVERB

Be Patient

Patience with others is Love, Patience with self is Hope, Patience with God is Faith.
~ ADEL BESTAVROS

No emergency excuses you from exercising tolerance.
~ PHYLLIS BOTTOME

I believe the sign of maturity is accepting deferred gratification.
~ PEGGY CAHN

I believe I was impatient with unintelligent people from the moment
I was born: a tragedy—for I am myself three-parts a fool.
~ MRS. PATRICK CAMPBELL

In prayer, more is accomplished by listening than by talking.
~ JANE FRANCES DE CHANTAL

You can't have genius without patience.
~ MARGARET DELAND

Who longest waits most surely wins.
~ HELEN HUNT JACKSON

The most potent and sacred command which can be laid upon any
artist is the command: wait.
~ IRIS MURDOCH

No good work is ever done while the heart is hot and anxious and
fretted.
~ OLIVE SCHREINER

Panic is not an effective long-term organizing strategy.
~ STARHAWK

Self-denial is painful for a moment, but very agreeable in the end.
~ JANE TAYLOR

It is only mercenaries who expect to be paid by the day.
~ TERESA OF AVILA

Be Considerate of Others

The whole art of life is knowing the right time to say things.
~ MAEVE BINCHY

It is not until you become a mother that your judgment slowly turns to compassion and understanding.
~ ERMA BOMBECK

If we would build on a sure foundation in friendship, we must love friends for their sake rather than for our own.
~ CHARLOTTE BRONTË

The nice thing about teamwork is that you always have others on your side.
~ MARGARET CARTY

Friendship, which is of its nature a delicate thing, fastidious, slow of growth, is easily checked, will hesitate, demur, recoil where love, good old blustering love, bowls ahead and blunders through every obstacle.
~ COLETTE

It is all right to say exactly what you think if you have learned to think exactly.
~ MARCELENE COX

Silence sweeter is than speech.
~ DINAH MARIA MULOCK CRAIK

When we get to wishing a great deal for ourselves, whatever we get soon turns into mere limitation and exclusion.
~ GEORGE ELIOT

The opposite of talking isn't listening. The opposite of talking is waiting.
~ FRAN LEBOWITZ

Listening is not merely not talking, though even that is beyond most of our powers; it means taking a vigorous, human interest in what is being told us.

~ ALICE DEUR MILLER

Why is it that people who cannot show feeling presume that that is a strength and not a weakness?

~ MAY SARTON

True love grows by sacrifice and the more thoroughly the soul rejects natural satisfaction the stronger and more detached its tenderness becomes.

~ THÉRÈSE OF LISIEUX

If everyone were allowed to take from the world all her heart desired, there would be nothing left for anyone else.

~ YIDDISH PROVERB

Don't Give in to Temptation

One "no" averts seventy evils.

~ AMERICAN INDIAN PROVERB

No matter how lovesick a woman is, she shouldn't take the first pill that comes along.

~ DR. JOYCE BROTHERS

He that hath no rule over his own spirit is like a city that is broken down and without walls.

~ TAYLOR CALDWELL

We have learned that power is a positive force if it is used for positive purposes.

~ ELIZABETH DOLE

You must learn to be still in the midst of activity, and to be vibrantly alive in repose.

~ INDIRA GANDHI

Silence Is Golden

The less said the better.

~ JANE AUSTEN

The fool shouts loudly, thinking to impress the world.

~ MARIE DE FRANCE

Blessed is the man who, having nothing to say, abstains from giving wordy evidence of the fact.

~ GEORGE ELIOT

It was enough just to sit there without words.

~ LOUISE ERDRICH

A closed mouth catches no flies.

~ FRENCH PROVERB

A word out of season may mar a whole lifetime.

~ GREEK PROVERB

Talking too much, too soon, and with too much self-satisfaction has always seemed to me a sure way to court disaster.

~ MEG GREENFIELD

A story is told as much by silence as by speech.

~ SUSAN GRIFFIN

Talk uses up ideas.... Once I have spoken them aloud, they are lost to me, dissipated into the noisy air like smoke. Only if I bury them, like bulbs, in the rich soil of silence do they grow.

~ DORIS GRUMBACH

Next to entertaining or impressive talk, a thoroughgoing silence manages to intrigue most people.

~ FLORENCE HURST HARRIMAN

Love understands love; it needs no talk.

~ FRANCES RIDLEY HAVERGAL

I like people who refuse to speak until they are ready to speak.

~ LILLIAN HELLMAN

The strokes of the pen need deliberation as much as the sword needs swiftness.

~ JULIA WARD HOWE

Handle them carefully, for words have more power than atom bombs.

~ PEARL STRACHAN HURD

One sees intelligence far more than one hears it. People do not always say transcendental things, but if they are capable of saying them, it is always visible.

~ MARIE LENÉRU

The silence of a man who loves to praise is a censure sufficiently severe.

~ CHARLOTTE LENNOX

Silence is one of the great arts of conversation.

~ HANNAH MOORE

Silence and reserve will give anyone a reputation for wisdom.

~ MYRTLE REED

It is impossible to persuade a man who does not disagree, but smiles.

~ MURIEL SPARK

All the feeling which my father could not put into words was in his hand—any dog, child, or horse would recognize the kindness of it.

~ FREYA STARK

Nothing could bother me more than the way a thing goes dead once it has been said.

~ GERTRUDE STEIN

Be Careful What You Say

A statement once let loose cannot be caught by four horses.

~ JAPANESE PROVERB

Minimum information given with maximum politeness.

~ JACQUELINE KENNEDY ONASSIS

A gossip is one who talks to you about others; a bore is one who talks to you about himself; and a brilliant conversationalist is one who talks to you about yourself.

~ LISA KIRK

Almost anything carried to its logical extreme becomes depressing, if not carcinogenic.

~ URSULA K. LE GUIN

The body pays for a slip of the foot, and gold pays for a slip of the tongue.

~ MALAYSIAN PROVERB

Beware of allowing a tactless word, rebuttal, a rejection to obliterate the whole sky.

~ ANAÏS NIN

Violence of the tongue is very real—sharper than any knife.

~ MOTHER TERESA

Don't confuse being stimulating with being blunt.

~ BARBARA WALTERS

Taking Control of Your Life

Expect More from Life

I don't want to get to the end of my life and find that I lived just the length of it. I want to have lived the width of it as well.
~ DIANE ACKERMAN

With renunciation life begins.
~ AMELIA BARR

As I grow older, part of my emotional survival plan must be to actively seek inspiration instead of passively waiting for it to find me.
~ BEBE MOORE CAMPBELL

There is only one big thing—desire. And before it, when it is big, all is little.
~ WILLA CATHER

Boredom is the fear of self.
~ COMTESSE DIANE

It is not opposition but indifference which separates men.
~ MARY PARKER FOLLETT

I have always had a dread of becoming a passenger in life.

    ~ MARGARETH II, QUEEN OF DENMARK

A continued atmosphere of hectic passion is very trying if you haven't got any of your own.

    ~ DOROTHY L. SAYERS

The clue is not to ask in a miserly way—the key is to ask in a grand manner.

    ~ ANN WIGMORE

Have a Vision of What You Want

Energy is equal to desire and purpose.

    ~ SHERYL ADAMS

Have regular hours for work and play; make each day both useful and pleasant, and prove that you understand the worth of time by employing it well. Then youth will be delightful, old age will bring few regrets, and life will become a beautiful success.

    ~ LOUISA MAY ALCOTT

Talent isn't genius and no amount of energy can make it so. I want to be great, or nothing. I won't be a commonplace dauber, so I don't intend to try any more.

    ~ LOUISA MAY ALCOTT

A stale mind is the devil's breadbox.

    ~ MARY BLY

If you really want something you can figure out how to make it happen.

    ~ CHER

Never be afraid to sit awhile and think.

    ~ LORRAINE HANSBURY

Genius is an infinite capacity for taking life by the scruff of the neck.

~ KATHARINE HEPBURN

I will not be just a tourist in the world of images, just watching images passing by which I cannot live in, make love to, possess as permanent sources of joy and ecstasy.

~ ANAÏS NIN

Find a need and fill it.

~ RUTH STAFFORD PEALE

What an immense power over the life is the power of possessing distinct aims. The voice, the dress, the look, the very motions of a person, define and alter when he or she begins to live for a reason.

~ ELIZABETH STUART PHELPS

You should always know when you're shifting gears in life. You should leave your era; it should never leave you.

~ LEONTYNE PRICE

Only the thinking man lives his life, the thoughtless man's life passes him by.

~ MARIE VON EBNER-ESCHENBACH

Don't Leave Your Future in the Hands of Others

I don't want to be a passenger in my own life.

~ DIANE ACKERMAN

Independence is happiness.

~ SUSAN B. ANTHONY

Woman must not depend upon the protection of man, but must be taught to protect herself.

~ SUSAN B. ANTHONY

I leave before being left. I decide.

~ BRIGITTE BARDOT

Living by proxy is always a precarious expedient.

~ SIMONE DE BEAUVOIR

When I saw something that needed doing, I did it.

~ NELLIE CASHMAN

We need to find the courage to say NO to the things and people that are not serving us if we want to rediscover ourselves and live our lives with authenticity.

~ BARBARA DE ANGELIS

No one is in control of your happiness but you; therefore, you have the power to change anything about yourself or your life that you want to change.

~ BARBARA DE ANGELIS

Women share with men the need for personal success, even the taste for power, and no longer are we willing to satisfy those needs through the achievements of surrogates, whether husbands, children, or merely role models.

~ ELIZABETH DOLE

I never really address myself to any image anybody has of me. That's like fighting with ghosts.

~ SALLY FIELD

There is no such thing as vicarious experience.

~ MARY PARKER FOLLETT

I love being single. It's almost like being rich.

~ SUE GRAFTON

It is better to be tied to any thorny bush than to be with a cross man.

~ AUGUSTA GREGORY

I don't follow precedent, I establish it.

~ FANNY ELLEN HOLTZMAN

Anything is better than a bad marriage.

~ IRISH PROVERB

Our concern must be to live while we're alive ... to release our inner selves from the spiritual death that comes with living behind a facade designed to conform to external definitions of who and what we are.

~ ELISABETH KUBLER-ROSS

Intimate relationships cannot substitute for a life plan. but to have any meaning or viability at all, a life plan must include intimate relationships.

~ HARRIET LERNER

Do not rely completely on any other human being ... we meet all of life's greatest tests alone.

~ AGNES MACPHAIL

If we do not rise to the challenge of our unique capacity to shape our lives, to seek the kinds of growth that we find individually fulfilling, then we can have no security: we will live in a world of sham, in which our selves are determined by the will of others, in which we will be constantly buffeted and increasingly isolated by the changes round us.

~ NENA O'NEIL

The great law of denial belongs to the powerful forces of life, whether the case be one of coolish baked beans, or an unrequited affection.

~ ELIZABETH STUART PHELPS

The thing women have got to learn is that nobody gives you power. You just take it.

~ ROSEANNE

Who ever walked behind anyone to freedom?

~ HAZEL SCOTT

I do not wish women to have power over men; but over themselves.

～ MARY WOLLSTONECRAFT SHELLEY

Do not wait for ideal circumstances, nor the best opportunities; they will never come.

～ JANET ERSKINE STUART

I am learning that if I just go on accepting the framework for life that others have given me, if I fail to make my own choices, the reason for my life will be missing. I will be unable to recognize that which I have the power to change.

～ LIV ULLMANN

Don't Be Fatalistic

I resolved to take Fate by the throat and shake the living out of her.

～ LOUISA MAY ALCOTT

I must have something to engross my thoughts, some object in life which will fill this vacuum and prevent this sad wearing away of the heart.

～ ELIZABETH BLACKWELL

He alone is great
Who by a life heroic conquers fate.

～ SARAH KNOWLES BOLTON

A life of reaction is a life of slavery, intellectually and spiritually. One must fight for a life of action, not reaction.

～ RITA MAE BROWN

When it comes time to do your own life, you either perpetuate your childhood or you stand on it and finally kick it out from under.

～ ROSELLEN BROWN

I got well by talking. Death could not get a word in edgewise, grew
discouraged, and traveled on.
~ LOUISE ERDRICH

You are in the driver's seat of your life and can point your life down
any road you want to travel. You can go as fast or as slow as you want
to go ... and you can change the road you're on at any time.
~ JINGER HEATH

I was forced to live far beyond my years when just a child, now I
have reversed the order and I intend to remain young indefinitely.
~ MARY PICKFORD

Overcome Your Fears

I am not afraid of storms, for I am learning how to sail my ship.
~ LOUISA MAY ALCOTT

No pressure, no diamonds.
~ MARY CASE

[A difficult childhood gave me] a kind of cocky confidence.... I
could never have so little that I hadn't had less. It took away my fear
~ JACQUELINE COCHRAN

I have not ceased being fearful, but I have ceased to let fear control me.
~ ERICA JONG

Life Is What You Make It

The door of opportunity won't open unless you do some pushing.

~ ANON.

Every tomorrow has two handles. We can take hold if it by the handle of anxiety, or by the handle of faith.

~ ANON.

If it is to be, it is up to me.

~ ANON.

Some pursue happiness—others create it.

~ ANON.

Boredom, like necessity, is very often the mother of invention.

~ ANON.

Boredom is a sickness of the soul.

~ ANON.

Luck serves ... as rationalization for every people that is not master of its own destiny.

~ HANNAH ARENDT

I was always looking outside myself for strength and confidence, but it comes from within. It is there all the time.

~ ANNA FREUD

A woman who is willing to be herself and pursue her own potential runs not so much the risk of loneliness as the challenge of exposure to more interesting men—and people in general.

~ LORRAINE HANSBURY

Take your life in your own hands, and what happens? A terrible thing: no one to blame.

~ ERICA JONG

There is no scientific answer for success. You can't define it. You've simply got to live it and do it.
～ ANITA RODDICK

You need to claim the events in your life to make yourself yours. When you truly possess all you have been and done, which may take some time, you are fierce with reality.
～ FLORIDA SCOTT-MAXWELL

As far as your self-control goes, as far goes your freedom.
～ MARIE VON EBNER-ESCHENBACH

I've learned from experience that the greater part of our happiness or misery depends on our dispositions and not on our circumstances.
～ MARTHA WASHINGTON

Don't Give Up

The best way out of a problem is through it.
～ ANON.

The secret of patience is to do something else in the meantime.
～ ANON.

The only difference between a rut and a grave is their dimensions.
～ ELLEN GLASGOW

We're swallowed up only when we are willing for it to happen.
～ NATHALIE SARRAUTE

Be Yourself

Borrowed thoughts, like borrowed money, only show the poverty of the borrower.

~ LADY MARGUERITE BLESSINGTON

You were once wild here. Don't let them tame you!

~ ISADORA DUNCAN

No person has the right to rain on your dreams.

~ MARIAN WRIGHT EDELMAN

Think wrongly, if you please, but in all cases think for yourself.

~ DORIS LESSING

My will shall shape my future. Whether I fail or succeed shall be no man's doing but my own. I am the force; I can clear any obstacle before me or I can be lost in the maze. My choice, my responsibility; win or lose, only I hold the key to my destiny.

~ ELAINE MAXWELL

She lacks confidence, she craves admiration insatiably. She lives on the reflections of herself in the eyes of others. She does not dare to be herself.

~ ANAÏS NIN

I had never been as resigned to ready-made ideas as I was to ready-made clothes, perhaps because although I couldn't sew, I could think.

~ JANE RULE

Self-reliance is the only road to true freedom, and being one's own person is its ultimate reward.

~ PATRICIA SAMPSON

The basic freedom of the world is woman's freedom.

~ MARGARET SANGER

I am a moonbeam, free to go whenever I choose.

~ MARINA TSVETAEVA

The fame you earn has a different taste from the fame that is forced upon you.

~ GLORIA VANDERBILT

Look Out for Number One

She soothed and solaced and celebrated, destroying her gift by maiming it to suit her hearers.

~ MARTHA BACON

Strong people don't need strong leaders.

~ ELLA BAKER

In a world that holds books and babies and canyon trails, why should one condemn oneself to live day in, day out with people one does not like, and sell oneself to chaperone and correct them?

~ RUTH BENEDICT

It is sometimes the man who opens the door who is the last to enter the room.

~ ELIZABETH ASQUITH BIBESCO

From self alone expect applause.

~ MARIAN L. BURTON

The first thing is to love your sport. Never do it to please someone else. It has to be yours.

~ PEGGY FLEMING

The pain of leaving those you grow to love is only the prelude to understanding yourself and others.

~ SHIRLEY MACLAINE

I don't tell the truth any more to those who can't make use of it. I tell it mostly to myself, because it always changes me.

~ ANAÏS NIN

Dedication to one's work in the world is the only possible sanctification. Religion in all its forms is dedication to Someone Else's work, not yours.

~ CYNTHIA OZICK

Real apprenticeship is ultimately always to the self.

~ CYNTHIA OZICK

Don't Waste Precious Moments

Still on it creeps,
Each little moment at another's heels,
Till hours, days, years, and ages are made up
Of such small parts as these, and men look back
Worn and bewilder'd, wondering how it is.

~ JOANNA BAILLIE

The biggest sin is sitting on your ass.

~ FLORYNCE KENNEDY

Don't agonize. Organize.

~ FLORYNCE KENNEDY

Regret is an appalling waste of energy; you can't build on it; it is only good for wallowing in.

~ KATHERINE MANSFIELD

Do not wait for ideal circumstances, nor the best opportunities; they will never come.

~ JANET ERSKINE STUART

Do not wait for leaders; do it alone, person to person.

~ MOTHER TERESA

If our education had included training to bear unpleasantness and to let the first shock pass until we could think more calmly, many an unbearable situation would become manageable, and many a nervous illness avoided. There is a proverb expressing this. It says, trouble is a tunnel through which we pass and not a brick wall against which we must break our head.

~ CLAIRE WEEKS

Make the Most of Every Day

It seems that we learn lessons when we least expect them but always when we need them the most, and, the true "gift" in these lessons always lies in the learning process itself.

~ CATHY LEE CROSBY

Getting fit is a political act—you are taking charge of your life.

~ JANE FONDA

I must govern the clock, not be governed by it.

~ GOLDA MEIR

I am optimistic and confident in all that I do. I affirm only the best for myself and others. I am the creator of my life and my world. I meet daily challenges gracefully and with complete confidence. I fill my mind with positive, nurturing, and healing thoughts.

~ ALICE POTTER

Knowing What Really Matters

Matters of the Spirit

You don't have to be dowdy to be a Christian.
~ TAMMY FAYE BAKKER

Spirit is the real and eternal; matter is the unreal and the temporal.
~ MARY BAKER EDDY

I need nothing but God, and to lose myself in the heart of God.
~ SAINT MARGARET MARY ALACOQUE

It is not my ability, but my response to God's ability, that counts.
~ CORRIE TEN BOOM

From silly devotions and from sour-faced saints, good Lord, deliver us.
~ TERESA OF AVILA

God prefers your health, and your obedience, to your penance.
~ TERESA OF AVILA

It is those who have a deep and real inner life who are best able to
deal with the irritating details of outer life.

∿ EVELYN UNDERHILL

The Little Pleasures of Life

Why not learn to enjoy the little things—there are so many of them.

∿ ANON.

Sooner or later we all discover that the important moments in life
are not the advertised ones, not the birthdays, the graduations, the
weddings, not the great goals achieved. The real milestones are less
prepossessing. They come to the door of memory.

∿ SUSAN B. ANTHONY

There is nothing like staying at home for real comfort.

∿ JANE AUSTEN

What would life be without art? Science prolongs life. To consist of
what—eating, drinking, and sleeping? What is the good of living
longer if it is only a matter of satisfying the requirements that sustain
life? All this is nothing without the charm of art.

∿ SARAH BERNHARDT

There are half hours that dilate to the importance of centuries.

∿ MARY CATHERWOOD

Anyone who's a great kisser I'm always interested in.

∿ CHER

Life is about enjoying yourself and having a good time.

∿ CHER

Moderation. Small helpings. Sample a little bit of everything. These
are the secrets of happiness and good health.

∿ JULIA CHILD

In violent and chaotic times such as these, our only chance for survival lies in creating our own little islands of sanity and order, in making little havens of our homes.

〜 SUSAN KAUFMAN

Small kindnesses, small courtesies, small considerations, habitually practiced in our social intercourse, give a greater charm to the character than the display of great talents and accomplishments.

〜 MARY ANN KELTY

Brevity is the soul of lingerie.

〜 DOROTHY PARKER

We women ought to put first things first. Why should we mind if men have their faces on the money, as long as we get our hands on it?

〜 IVY BAKER PRIEST

Eating is not merely a material pleasure. Eating well gives a spectacular joy to life and contributes immensely to goodwill and happy companionship. It is of great importance to the morale.

〜 ELSA SCHIAPIRELLI

I am beginning to learn that it is the sweet, simple things of life which are the real ones after all.

〜 LAURA INGALLS WILDER

Not Possessions, but a Life Well Lived

Judge each day not by the harvest, but by the seeds that you plant.

〜 ANON.

I think your whole life shows in your face and you should be proud of that.

〜 LAUREN BACALL

I wish I were with some of the wild people that run in the woods, and know nothing about accomplishments!

〜 JOANNA BAILLIE

It is sad to grow old but nice to ripen.

~ BRIGITTE BARDOT

Age is something that doesn't matter, unless you are a cheese.

~ BILLIE BURKE

If I had one wish for my children, it would be that each of them would reach for goals that have meaning for them as individuals.

~ LILLIAN CARTER

There are people who have money and people who are rich.

~ COCO CHANEL

I don't think about whether people will remember me or not. I've been an okay person. I've learned a lot. I've taught people a thing or two. That's what's important.

~ JULIA CHILD

I'm aiming by the time I'm fifty to stop being an adolescent.

~ WENDY COPE

Truth is like heat or light; its vibrations are endless, and are endlessly felt.

~ MARGARET DELAND

No one has yet had the courage to memorialize his wealth on his tombstone. A dollar mark would not look well there.

~ CORRA MAY HARRIS

My mother drew a distinction between achievement and success. She said that achievement is the knowledge that you have studied and worked hard and done the best that is in you. Success is being praised by others. That is nice but not as important or satisfying. Always aim for achievement and forget about success.

~ HELEN HAYES

So many of us define ourselves by what we have, what we wear, what kind of house we live in, and what kind of car we drive ... if you think of yourself as the woman in the Cartier watch and the Hermes scarf, a house fire will destroy not only your possessions but your self.

~ LINDA HENLEY

The externals are simply so many props; everything we need is within us.

~ ETTY HILLESUM

I want a busy life, a just mind, and a timely death.

~ ZORA NEALE HURSTON

Our last garment is made without pockets.

~ ITALIAN PROVERB

To me success means effectiveness in the world, that I am able to carry my ideas and values into the world—that I am able to change it in positive ways.

~ MAXINE HONG KINGSTON

The best things in life aren't things.

~ ANN LANDERS

If you have a good name, if you are right more often than you are wrong, if your children respect you, if your grandchildren are glad to see you, if your friends can count on you and you can count on them in time of trouble, if you can face your God and say "I have done my best," then you are a success.

~ ANN LANDERS

It is good to have an end to journey toward, but it is the journey that matters in the end.

~ URSULA K. LE GUIN

For the happiest life, days should be rigorously planned, nights left open to chance.

~ MIGNON MCLAUGHLIN

I don't want to make money. I just want to be wonderful.

      ～ MARILYN MONROE

Painting's not important. The important thing is keeping busy.

      ～ GRANDMA MOSES

Money never remains just coins and pieces of paper. Money can be translated into the beauty of living, a support in misfortune, an education, or future security.

      ～ SYLVIA PORTER

If I do have some success, I'd like to enjoy it, for heaven's sake! What is the point of having it otherwise?

      ～ LEONTYNE PRICE

There is a great difference between satisfaction and satiation.

      ～ MARY JANE SHERFEY

What you become is what counts.

      ～ LIZ SMITH

If my hands are fully occupied in holding on to something, I can neither give nor receive.

      ～ DOROTHY SÖLLE

From birth to age eighteen, a girl needs good parents. From eighteen to thirty-five, she needs good looks. From thirty-five to fifty-five, she needs a good personality. From fifty-five on, she needs good cash.

      ～ SOPHIE TUCKER

With every deed you are sowing a seed, though the harvest you may not see.

      ～ ELLA WHEELER WILCOX

Friends, Family, and the Respect of Others

We learn the inner secret of happiness when we learn to direct our inner drives, our interest, and our attention to something besides ourselves.

~ ETHEL PERCY ANDRUS

Friendship is a plant which must be often watered.

~ ANON.

The best rule of friendship is to keep your heart a little softer than your head.

~ ANON.

Better a hundred enemies outside the house than one inside.

~ ARABIC PROVERB

I figure if I have my health, can pay the rent and I have my friends, I call it "content."

~ LAUREN BACALL

You leave home to seek your fortune and, when you get it, you go home and share it with your family.

~ ANITA BAKER

It is not until you become a mother that your judgment slowly turns to compassion and understanding.

~ ERMA BOMBECK

The darn trouble with cleaning the house is it gets dirty the next day anyway, so skip a week if you have to. The children are the most important thing.

~ BARBARA BUSH

Power without [the people's] confidence is nothing.

~ CATHERINE THE GREAT

Reconciliation is more beautiful than victory.

~ VIOLETA BARRIOS DE CHAMORRO

The presidency is temporary—but the family is permanent.
~ YVONNE DE GAULLE

It's the friends you can call up at 4:00 a.m. that matter.
~ MARLENE DIETRICH

To nourish children and raise them against odds is in any time, any place, more valuable than to fix bolts in cars or design nuclear weapons.
~ MARILYN FRENCH

I believe that we are always attracted to what we need most, an instinct leading us towards the persons who are to open new vistas in our lives and fill them with new knowledge.
~ HELENE ISWOLSKY

If you bungle raising your children, I don't think whatever else you do matters very much.
~ JACQUELINE KENNEDY ONASSIS

If you have a good name, if you are right more often than you are wrong, if your children respect you, if your grandchildren are glad to see you, if your friends can count on you and you can count on them in time of trouble, if you can face your God and say "I have done my best," then you are a success.
~ ANN LANDERS

My darling little girl-child, after such a long and troublesome waiting I now have you in my arms. I am alone no more, I have my baby.
~ MARTHA MARTIN

You can't leave humanity out. If you didn't have humanity, you wouldn't have anything.
~ ALICE NEEL

Fame has only the span of the day, they say. But to live in the hearts of people—that is worth something.
~ OUIDA

There's a time when you have to explain to your children why they were born, and it's a marvelous thing if you know the reason by then.
~ HAZEL SCOTT

Is there any stab as deep as wondering where and how much you failed those you loved?
~ FLORIDA SCOTT-MAXWELL

Disorder in the society is the result of disorder in the family.
~ ELIZABETH ANN SETON

It seems to me that since I've had children, I've grown richer and deeper. They may have slowed down my writing for a while, but when I did write, I had more of a self to speak from.
~ ANNE TYLER

All love that has not friendship for its base is like a mansion built upon the sand.
~ ELLA WHEELER WILCOX

Biology is the least of what makes someone a mother.
~ OPRAH WINFREY

Being True to One's Vision and Principles

A puff of wind and popular praise weigh the same.
~ ENGLISH PROVERB

The most comprehensive formulation of therapeutic goals is the striving for wholeheartedness: to be without pretense, to be emotionally sincere, to be able to put the whole of oneself into one's feelings, one's work, one's beliefs.
~ KAREN HORNEY

Many persons have a wrong idea of what constitutes real happiness. It is not obtained through self-gratification but through fidelity to a worthy purpose.

~ HELEN KELLER

Man has no nobler function than to defend the truth.

~ MAHALIA JACKSON

We are traditionally rather proud of ourselves for having slipped creative work in there between the domestic chores and obligations. I'm not sure we deserve such big A-pluses for all that.

~ TONI MORRISON

Just because everything is different doesn't mean anything has changed.

~ IRENE PETER

Nothing is less important than which fork you use. Etiquette is the science of living. It embraces everything. It is ethics. It is honor.

~ EMILY POST

The attributes of a great lady may still be found in the rule of the four S's: Sincerity, Simplicity, Sympathy, and Serenity.

~ EMILY POST

The ultimate of being successful is the luxury of giving yourself the time to do what you want to do.

~ LEONTYNE PRICE

Someone once asked me what I regarded as the three most important requirements for happiness. My answer was: "A feeling that you have been honest with yourself and those around you; a feeling that you have done the best you could both in your personal life and in your work; and the ability to love others."

~ ELEANOR ROOSEVELT

I think God rarely gives to one man, or one set of men, more than one great moral victory to win.

~ LUCY STONE

From silly devotions and from sour-faced saints, good Lord, deliver us.

~ TERESA OF AVILA

Truth has beauty, power, and necessity.

~ SYLVIA TOWNSEND WARNER

Theories are like scaffolding: they are not the house, but you cannot build the house without them.

~ CONSTANCE FENIMORE WOOLSON

A good name is better than a precious stone.

~ YIDDISH PROVERB

Doing the Best We Can

Getting what you go after is success; but liking it while you are getting it is happiness.

~ BERTHA DAMON

To fulfill a dream, to be allowed to sweat over lonely labor, to be given the chance to create, is the meat and potatoes of life. The money is the gravy.

~ BETTE DAVIS

The only courage that matters is the kind that gets you from one moment to the next.

~ MIGNON MCLAUGHLIN

I was brought up to believe that the only thing worth doing was to add to the sum of accurate information in the world.

~ MARGARET MEAD

The power I exert on the court depends on the power of my arguments, not on my gender.

~ SANDRA DAY O'CONNOR

Ambition is destruction, only competence matters.

~ JILL ROBINSON

Someone once asked me what I regarded as the three most important requirements for happiness. My answer was: "A feeling that you have been honest with yourself and those around you; a feeling that you have done the best you could both in your personal life and in your work; and the ability to love others."

~ ELEANOR ROOSEVELT

There are only three colors, ten digits, and seven notes; it's what we do with them that's important.

~ RUTH ROSS

Wisdom and Peace of Mind

Knowledge is the prime need of the hour.

~ MARY MCLEOD BETHUNE

There is a gigantic difference between earning a great deal of money and being rich.

~ MARLENE DIETRICH

She could not separate success from peace of mind. The two must go together.

~ DAPHNE DU MAURIER

Happiness is not a possession to be prized, it is a quality of thought, a state of mind.

~ DAPHNE DU MAURIER

There are many excuses for the person who made the mistake of confounding money and wealth. Like many others they mistook the sign for the thing signified.

~ MILLICENT GARRETT FAWCETT

People in big empty places are likely to behave very much as the gods did on Olympus.

~ EDNA FERBER

Success based on anything but internal fulfillment is bound to be empty.

~ DR. MARTHA FRIEDMAN

A house is not a home unless it contains food and fire for the mind as well as the body.

~ MARGARET FULLER

There's more learning than is taught in books.

~ AUGUSTA GREGORY

Success doesn't necessarily make you a happy person ... but without the confidence and security that comes from being totally happy, I believe you cannot achieve your true potential and ultimate success.

~ JINGER HEATH

It is the mark of great people to treat trifles as trifles and important matters as important.

~ DORIS LESSING

What matters most is that we learn from living.

~ DORIS LESSING

Duration is not a test of true or false.

~ ANNE MORROW LINDBERGH

A BMW can't take you as far as a diploma.

~ JOYCE A. MYERS

There are only two things that are absolute realities, love and knowledge, and you can't escape them.

~ OLIVE SCHREINER

There's a time when you have to explain to your children why they were born, and it's a marvelous thing if you know the reason by then.

~ HAZEL SCOTT

Each person has a literature inside them. But when people lose language, when they have to experiment with putting their thoughts together on the spot—that's what I love most. That's where character lives.

~ ANNA DEAVERE SMITH

Existence is no more than the precarious attainment of relevance in an intensely mobile flux of past, present, and future.

~ SUSAN SONTAG

The real evidence of growing older is that things level off in importance.

~ GLADYS TABER

I have no riches but my thoughts. Yet these are wealth enough for me.

~ SARA TEASDALE

The only real elegance is in the mind; if you've got that, the rest really comes from it.

~ DIANA VREELAND

Love and Compassion

The Eskimos had fifty-two names for snow because it was important to them; there ought to be as many for love.

~ MARGARET ATWOOD

Not all of us have to possess earthshaking talent. Just common sense and love will do.

~ MYRTLE AUVIL

A woman who is loved always has success.

~ VICKI BAUM

There is a time for work. And a time for love. That leaves no other time.

~ COCO CHANEL

The secret of a happy marriage is finding the right person. You know they're right if you love to be with them all of the time.
~ JULIA CHILD

To serve thy generation, this thy fate:
"Written in water," swiftly fades thy name;
But he who loves his kind does, first or late,
A work too great for fame.
~ MARY CLEMMER

Real charity and a real ability never to condemn—the one real virtue—is so often the result of a waking experience that gives a glimpse of what lies beneath things.
~ IVY COMPTON-BURNETT

I don't want to live—I want to love first, and live incidentally.
~ ZELDA FITZGERALD

Love and respect are the most important aspects of parenting, and of all relationships.
~ JODIE FOSTER

Just pray for a tough hide and a tender heart.
~ RUTH GRAHAM

Nor need we power or splendor, wide hall or lordly dome; the good, the true, the tender—these form the wealth of home.
~ SARAH JOSEPHA HALE

Love, I find, is like singing. Everybody can do enough to satisfy themselves, though it may not impress the neighbors as being very much.
~ ZORA NEALE HURSTON

A caress is better than a career.
~ ELIZABETH MARBURY

I personally measure success in terms of the contributions an individual makes to his or her fellow human beings.

~ MARGARET MEAD

What is it that love does to a woman? Without it, she only sleeps; with it alone, she lives.

~ OUIDA

What a richly colored strong warm coat is woven when love is the warp and work is the woof.

~ MARGE PIERCY

We cannot really love anybody with whom we never laugh.

~ AGNES REPPLIER

Someone once asked me what I regarded as the three most important requirements for happiness. My answer was: "A feeling that you have been honest with yourself and those around you; a feeling that you have done the best you could both in your personal life and in your work; and the ability to love others."

~ ELEANOR ROOSEVELT

There is only one happiness in life, to love and be loved.

~ GEORGE SAND

There are only two things that are absolute realities, love and knowledge, and you can't escape them.

~ OLIVE SCHREINER

There is nothing ridiculous in love.

~ OLIVE SCHREINER

Our society allows people to be absolutely neurotic and totally out of touch with their feelings and everyone else's feelings, and yet be very respectable.

~ NTOZAKE SHANGE

He has achieved success, who has lived well, laughed often, and loved much; who has gained the respect of intelligent men and the love of little children.

∼ BESSIE A. STANLEY

Nothing has happened today except kindness.

∼ GERTRUDE STEIN

Some pray to marry the man they love, my prayer will somewhat vary; I humbly pray to Heaven above that I love the man I marry.

∼ ROSE PASTOR STOKES

If a man is pictured chopping off a woman's breast, it only gets an R rating, but if, God forbid, a man is pictured kissing a woman's breast, it gets an X rating. Why is violence more acceptable than tenderness?

∼ SALLY STRUTHERS

We are rich only through what we give, and poor only through what we refuse.

∼ ANNE-SOPHIE SWETCHINE

Infatuation is when you think that he's as sexy as Robert Redford, as smart as Henry Kissinger, as noble as Ralph Nader, as funny as Woody Allen, and as athletic as Jimmy Conners. Love is when you realize that he's as sexy as Woody Allen, as smart as Jimmy Conners, as funny as Ralph Nader, as athletic as Henry Kissinger, and nothing like Robert Redford—but you'll take him anyway.

∼ JUDITH VIORST

It's not the men in my life that count, it's the life in my men.

∼ MAE WEST

Good Health

I figure if I have my health, can pay the rent and I have my friends, I call it "content."

~ LAUREN BACALL

Happiness is good health and a bad memory.

~ INGRID BERGMAN

After you're older, two things are possibly more important than any others: health and money.

~ HELEN GURLEY BROWN

The best course was to buy a house across a road from a cemetery and look at it every morning. Reminding yourself where it all ended anyway, you'd never get upset about anything again.

~ MILDRED DAVIS

Tragedy had its compensations. Once the worst misfortune occurred, one never worried about the minor ones.

~ MILDRED DAVIS

A healthy woman is a successful woman.

~ FRENCH PROVERB

Vitality! That's the pursuit of life, isn't it?

~ KATHARINE HEPBURN

Give me good health and I'll take care of the rest.

~ MARILYN HORNE

My gift is that I'm not beautiful. My career was never about looks. It's about health and being in good shape.

~ SHIRLEY MACLAINE

God prefers your health, and your obedience, to your penance.

~ TERESA OF AVILA

It's What Inside That Counts

It doesn't help your five-iron if you're pretty.
~ LAURA BAUGH

I've never sought success in order to get fame and money; it's the talent and the passion that count in success.
~ INGRID BERGMAN

We all lose our looks eventually, better develop your character and interest in life.
~ JACQUELINE BISSET

There is only one history of any importance, and it is the history of what you once believed in, and the history of what you came to believe in.
~ KAY BOYLE

The only thing that makes one place more attractive to me than another is the quantity of heart I find in it.
~ JANE WELSH CARLYLE

Crooked logs make straight fires.
~ ENGLISH PROVERB

Toughness doesn't have to come in a pinstripe suit.
~ DIANNE FEINSTEIN

A woman may develop wrinkles and cellulite, lose her waistline, her bustline, her ability to bear a child, even her sense of humor, but none of that implies a loss of her sexuality, her femininity.
~ BARBARA GORDON

How long can you be cute?
~ GOLDIE HAWN

Being pretty on the inside means you don't hit your brother and you eat all your peas—that's what my grandma taught me.
~ ELIZABETH HELLER

Beauty is in the eye of the beholder.

~ MARGARET WOLFE HUNGERFORD

When you're fifty, you start thinking about things you haven't thought about before. I used to think getting old was about vanity—but actually it's about losing people you love. Getting wrinkles is trivial.

~ JOYCE CAROL OATES

After a certain number of years, our faces become our biographies.

~ CYNTHIA OZICK

Beauty to me is being comfortable in your own skin.

~ GWYNETH PALTROW

Not always the fanciest cake that's there
Is the best to eat!

~ MARGARET ELIZABETH SANGSTER

When you've got the personality, you don't need the nudity.

~ MAE WEST

A man can be short and dumpy and getting bald but if he has fire, women will like him.

~ MAE WEST

Everything's in the mind. That's where it all starts. Knowing what you want is the first step toward getting it.

~ MAE WEST

Experience and Achievement

Experience isn't interesting till it begins to repeat itself—in fact, till it does that, it hardly is experience.

~ ELIZABETH BOWEN

That is happiness; to be dissolved into something complete and great.

~ WILLA CATHER

We can't take any credit for our talents. It's how we use them that counts.
~ MADELEINE L'ENGLE

What really matters is what you do with what you have.
~ SHIRLEY LORD

Age is totally unimportant. The years are really irrelevant. It's how you cope with them.
~ SHIRLEY LORD

Where I was born and where and how I have lived is unimportant. It is what I have done with where I have been that should be of interest.
~ GEORGIA O'KEEFE

Experience is what really happens to you in the long run; the truth that finally overtakes you.
~ KATHERINE ANNE PORTER

Skilled labor teaches something not to be found in books or in colleges.
~ LAURA TOWNE

Work, Career, and Loving What You Do

The measure of achievement is not winning awards. It's doing something that you appreciate, something you believe is worthwhile. I think of my strawberry soufflé. I did that at least twenty-eight times before I finally conquered it.
~ JULIA CHILD

Duties are what make life most worth living. Lacking them, you are not necessary to anyone.
~ MARLENE DIETRICH

Neither woman nor man lives by work, or love, alone....The human self defines itself and grows through love AND work: All psychology before and after Freud boils down to that.
~ BETTY FRIEDAN

Work is creativity accompanied by the comforting realization that one is bringing forth something really good and necessary, with a conviction that a sudden, arbitrary cessation would cause a sensitive void, produce a loss.

~ JENNY HEYNRICHS

The medals don't mean anything and the glory doesn't last. It's all about your happiness. The rewards are going to come, but my happiness is just loving the sport and having fun performing.

~ JACKIE JOYNER-KERSEE

The simple idea that everyone needs a reasonable amount of challenging work in his or her life, and also a personal life, complete with noncompetitive leisure, has never really taken hold.

~ JUDITH MARTIN (MISS MANNERS)

What a richly colored strong warm coat is woven when love is the warp and work is the woof.

~ MARGE PIERCY

Like plowing, housework makes the ground ready for the germination of family life. The kids will not invite a teacher home if beer cans litter the living room. The family isn't likely to have breakfast together if somebody didn't remember to buy eggs, milk, or muffins. Housework maintains an orderly setting in which family life can flourish.

~ LETTY COTTIN POGREBIN

To find in ourselves what makes life worth living is risky business, for it means that once we know we must seek it. It also means that without it life will be valueless.

~ MARSHA SINETAR

To deny we need and want power is to deny that we hope to be effective.

~ LIZ SMITH

When I die, my epitaph should read: She Paid the Bills.

~ GLORIA SWANSON

Style and Grace

Fashion can be bought. Style one must possess.
~ EDNA WOOLMAN CHASE

Fashion is general; style is individual.
~ EDNA WOOLMAN CHASE AND ILKA CHASE

Styles, like everything else, change. Style doesn't.
~ LINDA ELLERBEE

I base most of my fashion taste on what doesn't itch.
~ GILDA RADNER

Spend all you have for loveliness.
~ SARA TEASDALE

The only real elegance is in the mind; if you've got that, the rest really comes from it.
~ DIANA VREELAND

Elegance is innate.... It has nothing to do with being well dressed.
~ DIANA VREELAND

Of two evils choose the prettier.
~ CAROLYN WELLS

Memories

How we remember, what we remember, and why we remember form the most personal map of our individuality.
~ CHRISTINA BALDWIN

Heirlooms we don't have in our family. But stories we've got.
~ ROSE CHERNIN

These are the stories that never, never die, that are carried like seed
into a new country, are told to you and me and make in us new and
lasting strengths.

~ MERIDEL LE SUEUR

What one loves in childhood stays in the heart forever.

~ MARY JO PUTNEY

The universe is made of stories, not of atoms.

~ MURIEL RUKEYSER

It's a pleasure to share one's memories. Everything remembered is
dear, endearing, touching, precious. At least the past is safe—though
we didn't know it at the time. We know it now. Because it's in the
past; because we have survived.

~ SUSAN SONTAG

The events in our lives happen in a sequence in time, but in their
significance to ourselves, they find their own order ... the
continuous thread of revelation.

~ EUDORA WELTY

Being Content with a Little

Fame is a pearl many dive for and only a few bring up. Even when
they do, it is not perfect, and they sigh for more, and lose better
things in struggling for them.

~ LOUISA MAY ALCOTT

The greatest wealth is contentment with a little.

~ ANON.

Economy, prudence, and a simple life are the sure masters of need,
and will often accomplish that which their opposites, with a fortune
at hand, will fail to do.

~ CLARA BARTON

A sure way to lose happiness, I found, is to want it at the expense of everything else.

~ BETTE DAVIS

Wealth consists not in having great possessions but in having few wants.

~ ESTHER DE WAAL

When we start deceiving ourselves into thinking not that we want something or need something, not that it is a pragmatic necessity for us to have it, but that it is a moral imperative that we have it, then is when we join the fashionable madmen, and then is when the thin whine of hysteria is heard in the land, and then is when we are in bad trouble.

~ JOAN DIDION

It's a grand thing to be able to take your money in your hand and to think no more of it when it slips away from you than you would a trout that would slip back into the stream.

~ AUGUSTA GREGORY

A speech does not need to be eternal to be immortal.

~ MURIEL HUMPHREY

The things people discard tell more about them than the things they keep.

~ HILDA LAWRENCE

A man who accustoms himself to buy superfluities is often in want of necessities.

~ HANNAH FARNHAM LEE

The best thing that can come with success is the knowledge that it is nothing to long for.

~ LIV ULLMANN

TWO

Developing Positive Habits

*A*ccepting Responsibility

Life Is What You Make It

I don't want to be a passenger in my own life.
~ DIANE ACKERMAN

What we say and what we do ultimately comes back to us so let us
own our responsibility, place it in our hands, and carry it with
dignity and strength.
~ GLORIA EVANGELINA ANZALDUA

The less I behave like Whistler's mother the night before, the more I
look like her the morning after.
~ TALLULAH BANKHEAD

Marriage is not just spiritual communication and passionate
embraces; marriage is also three meals a day, sharing the workload,
and remembering to carry out the trash.
~ DR. JOYCE BROTHERS

Every action we take, everything we do, is either a victory or defeat in the struggle to become what we want to be.

~ ANNE BYRHHE

Happiness is not something you get, but something you do.

~ MARCELENE COX

We are free up to the point of choice, then the choice controls the chooser.

~ MARY CROWLEY

To be born free is an accident; to live free a responsibility; to die free is an obligation.

~ MRS. HUBBARD DAVIS

When you make a commitment to a relationship, you invest your attention and energy in it more profoundly because you now experience ownership of that relationship.

~ BARBARA DE ANGELIS

Getting fit is a political act—you are taking charge of your life.

~ JANE FONDA

I was always looking outside myself for strength and confidence, but it comes from within. It is there all the time.

~ ANNA FREUD

It is easier to live life through someone else than to become complete yourself.

~ BETTY FRIEDAN

God gives the nuts, but He does not crack them.

~ GERMAN PROVERB

Being black does not stop you. You can sit out in the world and say, "Well, white people kept me back, and I can't do this." Not so. You can have anything you want if you make up your mind and you want it.

~ CLARA MCBRIDE HALE

No man may make another free.

~ ZORA NEALE HURSTON

As far as beauty is concerned, in order to be confident we must accept that the way we look and feel is our own responsibility.

~ SOPHIA LOREN

Exude happiness and you will feel it back a thousand times.

~ JOAN LUNDEN

What you have become is the price you paid to get what you used to want.

~ MIGNON MCLAUGHLIN

In dreams begins responsibility.

~ EDNA O'BRIEN

Real apprenticeship is ultimately always to the self.

~ CYNTHIA OZICK

Ask God's blessing on your work, but don't ask him to do it for you.

~ DAME FLORA ROBSON

Nothing strengthens the judgment and quickens the conscience like individual responsibility.

~ ELIZABETH CADY STANTON

You are the product of your own brainstorm.

~ ROSEMARY KONNER STEINBAUM

I long to put the experience of fifty years at once into your young lives, to give you at once the key to that treasure chamber every gem of which has cost me tears and struggles and prayers, but you must work for these inward treasures yourselves.

~ HARRIET BEECHER STOWE

The best place to find a helping hand is at the end of your own arm.

~ SWEDISH PROVERB

Do not wait for leaders; do it alone, person to person.

~ MOTHER TERESA

Seek not good from without: seek it within yourselves, or you will never find it.

~ BERTHA VON SUTTNER

My satisfaction comes from my commitment to advancing a better world.

~ FAYE WATTLETON

You end up as you deserve. In old age you must put up with the face, the friends, the health, and the children you have earned.

~ FAY WELDON

How you run your life, that's how your clock will run.

~ YIDDISH PROVERB

It's Up to You to Make Things Happen

We have too many sounding words and too few actions that correspond with them.

~ ABIGAIL ADAMS

Liberty cannot be caged into a charter and handed on ready-made to the next generation. Each generation must recreate liberty for its own times. Whether or not we establish freedom rests with ourselves.

~ FLORENCE ELLINWOOD ALLEN

I am one of those people who are blessed ... with a nature which has to interfere. If I see a thing that needs doing I do it.

~ MARGERY ALLINGHAM

Happiness is a conscious choice, not an automatic response.

~ MILDRED BARTHEL

Carry on, carry on, for the men and boys are gone,
But the furrow shan't lie fallow while the women carry on.
〜 JANET BEGBIE

I must have something to engross my thoughts, some object in life which
will fill this vacuum and prevent this sad wearing away of the heart.
〜 ELIZABETH BLACKWELL

The willingness to accept responsibility for one's own life is the
source from which self-respect springs.
〜 JOAN DIDION

If you don't like the way the world is, you change it. You have an
obligation to change it. You just do it one step at a time.
〜 MARIAN WRIGHT EDELMAN

To heal ourselves we also have to heal society.
〜 RIANE EISLER

To attain happiness in another world we need only to believe
something; to secure it in this world, we must do something.
〜 CHARLOTTE P. GILMAN

It is not our circumstances that create our discontent or
contentment. It is us.
〜 VIVIAN GREENE

Fortunately the family is a human institution: humans made it and
humans can change it.
〜 SHERE HITE

Any committee is only as good as the most knowledgeable,
determined, and vigorous person on it. There must be somebody
who provides the flame.
〜 LADY BIRD JOHNSON

My father instilled in me that if you don't see things happening the
way you want them to, you get out there and make them happen.
〜 SUSAN POWTER

Here is where some entrepreneurs fail. They are filled with creative juices and total commitment to their business, but too often they don't understand that they must also be managers, administrators, even gofers—at least for a while.

～ LILLIAN VERNON

Sometimes you gotta create what you want to be a part of.

～ GERI WEITZMAN

Don't Point Fingers

It takes two flints to make a fire.

～ LOUISA MAY ALCOTT

It is no use blaming the men—we made them what they are—and now it is up to us to try and make ourselves—the makers of men—a little more responsible.

～ NANCY ASTOR

Revolution begins with the self, in the self.

～ TONI CADE BAMBARA

Lead me not into temptation; I can find the way myself.

～ RITA MAE BROWN

We need to restore the full meaning of that old word, duty. It is the other side of rights.

～ PEARL S. BUCK

The way to achieve happiness is to have a high standard for yourself and a medium one for everyone else.

～ MARCELENE COX

Every person is responsible for all the good within the scope of his abilities, and for no more, and none can tell whose sphere is the largest.

～ GAIL HAMILTON

We make our own criminals, and their crimes are congruent with the national culture we all share. It has been said that a people get the kind of political leadership they deserve. I think they also get the kinds of crime and criminals they themselves bring into being.

$\sim$ MARGARET MEAD

We are accountable only to ourselves for what happens to us in our lives.

$\sim$ MILDRED NEWMAN

I attribute my success to this: I never gave or took an excuse.

$\sim$ FLORENCE NIGHTINGALE

Believe there is a great power silently working all things for good, behave yourself and never mind the rest.

$\sim$ BEATRIX POTTER

I made the decision. I'm accountable.

$\sim$ JANET RENO

Remember That Others Rely On and Look Up to You

If you can't be a good example, then you'll just have to be a horrible warning.

$\sim$ CATHERINE AIRD

Let everyone who has the grace of intelligence fear that, because of it, he will be judged more heavily if he is negligent.

$\sim$ SAINT BRIDGET OF SWEDEN

Service to others is the rent you pay for living on this planet.

$\sim$ MARIAN WRIGHT EDELMAN

To be a revolutionary you have to be a human being. You have to care about people who have no power.

$\sim$ JANE FONDA

Never reach out your hand unless you're willing to extend an arm.

~ ELIZABETH FULLER

It is not who you attend school with but who controls the school you attend.

~ NIKKI GIOVANNI

What is buried in the past of one generation falls to the next to claim.

~ SUSAN GRIFFIN

We've got to work to save our children and do it with full respect for the fact that if we do not, no one else is going to do it.

~ DOROTHY HEIGHT

No matter how lofty you are in your department, the responsibility for what your lowliest assistant is doing is yours.

~ BESSIE ROWLAND JAMES

Until the great mass of the people shall be filled with the sense of responsibility for each other's welfare, social justice can never be attained.

~ HELEN KELLER

We need to teach the next generation of children from day one that they are responsible for their lives.

~ ELISABETH KUBLER-ROSS

When you are a mother, you are never really alone in your thoughts.... A mother has to think twice, once for herself and once for her child.

~ SOPHIA LOREN

The oppressed never free themselves—they do not have the necessary strengths.

~ CLARE BOOTHE LUCE

My voice has been raised not only in song, but to make the big world outside Through me, understand something of the spirit of my beloved country.

~ NELLIE MELBA

I shall not pass this way again:
Then let me now relieve some pain,
Remove some barrier from the road,
Or brighten some one's heavy load.

~ EVA ROSE PARK

I think if I were dying and I heard of an act of injustice, it would
start me up to a moment's life again.

~ OLIVE SCHREINER

I am glad to see that men are getting their rights, but I want women
to get theirs, and while the water is stirring I will step into the pool.

~ SOJOURNER TRUTH

Don't Complain or Criticize

If you have no will to change it, you have no will to criticize it.

~ ANON.

It's better to light a candle than curse the darkness.

~ ELEANOR ROOSEVELT

It was completely fruitless to quarrel with the world, whereas the
quarrel with oneself was occasionally fruitful and always, she had to
admit, interesting.

~ MAY SARTON

Don't Just Talk—Act

We have too many sounding words and too few actions that correspond with them.

~ ABIGAIL ADAMS

A woman of words and not of deeds is like a garden full of weeds.

~ ANON.

There are people who put their dreams in a little box and say, "Yes, I've got dreams, of course, I've got dreams." Then they put the box away and bring it out once in a while to look in it, and yep, they're still there. These are great dreams, but they never even get out of the box. It takes an uncommon amount of guts to put your dreams on the line, to hold them up and say, "How good or how bad am I?" That's where courage comes in.

~ ERMA BOMBECK

There is a need for heroism in American life today.

~ AGNES MEYER

It's where we go, and what we do when we get there, that tells us who we are.

~ JOYCE CAROL OATES

There can be no happiness if the things we believe in are different from the things we do.

~ FREYA STARK

Ef women want any rights more'n dey got, why don't dey jes' take 'em and not be talkin' about it.

~ SOJOURNER TRUTH

All talk of women's rights is moonshine. Women have every right. They have only to exercise them.

~ VICTORIA CLAFFIN WOODHULL

A meowing cat catches no mice.

~ YIDDISH PROVERB

The World Does Not Owe You Anything

One has to handle these negative experiences alone. You can't get help from your friends or family. You're finally alone with it, and you have to come to grips with misfortune and go on.

     ~ SHIRLEY TEMPLE BLACK

Self-pity is a death that has no resurrection, a sinkhole from which no rescuing hand can drag you because you have chosen to sink.

     ~ ELIZABETH ELLIOT

It is not our circumstances that create our discontent or contentment. It is us.

     ~ VIVIAN GREENE

You've got to do your own growing, not matter how tall your grandfather was.

     ~ IRISH PROVERB

Take your life in your own hands, and what happens? A terrible thing: no one to blame.

     ~ ERICA JONG

Life's under no obligation to give us what we expect.

     ~ MARGARET MITCHELL

Expect nothing. Live frugally on surprise.

     ~ ALICE WALKER

If you put in you can take out.

     ~ YIDDISH PROVERB

Don't Turn a Blind Eye to Problems

We run away all the time to avoid coming face to face with ourselves.
~ ANON.

Truth can be outraged by silence quite as cruelly as by speech.
~ AMELIA BARR

Most of our platitudes notwithstanding, self-deception remains the most difficult deception. The tricks that worked on others count for nothing in that very well-lit back alley where one keeps assignations with oneself: no winning smiles will do here, no prettily drawn list of good intentions.
~ JOAN DIDION

No matter where I run, I meet myself there.
~ DOROTHY FIELDS

You can do one of two things; just shut up, which is something I don't find easy, or learn an awful lot very fast, which is what I tried to do.
~ JANE FONDA

Anything in life that we don't accept will simply make trouble for us until we make peace with it.
~ SHAKTI GAWAIN

Science may have found a cure for most evils; but it has found no remedy for the worst of them all—the apathy of human beings.
~ HELEN KELLER

The accomplice to the crime of corruption is frequently our own indifference.
~ BESS MYERSON

Ignorance is no excuse—it's the real thing.
~ IRENE PETER

My doctrine is this, that if we see cruelty or wrong that we have the power to stop, and do nothing, we make ourselves sharers in the guilt.

~ ANNA SEWELL

Whenever two good people argue over principles, they are both right.

~ MARIE VON EBNER-ESCHENBACH

Don't Be Fatalistic

Keep doing what you're doing and you'll keep getting what you're getting.

~ ANON.

No age or time of life, no position or circumstance, has a monopoly on success. Any age is the right age to start doing!

~ ANON.

One is not born a genius, one becomes a genius.

~ SIMONE DE BEAUVOIR

If you haven't been happy very young, you can still be happy later on, but it's much harder. You need more luck.

~ SIMONE DE BEAUVOIR

To have a curable illness and to leave it untreated except for prayer is like sticking your hand in a fire and asking God to remove the flame.

~ SANDRA L. DOUGLAS

It is not our circumstances that create our discontent or contentment. It is us.

~ VIVIAN GREENE

Mankind's greatest gift ... is that we have free choice.

~ ELISABETH KUBLER-ROSS

The process of maturing is an art to be learned, an effort to be sustained. By the age of fifty, you have made yourself what you are, and if it is good, it is better than your youth.

~ MARYA MANNES

Choice is the essence of what I believe it is to be human.

~ LIV ULLMANN

Don't Shrink from a Challenge

I wish I were with some of the wild people that run in the woods, and know nothing about accomplishments!

~ JOANNA BAILLIE

You have to do what you love to do, not get stuck in that comfort zone of a regular job. Life is not a dress rehearsal. This is it.

~ LUCINDA BASSET

I used to believe that marriage would diminish me, reduce my options. That you had to be someone less to live with someone else when, of course, you have to be someone more.

~ CANDICE BERGEN

Borrowed thoughts, like borrowed money, only show the poverty of the borrower.

~ LADY MARGUERITE BLESSINGTON

There are people who put their dreams in a little box and say, "Yes, I've got dreams, of course, I've got dreams." Then they put the box away and bring it out once in a while to look in it, and yep, they're still there. These are great dreams, but they never even get out of the box. It takes an uncommon amount of guts to put your dreams on the line, to hold them up and say, "How good or how bad am I?" That's where courage comes in.

~ ERMA BOMBECK

He who walks in another's tracks leaves no footprints.

～ JOAN L. BRANNON

The human mind prefers to be spoon-fed with the thoughts of others, but deprived of such nourishment it will, reluctantly, begin to think for itself—and such thinking, remember, is original thinking and may have valuable results.

～ AGATHA CHRISTIE

If we choose to be no more than clods of clay, then we shall be used as clods of clay for braver feet to tread on.

～ MARIE CORELLI

I'll have to, as you say, take a stand, do something toward shaking up that system.... Despair ... is too easy an out.

～ PAULE MARSHALL

Hiding leads nowhere except to more hiding.

～ MARGARET A. ROBINSON

There is no movement without our own resistance.

～ DR. LAURA SCHLESSINGER

If the sky falls, hold up your hands.

～ SPANISH PROVERB

If the first woman God ever made was strong enough to turn the world upside down, these women together ought to be able to turn it right side up again.

～ SOJOURNER TRUTH

Fear not those who argue but those who dodge.

～ MARIE VON EBNER-ESCHENBACH

We must prepare and study truth under every aspect, endeavoring to ignore nothing, if we do not wish to fall into the abyss of the unknown when the hour shall strike.

～ MARIE VON EBNER-ESCHENBACH

It is a fact of history that those who seek to withdraw from its great experiments usually end up being overwhelmed by them.

⁓ BARBARA WARD

Admit When You're Wrong

Grant us peace, Almighty Father, so to pray as to deserve to be heard.

⁓ JANE AUSTEN

Ah, how steadily do they who are guilty shrink from reproof!

⁓ AMELIA JENKS BLOOMER

I've arrived at this outermost edge of my life by my own actions. Where I am is thoroughly unacceptable. Therefore, I must stop doing what I have been doing.

⁓ ALICE KOLLER

I believe we are solely responsible for our choices, and we have to accept the consequences of every deed, word, and thought throughout our lifetime.

⁓ ELISABETH KUBLER-ROSS

Doing the Right Thing

Acting Ethically

Social advance depends as much upon the process through which it
is secured as upon the result itself.

~ JANE ADDAMS

Do all the good you can,
By all the means you can,
In all the ways you can,
In all the places you can,
At all the times you can.

~ ANON.

Children use the fist
Until they are of the age to use the brain.

~ ELIZABETH BARRETT BROWNING

Those who set their minds on virtue will do no evil.

~ CHINESE PROVERB

Crime seems to change character when it crosses a bridge or a tunnel. In the city, crime is taken as emblematic of class and race. In the suburbs, though, it's intimate and psychological—resistant to generalization, a mystery of the individual soul.

~ BARBARA EHRENREICH

Since when do grown men and women, who presume to hold high government office and exercise what they think of as "moral leadership," require ethics officers to tell them whether it is or isn't permissible to grab the secretary's behind or redirect public funds to their own personal advantage?

~ MEG GREENFIELD

Wisdom and virtue are like the two wheels of a cart.

~ JAPANESE PROVERB

Vice
Is nice
But a little virtue
Won't hurt you.

~ FELICIA LAMPORT

The lesser evil is also evil.

~ NAOMI MITCHISON

The great majority of successful business men and women have been and are possessors of strong personalities of the right sort, and by analyzing their climb to success it is amazing to discover how large a part good manners, good breeding, and correct behavior have had in helping them to win the goal.

~ IDA WHITE PARKER

I don't eat junk food and I don't think junk thoughts.

~ PEACE PILGRIM

The Department of Justice is committed to asking one central question of everything we do: What is the right thing to do? Now that can produce debate, and I want it to be spirited debate. I want the lawyers of America to be able to call me and tell me: Janet, have you lost your mind?

~ JANET RENO

You have to count on living every single day in a way you believe will make you feel good about your life, so that if it were over tomorrow, you'd be content.

~ JANE SEYMOUR

Noble deeds and hot baths are the best cures for depression.

~ DODIE SMITH

The voice of conscience is so delicate that it is easy to stifle it; but it is also so clear that it is impossible to mistake it.

~ MADAME DE STAËL

The act of acting morally is behaving as if everything we do matters.

~ GLORIA STEINEM

I place a high moral value on the way people behave. I find it repellent to have a lot, and to behave with anything other than courtesy in the old sense of the word—politeness of the heart, a gentleness of the spirit.

~ EMMA THOMPSON

Happy is she who conducts herself honorably.

~ YIDDISH PROVERB

Following a Divine Example

Christ has made my soul beautiful with the jewels of grace and virtue.
~ SAINT AGNES

Our awesome responsibility to ourselves, to our children, and to the future is to create ourselves in the image of goodness, because the future depends on the nobility of our imaginings.
~ BARBARA GRIZZUTI HARRISON

Charity. To love human beings in so far as they are nothing. That is to love them as God does.
~ SIMONE WEIL

Being Truthful

Truth is the vital breath of Beauty; Beauty the outward form of Truth.
~ GRACE AGUILAR

The trouble with lying and deceiving is that their efficiency depends entirely upon a clear notion of the truth that the liar and deceiver wishes to hide.
~ HANNAH ARENDT

There is at least one thing more brutal than the truth, and that is the consequence of saying less than the truth.
~ TI-GRACE ATKINSON

Defending the truth is not something one does out of a sense of duty or to allay guilt complexes, but is a reward in itself.
~ SIMONE DE BEAUVOIR

No blame should attach to telling the truth.
~ ANITA BROOKNER

The elegance of honesty needs no adornment.
~ MERRY BROWNE

Truth is always exciting. Speak it, then; life is dull without it.
~ PEARL S. BUCK

You cannot weave truth on a loom of lies.
~ SUZETTE HADEN ELGIN

A lie travels round the world while truth is putting her boots on.
~ FRENCH PROVERB

Earnestness and sincerity are synonymous.
~ CORITA KENT

The naked truth is always better than the best-dressed lie.
~ ANN LANDERS

The ultimate umpire of all things in life is—fact.
~ AGNES C. LAUT

The most exhausting thing in life is being insincere.
~ ANNE MORROW LINDBERGH

If the word *frankly* or *sincerely* is not uttered in the first ten minutes—
or *let us speak openly*—then you are not in the presence of a genuine
businessman, and he will certainly go bankrupt.
~ FRANÇOISE MALLET-JORIS

If I ever said in grief or pride,
I tired of honest things, I lied.
~ EDNA ST. VINCENT MILLAY

Truth, that fair goddess who comes always with healing in her wings.
~ ANNE SHANNON MONROE

There is in the end no remedy but truth. It is the one course that
cannot be evil.
~ ELLIS PETERS

There is no power on earth more formidable than the truth.
~ MARGARET LEE RUNBECK

If one cannot invent a really convincing lie, it is often better to stick to the truth.

~ ANGELA THIRKELL

If you tell the truth, you don't have to swear.

~ YIDDISH PROVERB

Setting a Good Example

If you can't be a good example, then you'll just have to be a horrible warning.

~ CATHERINE AIRD

You find yourself refreshed by the presence of cheerful people. Why not make an honest effort to confer that pleasure on others? Half the battle is gained if you never allow yourself to say anything gloomy.

~ LYDIA MARIA CHILD

What is buried in the past of one generation falls to the next to claim.

~ SUSAN GRIFFIN

We can be wise from goodness and good from wisdom.

~ MARIE VON EBNER-ESCHENBACH

Sticking to Your Principles

The attainment of justice is the highest human endeavor.

~ FLORENCE ELLINWOOD ALLEN

When one bases her life on principle, 99 percent of her decisions are already made.

~ ANON.

A good message will always find a messenger.

~ AMELIA BARR

It's no good saying one thing and doing another.
~ CATHERINE COOKSON

Decide on what you think is right, and stick to it.
~ GEORGE ELIOT

Let how you live your life stand for something, no matter how small and incidental it may seem.
~ JODIE FOSTER

Conscience, as I understand it, is the impulse to do the right thing because it is right, regardless of personal ends, and has nothing whatever to do with the ability to distinguish between right and wrong.
~ MARGARET COLLIER GRAHAM

I cannot and will not cut my conscience to fit this year's fashions.
~ LILLIAN HELLMAN

What's got badly, goes badly.
~ IRISH PROVERB

Don't compromise yourself. You're all you've got.
~ JANIS JOPLIN

Being Socially Responsible

It is human nature that rules the world, not governments and regimes.
~ SVETLANA ALLILUYEVA

Injustice is a sixth sense, and rouses all the others.
~ AMELIA BARR

An institution or reform movement that is not selfish, must originate in the recognition of some evil that is adding to the sum of human suffering, or diminishing the sum of happiness. I suppose it is a philanthropic movement to try to reverse the process.
~ CLARA BARTON

The true worth of a race must be measured by the character of its womanhood.

~ MARY MCLEOD BETHUNE

It is well worth the efforts of a lifetime to have attained knowledge which justifies an attack on the root of all evil ... which asserts that because forms of evil have always existed in society, therefore they must always exist.

~ ELIZABETH BLACKWELL

Most Americans have never seen the ignorance, degradation, hunger, sickness, and the futility in which many other Americans live....They won't become involved in economic or political change until someone brings the seriousness of the situation home to them.

~ SHIRLEY CHISHOLM

Sow good services; sweet remembrances will grow from them.

~ MADAME DE STAËL

Make the world better.

~ LUCY STONE

Respecting Others

As long as you keep a person down, some part of you has to be down there to hold him down, so it means you cannot soar as you otherwise might.

~ MARIAN ANDERSON

Power is the ability to do good things for others.

~ BROOKE ASTOR

Character builds slowly, but it can be torn down with incredible swiftness.

~ FAITH BALDWIN

Never say anything on the phone that you wouldn't want your
mother to hear at your trial.
~ SYDNEY BIDDLE BARROWS

Better to be without logic than without feeling.
~ CHARLOTTE BRONTË

You cannot make yourself feel something you cannot feel, but you
can make yourself do right in spite of your feelings.
~ PEARL S. BUCK

Be pretty if you can, be witty if you must, but be gracious if it kills you.
~ ELSIE DE WOLFE

The whole human race loses by every act of personal vengeance.
~ RAE FOLEY

Nothing is as burdensome as a secret.
~ FRENCH PROVERB

Cruelty is the only sin.
~ ELLEN GLASGOW

Before a secret is told, one can often feel the weight of it in the
atmosphere.
~ SUSAN GRIFFIN

To be meek, patient, tactful, modest, honorable, brave, is not to be
either manly or womanly, it is to be humane.
~ JANE HARRISON

Who sows thorns should not go barefoot.
~ ITALIAN PROVERB

I never fight, except against difficulties.
~ HELEN KELLER

Not observation of a duty but liberty itself is the pledge that assures fidelity.

~ ELLEN KEY

A cruel story runs on wheels, and every hand oils the wheels as they run.

~ OUIDA

Justice and judgment lie often a world apart.

~ EMMELINE PANKHURST

He that despiseth his neighbor sinneth; but he that hath mercy on the poor, happy is he.

~ PROVERBS

If you give your life as a wholehearted response to love, then love will wholeheartedly respond to you.

~ MARIANNE WILLIAMSON

Realizing the Consequences of Your Actions

History is a stern judge.

~ SVETLANA ALLILUYEVA

I get a little angry about this high-handed scrapping of the look of things. What else have we to go by? How else can the average person form an opinion of a girl's sense of values or even of her chastity except by the looks of her conduct?

~ MARGARET CULKIN BANNING

You wouldn't want to be caught wearing cheap perfume, would you? Then why do you want to wear cheap perfume on your conduct?

~ MARGARET CULKIN BANNING

The difference between weakness and wickedness is much less than people suppose; and the consequences are nearly always the same.

~ LADY MARGUERITE BLESSINGTON

Authority without wisdom is like a heavy axe without an edge, fitter to bruise than to polish.

~ ANNE BRADSTREET

One faces the future with one's past.

~ PEARL S. BUCK

Our deeds still travel with us from afar, and what we have been makes us what we are.

~ GEORGE ELIOT

The beginning of compunction is the beginning of a new life.

~ GEORGE ELIOT

Character is easier kept than recovered.

~ ENGLISH PROVERB

Add not fire to fire.

~ GREEK PROVERB

Life is for one generation. A good name is forever.

~ JAPANESE PROVERB

You must not change one thing, one pebble, one grain of sand, until you know what good and evil will follow on that act.

~ URSULA K. LE GUIN

Making Good Choices

Where bad is best, bad must be the only choice.

~ ANON.

Here's a rule I recommend. Never practice two vices at once.

~ TALLULAH BANKHEAD

Of course, fortune has its part in human affairs, but conduct is really much more important.

~ JEAN DETOURBEY

A clear conscience is a soft pillow.

~ GERMAN PROVERB

The only causes of regret are laziness, outbursts of temper, hurting others, prejudice, jealousy, and envy.

~ GERMAINE GREER

There is always a time to make right what is wrong.

~ SUSAN GRIFFIN

Lawlessness is a self-perpetuating, ever-expanding habit.

~ DOROTHY THOMPSON

All sins are attempts to fill voids.

~ SIMONE WEIL

Rob not, repent not.

~ YIDDISH PROVERB

Being True to Yourself

A guilty conscience is a hidden enemy.

~ AMERICAN INDIAN PROVERB

The first and worst of all frauds is to cheat one's self. All sin is easy after that.

~ PEARL BAILEY

Rules of society are nothing; one's conscience is the umpire.

~ MADAME DUDEVANT

Our deeds determine us, as much as we determine our needs.

~ GEORGE ELIOT

Crime is naught but misdirected energy. So long as every institution of today—economic, political, social, and moral—conspires to misdirect human energy into wrong channels; so long as most people are out of place doing the things they hate to do, living a life they loathe to live, crime will be inevitable.

~ EMMA GOLDMAN

To keep your character intact you cannot stoop to filthy acts. It makes it easier to stoop the next time.

~ KATHARINE HEPBURN

Keep integrity and your work ethics intact. So what if that means working a little harder; an honorable character is your best calling card, and that's something anyone can have!

~ KATHY IRELAND

Your own deeds will long be baptized on you.

~ IRISH PROVERB

The world may take your reputation from you, but it cannot take your character.

~ EMMA DUNHAM KELLEY

Put your ear down close to your soul and listen hard.

~ ANNE SEXTON

It's the soul's duty to be loyal to its own desires.

~ REBECCA WEST

Like the winds of the sea are the ways of fate;
As the voyage along thru life;
'Tis the will of the soul
That decides its goal,
And not the calm or the strife.

~ ELLA WHEELER WILCOX

Learning to Share and Give

[Our children] had the privilege of growing up where they'd raised a lot of food. They were never hungry. They could share their food with people. And so, you share your lives with people.

~ ELLA BAKER

In necessary things, unity; in doubtful things, liberty; in all things, charity.

~ ANNE BAXTER

The results of philanthropy are always beyond calculation.

~ MIRIAM BEARD

That's what I consider true generosity. You give your all and yet you always feel as if it costs you nothing.

~ SIMONE DE BEAUVOIR

A cup that is already full cannot have more added to it. In order to receive the further good to which we are entitled, we must give of that which we have.

~ MARGARET BECKER

The fragrance always stays in the hand that gives the rose.

~ HEDA BEJAR

You can give without loving, but you cannot love without giving.

~ AMY CARMICHAEL

Better give a penny than lend twenty.

~ ITALIAN PROVERB

Measure thy life by loss instead of gain,
Not by the wine drunk, but by the wine poured forth.

~ HARRIET KING

Purposeful giving is not as apt to deplete one's resources; it belongs to that natural order of giving that seems to renew itself even in the act of depletion.

~ ANNE MORROW LINDBERGH

Generosity with strings is not generosity: it is a deal.

~ MARYA MANNES

Almsgiving leaves a man just where he was before. Aid restores him to society as an individual worthy of all respect and not as a man with a grievance.

~ EVA PERÓN

You have not lived a perfect day … unless you have done something for someone who will never be able to repay you.

~ RUTH SMELTZER

To have and not to give is often worse than to steal.

~ MARIE VON EBNER-ESCHENBACH

Forgiving Others

Forgiveness is the act of admitting we are like other people.

~ CHRISTINA BALDWIN

Forgiveness is an act of the will, and the will can function regardless of the temperature of the heart.

~ CORRIE TEN BOOM

Living Your Ideals

You cannot contribute anything to the ideal condition of mind and heart known as Brotherhood, however much you preach, posture, or agree, unless you live it.

~ FAITH BALDWIN

The secret of staying young is to live honestly, eat slowly, and lie about your age.

~ LUCILLE BALL

Virtue, like a dowerless beauty, has more admirers than followers.

~ LADY MARGUERITE BLESSINGTON

We can build upon foundations anywhere, if they are well and truly laid.

~ IVY COMPTON-BURNETT

Though language forms the preacher,
'Tis "good works" make the man.

~ ELIZA COOK

When you're in your nineties and looking back, it's not going to be how much money you made or how many awards you've won. It's really what did you stand for. Did you make a positive difference for people?

~ ELIZABETH DOLE

For attractive lips, speak words of kindness.
For lovely eyes, seek out the good in people.
For a slim figure, share your food with the hungry.
For beautiful hair, let a child run his or her fingers through it once a day.
For poise, walk with the knowledge you'll never walk alone.

~ AUDREY HEPBURN

I am convinced that we must train not only the head, but the heart and hand as well.

~ MADAME CHIANG KAI-SHEK

Remember, no effort that we make to attain something beautiful is ever lost.

~ HELEN KELLER

It's what you do that makes your soul, not the other way around.

~ BARBARA KINGSOLVER

There is no other solution to man's progress but the day's honest work, the day's honest decisions, the day's generous utterances, and the day's good deed.

~ CLARE BOOTHE LUCE

You have much more power when you are working for the right thing than when you are working for the wrong thing.

~ PEACE PILGRIM

Live virtuously, and you cannot die too soon, or live too long.

~ LADY R. RUSSELL

Changing the Way You Look at Things

Don't Dwell on the Past

Forgetting is the cost of living cheerfully.

~ ZOË AKINS

I used to store my anger and it affected my play. Now I get it out. I'm never rude to my playing partner. I'm very focused on the ball. Then it's over.

~ HELEN ALFREDSSON

Those who can't forget are worse off than those who can't remember.

~ ANON.

Just do your best today and tomorrow will come ... tomorrow's going to be a busy day, a happy day.

~ HELEN BOEHM

"The good old days." The only good days are ahead.

~ ALICE CHILDRESS

There are two kinds of stones, as everyone knows, one which rolls.

～ AMELIA EARHART

When one door of happiness closes, another opens; but often we look so long at the closed door that we do not see the one which has opened for us.

～ HELEN KELLER

Accept the pain, cherish the joys, resolve the regrets; then can come the best of benedictions—"If I had my life to live over, I'd do it all the same."

～ JOAN MCINTOSH

Better by far you should forget and smile, than you should remember and be sad.

～ CHRISTINA GEORGINA ROSETTI

How pleasant it is, at the end of the day,
No follies to have to repent;
But reflect on the past, and be able to say,
That my time has been properly spent.

～ ANN TAYLOR

Shrug It Off

Keep your sense of humor. There's enough stress in the rest of your life to let bad shots ruin a game you're supposed to enjoy.

～ AMY ALCOTT

Things turn out best for people who make the best of the way things turn out.

～ ANON.

Faith sees the invisible, believes the unbelievable, and receives the impossible.

～ CORRIE TEN BOOM

Our family never had any hard luck, because nothing seemed hard luck to it, nor was it ever disgraced for there was nothing which it would acknowledge as disgrace.

~ BOXCAR BERTHA

Total absence of humor renders life impossible.

~ COLETTE

Learn to laugh at your troubles and you'll never run out of things to laugh at.

~ LYN KAROL

WARNING: Humor may be hazardous to your illness.

~ ELLIE KATZ

Stay Optimistic

The optimism of a healthy mind is indefatigable.

~ MARGERY ALLINGHAM

One of the things I learned the hard way was that it doesn't pay to get discouraged. Keeping busy and making optimism a way of life can restore your faith in yourself.

~ LUCILLE BALL

It is only in sorrow bad weather masters us; in joy we face the storm and defy it.

~ AMELIA BARR

There is no justification for present existence other than its expansion into an indefinitely open future.

~ SIMONE DE BEAUVOIR

There is hope for all of us. Well, anyway, if you don't die you live through it, day in, day out.

~ MARY BECKETT

Our faith in the present dies out long before our faith in the future.

~ RUTH BENEDICT

We grow in time to trust the future for our answers.

~ RUTH BENEDICT

Opportunities are everywhere.

~ LUCY BENINGTON

I see not a step before me as I tread on another year;
But I've left the Past in God's keeping, the Future
His mercy shall clear;
And what looks dark in the distance may brighten as I draw near.

~ MARY GARDINER BRAINARD

It is astonishing how short a time it takes for very wonderful things
to happen.

~ FRANCES HODGSON BURNETT

I have found adventure in flying, in world travel, in business, and
even close at hand.... Adventure is a state of mind—and spirit. It
comes with faith, for with complete faith there is no fear of what
faces you in life or death.

~ JACQUELINE COCHRAN

There never was night that had no morn.

~ DINAH MARIA MULOCK CRAIK

Hope is the thing with feathers
That perches in the soul,
And sings the tune without the words,
And never stops at all.

~ EMILY DICKINSON

Faith walks simply, childlike, between the darkness of human life and
the hope of what is to come.

~ CATHERINE DE HUECK DOHERTY

Stars will blossom in the darkness,
Violets bloom beneath the snow.

~ JULIA DORR

Grass grows at last above all graves.

~ JULIA DORR

Am I like the optimist who, while falling ten stories from a building,
says at each story, "I'm all right so far"?

~ GRETEL EHRLICH

My faith is important. I have nothing without it.

~ KATHY IRELAND

Someday the sun is going to shine down on me in some faraway place.

~ MAHALIA JACKSON

All shall be well, and all shall be well, and all manner of things shall
be well.

~ JULIAN OF NORWICH

Optimism is the faith that leads to achievement. Nothing can be
done without hope and confidence.

~ HELEN KELLER

No pessimist ever discovered the secret of the stars, or sailed to an
uncharted land, or opened a new doorway for the human spirit.

~ HELEN KELLER

Clouds and darkness surround us, yet heaven is just, and the day of
triumph will surely come, when justice and truth will be vindicated.
Our wrongs will be made right, and we will once more taste the
blessings of freedom.

~ MARY TODD LINCOLN

It is characteristic of genius to be hopeful and aspiring.

~ HARRIET MARTINEAU

The happy ending is our national belief.

~ MARY MCCARTHY

Pessimism is a luxury that a Jew can never afford himself.

~ GOLDA MEIR

Nobody really cares if you're miserable, so you might as well be happy.

~ CYNTHIA NELMS

Rosiness is not a worse windowpane than gloomy gray when viewing the world.

~ GRACE PALEY

She knew in her heart that to be without optimism, that core of reasonless hope in the spirit, rather than the brain, was a fatal flaw, the seed of death.

~ ANNE PERRY

The real winners in life are the people who look at every situation with an expectation that they can make it work or make it better.

~ BARBARA PLETCHER

I have become my own version of an optimist. If I can't make it through one door, I'll go through another door—or I'll make a door. Something terrific will come no matter how dark the present.

~ JOAN RIVERS

If you think you're too small to have an impact, try going to bed with a mosquito.

~ ANITA RODDICK

Gardening is an exercise in optimism.

~ MARIA SCHINZ

Optimism is an intellectual choice.

~ DIANA SCHNEIDER

Faith is like radar that sees through the fog—the reality of things at a distance that the human eye cannot see.

~ CORRIE TEN BOOM

Look to the East, where up the lucid sky
The morning climbs! The day shall yet be fair.

~ CELIA THAXTER

'Tis easy enough to be pleasant, when life flows like a song. But the man worthwhile is the one who will smile when everything goes dead wrong.

~ ELLA WHEELER WILCOX

When I look to the future, it's so bright, it burns my eyes.

~ OPRAH WINFREY

Don't Worry about Things You Can't Control

We cannot alter facts, but we can alter our ways of looking at them.

~ PHYLLIS BOTTOME

It had been my repeated experience that when you said to life calmly and firmly (but very firmly!) "I trust you, do what you must," life had an uncanny way of responding to your need.

~ OLGA ILYIN

Let us be of good cheer, remembering that the misfortunes hardest to bear are those which never come.

~ AMY LOWELL

It is easy and dismally enervating to think of opposition as merely perverse or actually evil—far more invigorating to see it as essential for honing the mind, and as a positive good in itself. For the day that moral issues cease to be fought over is the day the word "human" disappears from the race.

~ JILL TWEEDIE

Failure Is Not an Option

Be a "how" thinker, not an "if" thinker.
              ~ ANON.

Some of my best friends are illusions. Been sustaining me for years.
          ~ SHEILA BALLANTYNE

Without faith, nothing is possible. With it, nothing is impossible.
         ~ MARY MCLEOD BETHUNE

To some people, the impossible is impossible.
        ~ ELIZABETH ASQUITH BIBESCO

All that is necessary to break the spell of inertia and frustration is this: act as if it were impossible to fail. That is the talisman, the formula, the command of right-about-face that turns us from failure toward success.
        ~ DOROTHEA BRANDE

All things are possible until they are proved impossible—and even the impossible may only be so, as of now.
       ~ PEARL S. BUCK

At first people refuse to believe that a strange new thing can be done, then they begin to hope it can be done, then they see it can be done—then it is done and all the world wonders why it was not done centuries ago.
      ~ FRANCES HODGSON BURNETT

Ordinary people believe only in the possible. Extraordinary people visualize not what is possible or probable, but rather what is impossible. And by visualizing the impossible, they begin to see it as possible.
     ~ CHERIE CARTER-SCOTT

Success is often achieved by those who don't know that failure is inevitable.
     ~ COCO CHANEL

If folks can learn to be racist, then they can learn to be antiracist. If being sexist ain't genetic, then, dad gum, people can learn about gender equality.

~ JOHNNETTA BETSCH COLE

Oh! Much may be done by defying
The ghosts of Despair and Dismay
And much may be gained by relying
On "Where there's a Will There's a Way."

~ ELIZA COOK

When nothing is sure, everything is possible.

~ MARGARET DRABBLE

Adieu, my friends, I go on to glory!

~ ISADORA DUNCAN

Might, could, would—they are contemptible auxiliaries.

~ GEORGE ELIOT

When faith is supported by facts or by logic it ceases to be faith.

~ EDITH HAMILTON

The thought that we are enduring the unendurable is one of the things that keeps us going.

~ MOLLY HASKELL

What we have most to fear is failure of the heart.

~ SONIA JOHNSON

We have seen too much defeatism, too much pessimism, too much of a negative approach. The answer is simple: if you want something very badly, you can achieve it. It may take patience, very hard work, a real struggle, and a long time; but it can be done. That much faith is a prerequisite of any undertaking.

~ MARGO JONES

Faith is that quality or power by which the things desired become the things possessed.

~ KATHRYN KUHLMAN

Hope begins in the dark, the stubborn hope that if you just show up and try to do the right thing, the dawn will come. You wait and watch and work: you don't give up.

~ ANNE LAMOTT

There are no hopeless situations; there are only men who have grown hopeless about them.

~ CLARE BOOTHE LUCE

Truth, like the burgeoning of a bulb under the soil, however deeply sown, will make its way to the light.

~ ELLIS PETERS

We can never give up the belief that good guys always win. And that we are the good guys.

~ FAITH POPCORN

I know there will be spring, as surely as the birds know it when they see above the snow two tiny, quivering green leaves. Spring cannot fail us.

~ OLIVE SCHREINER

Never face facts; if you do you'll never get up in the morning.

~ MARLO THOMAS

Focus on the Good Things

The really happy woman is one who can enjoy the scenery on a detour.

~ ANON.

Work is either fun or drudgery. It depends on your attitude. I like fun.

~ COLLEEN C. BARRETT

Life is raw material. We are artisans. We can sculpt our existence into something beautiful, or debase it into ugliness. It's in our hands.

～ CATHY BETTER

Proust has pointed out that the predisposition to love creates its own objects: is that not also true of fear?

～ ELIZABETH BOWEN

If you look at life one way, there is always cause for alarm.

～ ELIZABETH BOWEN

It has never been, and never will be easy work! But the road that is built in hope is more pleasant to the traveler than the road built in despair, even though they both lead to the same destination.

～ MARION ZIMMER BRADLEY

Both abundance and lack exist simultaneously in our lives, as parallel realities. It is always our conscious choice which secret garden we will tend.... When we choose not to focus on what is missing from our lives but are grateful for the abundance that's present—love, health, family, friends, work, the joys of nature, and personal pursuits that bring us pleasure—the wasteland of illusion falls away and we experience heaven on earth.

～ SARAH BAN BREATHNACH

I invented my life by taking for granted that everything I did not like would have an opposite, which I would like.

～ COCO CHANEL

Being tall is an advantage, especially in business. People will always remember you. And if you're in a crowd, you'll always have some clean air to breathe.

～ JULIA CHILD

The pure, the beautiful, the bright,
That stirred our hearts in youth,
The impulse to a wordless prayer,
The dreams of love and truth,
The longings after something lost,
The spirit's yearning cry,
The strivings after better hopes,
These things can never die.

~ SARAH DOUDNEY

I actually remember feeling delight, at two o'clock in the morning,
when the baby woke for his feed, because I so longed to have
another look at him.

~ MARGARET DRABBLE

The human mind can bear plenty of reality, but not too much of
intermittent gloom.

~ MARGARET DRABBLE

But here's what I've learned in this war, in this country, in this city:
to love the miracle of having been born.

~ ORIANA FALLACI

Sometimes I found that in my happy moments I could not believe
that I had ever been miserable.

~ JOANNA FIELD

Teenagers travel in droves, packs, swarms.... To the librarian, they're a
gaggle of geese. To the cook, they're a scourge of locusts. To
department stores, they're a big beautiful exaltation of larks ... all
lovely and loose and jingly.

~ BERNICE FITZ-GIBBON

I keep my ideals, because in spite of everything I still believe that
people are really good at heart.

~ ANNE FRANK

I do think that being the second [female Supreme Court Justice] is wonderful, because it is a sign that being a woman in a place of importance is no longer extraordinary.

~ RUTH BADER GINSBERG

Women forget all the things they don't want to remember, and remember everything they don't want to forget.

~ ZORA NEALE HURSTON

Love conceals ugliness, and hate sees many faults.

~ IRISH PROVERB

Be of good cheer. Do not think of today's failures, but of the success that may come tomorrow.

~ HELEN KELLER

This is the art of courage: to see things as they are and still believe that the victory lies not with those who avoid the bad, but those who taste, in living awareness, every drop of the good.

~ VICTORIA LINCOLN

When you're in love, you put up with things that, when you're out of love you cite.

~ JUDITH MARTIN (MISS MANNERS)

What I cannot love, I overlook.

~ ANAÏS NIN

The coat is quite new, only the holes are old.

~ RUSSIAN PROVERB

I think there is a choice possible to us at any moment, as long as we live. But there is no sacrifice. There is a choice, and the rest falls away. Second choice does not exist. Beware of those who talk about sacrifice.

~ MURIEL RUKEYSER

Life has, indeed, many ills, but the mind that views every object in its most cheering aspect, and every doubtful dispensation as replete with latent good, bears within itself a powerful and perpetual antidote.

~ LYDIA H. SIGOURNEY

Some folks never exaggerate—they just remember big.

~ AUDREY SNEAD

I expect some new phases of life this summer, and shall try to get the honey from each moment.

~ LUCY STONE

Love is much nicer to be in than an automobile accident, a tight girdle, a higher tax bracket, or a holding pattern over Philadelphia.

~ JUDITH VIORST

Happiness is the ability to recognize it.

~ CAROLYN WELLS

The saddest day hath gleams of light,
The darkest wave hath bright foam beneath it,
The twinkles o'er the cloudiest night,
Some solitary star to cheer it.

~ SARAH WINNEMUCCA

Don't Look Outside Yourself for Hope

It isn't our position, but our disposition, that makes us happy.

~ ANON.

All happiness is in the mind.

~ ANON

All times are beautiful for those who maintain joy within them; but there is no happy or favorable time for those with disconsolate or orphaned souls.

~ ROSALIA CASTRO

Time, like money, is measured by our needs.

~ GEORGE ELIOT

Learn to get in touch with silence within yourself and know that everything in life has a purpose.

~ ELISABETH KUBLER-ROSS

People are like stained-glass windows. They sparkle and shine when the sun is out, but when the darkness sets in, their true beauty is revealed only if there is a light from within.

~ ELISABETH KUBLER-ROSS

If you can't change your fate, change your attitude.

~ AMY TAN

Set Your Goals Higher

It's expectation that differentiates you from the dead.

~ SHEILA BALLANTYNE

I have an almost complete disregard of precedent and a faith in the possibility of something better. It irritates me to be told how things always have been done.... I defy the tyranny of precedent. I cannot afford the luxury of a closed mind. I go for anything new that might improve the past.

~ CLARA BARTON

There is no justification for present existence other than its expansion into an indefinitely open future.

~ SIMONE DE BEAUVOIR

I am comforted by life's stability, by earth's unchangeableness. What has seemed new and frightening assumes its place in the unfolding of knowledge.

~ PEARL S. BUCK

Someday, someone will follow in my footsteps and preside over the White House as the President's spouse. And I wish him well.

~ BARBARA BUSH

I am always more interested in what I am about to do than in what I have already done.

~ RACHEL CARSON

We have believed—and we do believe now—that freedom is indivisible, that peace is indivisible, that economic prosperity is indivisible.

~ INDIRA GANDHI

I always ask the question, "Is this what I want in my life?"

~ KATHY IRELAND

Your world is as big as you make it.

~ GEORGIA DOUGLAS JOHNSON

I truly believe that before I retire from public office, I'll be voting for a woman for president.

~ BARBARA MIKULSKI

You're as Young as You Feel

Youth is not a question of years: one is young or old from birth.

~ NATALIE CLIFFORD BARNEY

When I was fourteen, I was the oldest I ever was.... I've been getting younger ever since.

~ SHIRLEY TEMPLE BLACK

A child's world is fresh and new and beautiful, full of wonder and excitement. It is our misfortune that for most of us that clear-eyed vision, that true instinct for what is beautiful and awe-inspiring, is dimmed and even lost before we reach adulthood.

~ RACHEL CARSON

Sure, I'm for helping the elderly. I'm going to be old myself someday.
～ LILLIAN CARTER

Youth is something very new: twenty years ago no one mentioned it.
～ COCO CHANEL

A comfortable old age is the reward of a well-spent youth. Instead of
its bringing sad and melancholy prospects of decay, it would give us
hopes of eternal youth in a better world.
～ LYDIA MARIA CHILD

We turn not older with years, but newer every day.
～ EMILY DICKINSON

Old age is when the liver spots show through your gloves.
～ PHYLLIS DILLER

The middle years, caught between children and parents, free of
neither: the past stretches back too densely, it is too thickly
populated, the future has not yet thinned out.
～ MARGARET DRABBLE

It is not how old you are, but how you are old.
～ MARIE DRESSLER

One of the many things nobody ever tells you about middle age is
that it's such a nice change from being young.
～ DOROTHY CANFIELD FISHER

When you become 100, life changes completely.
～ LADY WILLIE FORBUS

This is a youth-oriented society, and the joke is on them because
youth is a disease from which we all recover.
～ DOROTHY FULDHEIM

Discussing how old you are is the temple of boredom.
～ RUTH GORDON

Old age, believe me, is a good and pleasant thing. It is true you are gently shouldered off the stage, but then you are given such a comfortable front stall as spectator.

~ JANE HARRISON

I look forward to growing old and wise and audacious.

~ GLENDA JACKSON

It is so comical to hear oneself called old, even at ninety I suppose!

~ ALICE JAMES

I enjoy my wrinkles and regard them as badges of distinction—I've worked hard for them!

~ MAGGIE KUHN

The lovely thing about being forty is that you can appreciate twenty-five-year-old men more.

~ COLLEEN MCCULLOUGH

Old age is like a plane flying through a storm. Once you are aboard there is nothing you can do.

~ GOLDA MEIR

In youth the days are short and the years are long. In old age the years are short and day's long.

~ NIKITA IVANOVICH PANIN

Youth is not a time of life, it is a state of mind. You are as old as your doubt, your fear, your despair. The way to keep young is to keep your faith young. Keep your self-confidence young. Keep your hope young.

~ LUELLA F. PHEAN

No, Doctor, I don't want to grow young again. I just want to keep on growing old.

~ MADAME DE ROTHSCHILD

It is quite wrong to think of old age as a downward slope. On the contrary, one climbs higher and higher with the advancing years, and that, too, with surprising strides.

~ GEORGE SAND

Time—our youth—it never really goes, does it? It is all held in our minds.

~ HELEN HOOVER SANTMYER

Don't Be Fatalistic

Fatalism is a lazy man's way of accepting the inevitable.

~ NATALIE CLIFFORD BARNEY

To eat bread without hope is still slowly to starve to death.

~ PEARL S. BUCK

In this unbelievable universe in which we live, there are no absolutes. Even parallel lines, reaching into infinity, meet somewhere yonder.

~ PEARL S. BUCK

Instead of looking at life as a narrowing funnel, we can see it ever widening to choose the things we want to do, to take the wisdom we've learned and create something.

~ LIZ CARPENTER

Others may argue about whether the world ends with a bang or a whimper. I just want to make sure mine doesn't end with a whine.

~ BARBARA GORDON

I discovered I always have choices and sometimes it's only a choice of attitude.

~ JUDITH M. KNOWLTON

Experience shows that exceptions are as true as rules.

~ EDITH RONALD MIRRIELEES

What we call reality is an agreement that people have arrived at to make their lives more livable.

~ LOUISE NEVELSON

A change of heart is the essence of all other change, and it has brought about me a reeducation of the mind.

~ EMMELINE PETHICK-LAWRENCE

Death is a door life opens.

~ ADELA ROGERS ST. JOHNS

The incurable ills are the imaginary ills.

~ MARIE VON EBNER-ESCHENBACH

Don't Feel Sorry for Yourself

It has never been, and never will be easy work! But the road that is built in hope is more pleasant to the traveler than the road built in despair, even though they both lead to the same destination.

~ MARION ZIMMER BRADLEY

Pain is inevitable, suffering is optional.

~ M. KATHLEEN CASEY

Opposition may become sweet to a man when he has christened it persecution.

~ GEORGE ELIOT

If you believe, then you hang on. If you believe, it means you've got imagination, you don't need stuff thrown out on a blueprint, and don't face facts—what can stop you? If I don't make it today, I'll come in tomorrow.

~ RUTH GORDON

Children seldom have a proper sense of their own tragedy, discounting and keeping hidden the true horrors of their short lives, humbly imagining real calamity to be some prestigious drama of the grown-up world.
～ SHIRLEY HAZZARD

It's not the load that breaks you down, it's the way you carry it.
～ LENA HORNE

I'm not overweight, I'm just nine inches too short.
～ SHELLEY WINTERS

Make the Best of a Bad Situation

Make good use of bad rubbish.
～ ELIZABETH BERESFORD

A great wind is blowing, and that gives you either imagination or a headache.
～ CATHERINE THE GREAT

A clever person turns great troubles into little ones and little ones into none at all.
～ CHINESE PROVERB

Life is not always what one wants it to be, but to make the best of it as it is, is the only way of being happy.
～ JENNIE JEROME CHURCHILL

Though his beginnings be but poor and low,
Thank God a man can grow!
～ FLORENCE EARLE COATES

It seems that we learn lessons when we least expect them but always when we need them the most, and, the true "gift" in these lessons always lies in the learning process itself.
～ CATHY LEE CROSBY

Boys, this is only a game. But it's like life in that you will be dealt some bad hands. Take each hand, good or bad, and don't whine and complain, but play it out. If you're men enough to do that, God will help you and you will come out well.

      ⌒ IDA EISENHOWER

Sometimes only a change of viewpoint is needed to convert a tiresome duty into an interesting opportunity.

      ⌒ ALBERTA FLANDERS

Nothing in life is so hard that you can't make it easier by the way you take it.

      ⌒ ELLEN GLASGOW

Never regret. If it's good, it's wonderful. If it's bad, it's experience.

      ⌒ VICTORIA HOLT

I think we should look forward to death more than we do. Of course everybody hates to go to bed or miss anything but dying is really the only chance we'll get to rest.

      ⌒ FLORYNCE KENNEDY

What you can't get out of, get into wholeheartedly.

      ⌒ MIGNON MCLAUGHLIN

All that is necessary is to accept the impossible, do without the indispensable, and bear the intolerable.

      ⌒ KATHLEEN NORRIS

When all that hate energy was focused on me, it was transformed into a fantastic energy. It was supporting me. If you are centered and you can transform all this energy that comes in, it will help you. If you believe it is going to kill you, it will kill you.

      ⌒ YOKO ONO

The world is round and the place which may seem like the end may also be the beginning.

      ⌒ IVY BAKER PRIEST

I am dying, but otherwise I feel quite well.

～ DAME EDITH SITWELL

If you are being run out of town, get in front of the crowd and make it look like a parade.

～ SALLY STANFORD

One advantage of marriage, it seems to me, is that when you fall out of love with him, or he falls out of love with you, it keeps you together until you maybe fall in love again.

～ JUDITH VIORST

Don't Let Others Define Who You Are

I am not a glutton—I am an explorer of food.

～ ERMA BOMBECK

I'm just a person trapped inside a woman's body.

～ ELAYNE BOOSLER

Confronted by an absolutely infuriating review, it is sometimes helpful for the victim to do a little personal research on the critic. Is there any truth to the rumor that he had no formal education beyond the age of eleven? In any event, is he able to construct a simple English sentence? Do his participles dangle? When moved to lyricism, does he write "I had a fun time"? Was he ever arrested for burglary? I don't know that you will prove anything this way, but it is perfectly harmless and quite soothing.

～ JEAN KERR

It's just like magic. When you live by yourself, all your annoying habits are gone!

～ MERRILL MARKOE

When people say: she's got everything, I've only one answer: I haven't had tomorrow.

～ ELIZABETH TAYLOR

Cuteness in children is totally an adult perspective. The children themselves are unaware that the quality exists, let alone its desirability, until the reactions of grown-ups inform them.

~ LEONTINE YOUNG

A Positive Attitude Is Its Own Reward

Those who have easy, cheerful attitudes tend to be happier than those with less pleasant temperaments regardless of money, "making it," or success.

~ DR. JOYCE BROTHERS

When hope is taken away from the people moral degeneration follows swiftly after.

~ PEARL S. BUCK

Wonder ... music heard in the heart, is voiceless.

~ ROSEMARY DOBSON

Who soweth good seed shall surely reap; The year grows rich as it groweth old, And life's latest sands are its sands of gold!

~ JULIA DORR

Though outwardly a gloomy shroud,
The inner half of every cloud
Is bright and shining:
I therefore turn my clouds about
And always wear them inside out
To show the lining.

~ ELLEN THORNEYCROFT FOWLER

When we cannot get what we love, we must love what is within our reach.

~ FRENCH PROVERB

If you constantly think of illness, you eventually become ill; if you believe yourself to be beautiful, you become so.

~ SHAKTI GAWAIN

Misery is a communicable disease.

~ MARTHA GRAHAM

Enthusiasm is the divine particle in our composition: with it we are great, generous, and true; without it, we are little, false, and mean.

~ L.E. LANDON

If I had a party to attend and didn't want to be there, I would play the part of someone who was having a lovely time.

~ SHIRLEY MACLAINE

Take hope from the heart of man and you make him a beast of prey.

~ OUIDA

The name we give to something shapes our attitude toward it.

~ KATHERINE PATERSON

Always keep that happy attitude. Pretend that you are holding a beautiful fragrant bouquet.

~ CANDICE M. POPE

This I know. This I believe with all my heart. If we want a free and peaceful world, if we want to make the deserts bloom and man grow to greater dignity as a human being—we can do it!

~ ELEANOR ROOSEVELT

Cheerfulness prepares a glorious mind for all the noblest acts.

~ ELIZABETH ANN SETON

All you need is positivity.

~ THE SPICE GIRLS

Thoughts have power; thoughts are energy. And you can make your world or break it by your own thinking.

~ SUSAN TAYLOR

I've learned from experience that the greater part of our happiness
or misery depends on our dispositions and not on our circumstances.
〜 MARTHA WASHINGTON

Have Faith

I feel no need for any other faith than my faith in human beings.
〜 PEARL S. BUCK

No object is mysterious. The mystery is your eye.
〜 ELIZABETH BOWEN

Faith hasn't got no eyes, but she' long-legged.
〜 ZORA NEALE HURSTON

Faith is not a series of gilt-edged propositions that you sit down to
figure out, and if you follow all the logic and accept all the conclusions,
then you have it. It is crumpling and throwing away everything,
proposition by proposition, until nothing is left, and then writing a new
proposition, your very own, to throw in the teeth of despair.
〜 MARY JEAN IRION

Hope is the last thing ever lost.
〜 ITALIAN PROVERB

How desperately we wish to maintain our trust in those we love! In
the face of everything, we try to find reasons to trust. Because losing
faith is worse than falling out of love.
〜 SONIA JOHNSON

It's going to be a long, hard drag, but we'll make it.
〜 JANIS JOPLIN

The best and most beautiful things in the world cannot be seen or
even touched—they must be felt with the heart.
〜 HELEN KELLER

Not truth, but faith it is that keeps the world alive.

~ EDNA ST. VINCENT MILLAY

Hope is a song in a weary throat.

~ PAULI MURRAY

Hope … is not a feeling; it is something you do.

~ KATHERINE PATERSON

Not seeing is half-believing.

~ VITA SACKVILLE-WEST

Hope is a very unruly emotion.

~ GLORIA STEINEM

Hope for forces which you do not yet have.

~ RACHEL VARNHAGEN

Steady as a clock, busy as a bee, and cheerful as a cricket.

~ MARTHA WASHINGTON

$\mathcal{T}$aking Risks

View Risk as an Opportunity for Reward

If the risk-reward ratio is right, you can make big money buying trouble.
> $\sim$ ANON.

Women must think strategically about creating ongoing pressure for change.
> $\sim$ MARY BAKER EDDY

Anything I've ever done that ultimately was worthwhile … initially scared me to death.
> $\sim$ BETTY BENDER

Attempt the impossible in order to improve your work.
> $\sim$ BETTE DAVIS

When you make a commitment to a relationship, you invest your attention and energy in it more profoundly because you now experience ownership of that relationship.
> $\sim$ BARBARA DE ANGELIS

Security is not the meaning of my life. Great opportunities are worth the risks.

~ SHIRLEY HUFSTEDLER

It is better to die on your feet than to live on your knees!

~ DELORES IBARRURI

Security is mostly superstition. It does not exist in nature.

~ HELEN KELLER

Only in growth, reform, and change, paradoxically enough, is true security to be found.

~ ANNE MORROW LINDBERGH

Competition can damage self-esteem, create anxiety, and lead to cheating and hurt feelings. But so can romantic love.

~ MARIAH BURTON NELSON

I am willing to put myself through anything; temporary pain or discomfort means nothing to me as long as I can see that the experience will take me to a new level. I am interested in the unknown, and the only path to the unknown is through breaking barriers, an often painful process.

~ DIANA NYAD

Love, like a chicken salad or restaurant hash, must be taken with blind faith or it loses its flavor.

~ HELEN ROWLAND

Providence has hidden a charm in difficult undertakings, which is appreciated only by those who dare to grapple with them.

~ ANNE-SOPHIE SWETCHINE

Life is a risk.

~ DIANE VON FURSTENBERG

Failure Isn't Fatal

If I had to live my life again, I'd make the same mistakes, only sooner.
~ TALLULAH BANKHEAD

A peacefulness follows any decision, even the wrong one.
~ RITA MAE BROWN

If you don't accept failure as a possibility, you don't set high goals, you don't branch out, you don't try—you don't take the risk.
~ ROSALYNN CARTER

You must accept that you might fail; then, if you do your best and still don't win, at least you can be satisfied that you've tried.
~ ROSALYNN CARTER

Who would not rather trust and be deceived?
~ ELIZA COOK

Finite to fail, but infinite to venture.
~ EMILY DICKINSON

When in doubt, make a fool of yourself. There is a microscopically thin line between being brilliantly creative and acting like the most gigantic idiot on earth. So what the hell, leap.
~ CYNTHIA HEIMEL

It is better to be boldly decisive and risk being wrong than to agonize at length and be right too late.
~ MARILYN MOATS KENNEDY

Be bold. If you're going to make an error, make a doozy, and don't be afraid to hit the ball.
~ BILLIE JEAN KING

When I look at the kids training today … I can tell which ones are going to do well. It's not necessarily the ones who have the most natural talent or who fall the least. Sometimes it's the kids who fall the most, and keep pulling themselves up and trying again.

~ MICHELLE KWAN

Take chances, make mistakes. That's how you grow. Pain nourishes your courage. You have to fail in order to practice being brave.

~ MARY TYLER MOORE

Take risks. You can't fall off the bottom.

~ BARBARA PROCTOR

If I had to live my life over again, I'd dare to make more mistakes next time.

~ NADINE STAIR

You Must Take Risks to Realize Your Potential

Nothing ventured, nothing gained.

~ ANON.

Most people live and die with their music still unplayed. They never dare to try.

~ MARY KAY ASH

There are people who put their dreams in a little box and say, "Yes, I've got dreams, of course, I've got dreams." Then they put the box away and bring it out once in a while to look in it, and yep, they're still there. These are great dreams, but they never even get out of the box. It takes an uncommon amount of guts to put your dreams on the line, to hold them up and say, "How good or how bad am I?" That's where courage comes in.

~ ERMA BOMBECK

It is a very dangerous thing to have an idea that you will not practice.

~ PHYLLIS BOTTOME

If you risk nothing, then you risk everything.

~ GEENA DAVIS

To know that one has never really tried—that is the only death.

~ MARIE DRESSLER

If you play it safe in life, you've decided that you don't want to grow anymore.

~ SHIRLEY HUFSTEDLER

And the trouble is, if you don't risk anything, you risk even more.

~ ERICA JONG

The fearful are caught as often as the bold.

~ HELEN KELLER

Inaction, contrary to its reputation for being a refuge, is neither safe nor comfortable.

~ MADELEINE KUNIN

Deliberation often loses a good chance.

~ LATIN PROVERB

We have to keep trying things we're not sure we can pull off. If we just do the things we know we can do ... you don't grow as much. You gotta take those chances on making those big mistakes.

~ CYBIL SHEPHERD

In the past, few women have tried and even fewer have succeeded.

~ ROSALYN YALOW

Believe That Your Higher Power Will Help You

God does not ask your ability or your inability. He asks only your availability.
~ MARY KAY ASH

Heroic deeds, to use whatever dower
Heaven has bestowed, to test our utmost power.
~ SARAH KNOWLES BOLTON

Act boldly and unseen forces will come to your aid.
~ DOROTHEA BRANDE

Leap, and the net will appear.
~ JULIE CAMERON

Cowards falter, but danger is often overcome by those who nobly dare.
~ QUEEN ELIZABETH I

God Himself is not secure, having given man dominion over His works.
~ HELEN KELLER

Faith is kind of like jumping out of an airplane at 10,000 feet. If God doesn't catch you, you splatter. But how do you know whether or not he is going to catch you unless you jump out?
~ ANN KIEMEL

God will help you if you try, and you can if you think you can.
~ ANNA DELANEY PEALE

Significant Change May Require Significant Risk

If you don't place your foot on the rope, you'll never cross the chasm.
~ ANON.

We stand now where two roads diverge. but unlike the roads in Robert Frost's familiar poem, they are not equally fair. The road we have long been traveling is deceptively easy, a smooth superhighway on which we progress with great speed, but at its end lies disaster. The other fork of the road—the one less traveled by—offers our last, our only chance to reach a destination that assures the preservation of the earth.

~ RACHEL CARSON

To gain that which is worth having, it may be necessary to lose everything else.

~ BERNADETTE DEVLIN

Risk always brings its own rewards: the exhilaration of breaking through, of getting to the other side; the relief of a conflict healed; the clarity when a paradox dissolves.

~ MARILYN FERGUSON

Whenever you take a step forward, you are bound to disturb something.

~ INDIRA GANDHI

It is better to die on your feet than to live on your knees!

~ DELORES IBARRURI

Sometimes I think we can tell how important it is to risk by how dangerous it is to do so.

~ SONIA JOHNSON

Life is either a daring adventure or nothing.

~ HELEN KELLER

When something does not insist on being noticed, when we aren't grabbed by the collar or struck on the skull by a presence or an event, we take for granted the very things that most deserve our gratitude.

~ CYNTHIA OZICK

There are those who have discovered that fear is death in life, and have willingly risked physical death and loss of all that is considered valuable in order to live in freedom.

~ VIRGINIA BURDEN TOWER

I tore myself away from the safe comfort of certainties through my love for truth; and truth rewarded me.

～ SYLVIA ASHTON WARNER

In danger there is great power.

～ AGNES WHISTLING ELK

We Feel Most Alive When We Take a Chance

Our whole way of life today is dedicated to the removal of risk. Cradle to grave we are supported, insulated, and isolated from the risks of life—and if we fall, our government stands ready with Band-Aids of every size.

～ SHIRLEY TEMPLE BLACK

Borrowed thoughts, like borrowed money, only show the poverty of the borrower.

～ LADY MARGUERITE BLESSINGTON

Dancing on the edge is the only place to be.

～ TRISHA BROWN

It is so tempting to try the most difficult thing possible.

～ JENNIE JEROME CHURCHILL

To live without risk for me would be tantamount to death.

～ JACQUELINE COCHRAN

Traveling is like flirting with life. It's like saying, "I would stay and love you, but I have to go; this is my station."

～ LISA ST. AUBIN DE TERAN

Life has no romance without risk.

～ SARAH DOHERTY

What one has not experienced, one will never understand in print.

～ ISADORA DUNCAN

Only those who dare, truly live.

~ RUTH P. FREEDMAN

We love because it is the only true adventure.

~ NIKKI GIOVANNI

Life is either a daring adventure or nothing.

~ HELEN KELLER

It's better to be a lion for a day than a sheep all your life.

~ ELIZABETH KENNY

Be bold. If you're going to make an error, make a doozy, and don't be afraid to hit the ball.

~ BILLIE JEAN KING

I'm in love with the potential of miracles. For me, the safest place is out on a limb.

~ SHIRLEY MACLAINE

I never liked the middle ground—the most boring place in the world.

~ LOUISE NEVELSON

One must be thrust out of a finished cycle in life, and that leap is the most difficult to make—to part with one's faith, one's love, when one would prefer to renew the faith and recreate the passion.

~ ANAÏS NIN

Be Brave and Dive into Your Greatest Fear or Challenge

All glory comes from daring to begin.

~ ANON.

More powerful than the will to win is the courage to begin.

~ ANON.

I don't think about risks much. I just do what I want to do. If you gotta go, you gotta go.

~ LILLIAN CARTER

Ideas are powerful things, requiring not a studious contemplation but an action, even if it is only an inner action.

~ MIDGE DECTOR

It is better to begin in the evening than not at all.

~ ENGLISH PROVERB

A sharp knife cuts the quickest and hurts the least.

~ KATHARINE HEPBURN

It's only when we have nothing else to hold onto that we're willing to try something very audacious and scary.

~ SONIA JOHNSON

Avoiding danger is no safer in the long run than outright exposure.

~ HELEN KELLER

Fear to let spill a drop and you will spill a lot.

~ MALAYSIAN PROVERB

All reformations seem formidable before they are attempted.

~ HANNAH MOORE

Doing is a quantum leap from imagining. Thinking about swimming isn't much like actually getting in the water. Actually getting in the water can take your breath away. The defense force inside of us wants us to be cautious, to stay away from anything as intense as a new kind of action. Its job is to protect us, and it categorically avoids anything resembling danger. But it's often wrong. Anything worth doing is worth doing too soon.

~ BARBARA SHER

All serious daring starts from within.

~ EUDORA WELTY

Dream Big Dreams and Imagine Them Coming True

The young do not know enough to be prudent, and therefore they attempt the impossible—and achieve it, generation after generation.

~ PEARL S. BUCK

We owe something to extravagance, for thrift and adventure seldom go hand in hand.

~ JENNIE JEROME CHURCHILL

Creativity is inventing, experimenting, growing, taking risks, breaking rules, making mistakes, and having fun.

~ MARY LOU COOK

Finite to fail, but infinite to venture.

~ EMILY DICKINSON

You do not have to be superhuman to do what you believe in.

~ DEBBI FIELDS

We can only do what is possible for us to do. But still it is good to know what the impossible is.

~ MARIA IRENE FORNÉS

When I look at the kids training today ... I can tell which ones are going to do well. It's not necessarily the ones who have the most natural talent or who fall the least. Sometimes it's the kids who fall the most, and keep pulling themselves up and trying again.

~ MICHELLE KWAN

I love the challenge.

~ NANCY LOPEZ

Into the darkness they go, the wise and the lovely.

~ EDNA ST. VINCENT MILLAY

I am willing to put myself through anything; temporary pain or discomfort means nothing to me as long as I can see that the experience will take me to a new level. I am interested in the unknown, and the only path to the unknown is through breaking barriers, an often painful process.

⌒ DIANA NYAD

There was never a place for her in the ranks of the terrible, slow army of the cautious. She ran ahead, where there were no paths.

⌒ DOROTHY PARKER

It's Usually More Fun to Be Surprised

My favorite thing is to go where I have never gone.

⌒ DIANE ARBUS

The moment somebody says to me "This is very risky," is the moment it becomes attractive to me.

⌒ KATE CAPSHAW

The power of habit and the charm of novelty are the two adverse forces which explain the follies of mankind.

⌒ MARIA DE BEAUSACQ

The soul should always stand ajar, ready to welcome the ecstatic experience.

⌒ EMILY DICKINSON

Adventure is worthwhile in itself.

⌒ AMELIA EARHART

A dreamer—you know—it's a mind that looks over the edges of things.

⌒ MARY O'HARA

I feel very adventurous. There are so many doors to be opened, and I'm not afraid to look behind them.

⌒ ELIZABETH TAYLOR

Between two evils, I always picked the one I never tried before.
>   MAE WEST

Life is either always a tightrope or a feather bed. Give me the tightrope.
>   EDITH WHARTON

Not Knowing, and Being Ready for Anything, Can Be a Strength

A fool without fear is sometimes wiser than an angel with fear.
>   NANCY ASTOR

My success was not based so much on any great intelligence but on great common sense.
>   HELEN GURLEY BROWN

Beginnings are apt to be shadowy.
>   RACHEL CARSON

Lose yourself wholly; and the more you lose, the more you will find.
>   SAINT CATHERINE OF SIENA

Into the darkness they go, the wise and the lovely.
>   EDNA ST. VINCENT MILLAY

Heroes take journeys, confront dragons, and discover the treasure of their true selves.
>   CAROL PEARSON

Life's challenges are not supposed to paralyze you, they're supposed to help you discover who you are.
>   BERNICE JOHNSON REAGON

The rewards go to the risk-takers, those who are willing to put their egos on the line and reach out to other people and to a richer, fuller life for themselves.
>   SUSAN ROANE

It is best to learn as we go, not go as we have learned.

      ~ LESLIE JEANNE SAHLER

I make the most of all that comes and the least of all that goes.

      ~ SARA TEASDALE

Believe in Yourself—Don't Worry What Others May Say

Cautious, careful people, always casting about to preserve their reputation and social standing, never can bring about a reform.

      ~ SUSAN B. ANTHONY

Everybody wants to do something to help, but nobody wants to be first.

      ~ PEARL BAILEY

It is not easy to be a pioneer—but oh, it is fascinating! I would not trade one moment, even the worst moment, for all the riches in the world.

      ~ ELIZABETH BLACKWELL

The decision to speak out is the vocation and lifelong peril by which the intellectual must live.

      ~ KAY BOYLE

Let us not forget that among [women's] rights is the right to speak freely.

      ~ HILLARY RODHAM CLINTON

In my business, you measure your respect by the enemies you make.

      ~ THEO E. COLBORN

Not knowing when the dawn will come, I open every door.

      ~ EMILY DICKINSON

I went for years not finishing anything. Because, of course, when you finish something you can be judged.... I had poems which were rewritten so many times I suspect it was just a way of avoiding sending them out.

~ ERICA JONG

I have come to believe over and over again that what is most important to me must be spoken, made verbal and shared, even at the risk of having it bruised or misunderstood.

~ AUDRE LORDE

Risk! Risk anything! Care no more for the opinion of others, for those voices. Do the hardest thing on earth for you. Act for yourself. Face the truth.

~ KATHERINE MANSFIELD

Standing in the middle of the road is very dangerous; you get knocked down by the traffic from both sides.

~ MARGARET THATCHER

Take the First Step—And Find That Your Fear Was Unfounded

Danger itself is the best remedy for danger.

~ ANON.

Bad weather always looks worse through a window.

~ ANON.

Whatever you are trying to avoid won't go away until you confront it.

~ ANON.

I think we should follow a simple rule: if we can take the worst, take the risk.

~ DR. JOYCE BROTHERS

In soloing—as in other activities—it is far easier to start something than it is to finish it.

~ AMELIA EARHART

Ultimately we know deeply that the other side of every fear is freedom.

~ MARILYN FERGUSON

Happiness is to take up the struggle in the midst of the raging storm, not to pluck the lute in the moonlight or recite poetry among the blossoms.

~ DING LING

I am willing to put myself through anything; temporary pain or discomfort means nothing to me as long as I can see that the experience will take me to a new level. I am interested in the unknown, and the only path to the unknown is through breaking barriers, an often painful process.

~ DIANA NYAD

Winners take chances. Like everyone else, they fear failing, but they refuse to let fear control them.

~ NANCY SIMMS

If I had to live my life over again, I'd dare to make more mistakes next time.

~ NADINE STAIR

Staying Focused on Your Goals

You Must Dream Your Dream Before You Can Achieve It

Aim at nothing and you'll succeed.

~ ANON.

If I had one wish for my children, it would be that each of them would reach for goals that have meaning for them as individuals.

~ LILLIAN CARTER

If we have not achieved our early dreams, we must either find new ones or see what we can salvage from the old. If we have accomplished what we set out to do in our youth, we need not weep like Alexander the Great that we have no more worlds to conquer.

~ ROSALYNN CARTER

One must desire something to be alive: perhaps absolute satisfaction is only another name for Death.

~ MARGARET DELAND

You know, my children, that humanity advances only by forming itself an ideal and endeavoring to realize it. Every passion has its ideal, which is modified by that of the whole.

       ~ JENNY P. D'HERICOURT

Death does not frighten me, but dying obscurely and above all uselessly does.

       ~ ISABELLE EBERHARDT

What makes life dreary is want of motive.

       ~ GEORGE ELIOT

It seems to me we can never give up longing and wishing while we are alive. There are certain things we feel to be beautiful and good, and we must hunger for them.

       ~ GEORGE ELIOT

The best antidote I have found is to yearn for something. As long as you yearn, you can't congeal: there is a forward motion to yearning.

       ~ GAIL GODWIN

Every woman dreams of her own political career and her own place in life.

       ~ RAISA M. GORBACHEV

The truth isn't always beauty, but the hunger for it is.

       ~ NADINE GORDIMER

To have a reason to get up in the morning, it is necessary to possess a guiding principle.

       ~ JUDITH GUEST

When your dreams tire, they go underground and out of kindness that's where they stay.

       ~ LIBBY HOUSTON

The very least you can do in your life is to figure out what you hope for. And the most you can do is live inside that hope. Not admire it from a distance but live right in it, under its roof.

~ BARBARA KINGSOLVER

We can do whatever we wish to do provided our wish is strong enough.... What do you want most to do? That's what I have to keep asking myself, in the face of difficulties.

~ KATHERINE MANSFIELD

The history of all times, and of today especially, teaches that ... women will be forgotten if they forget to think about themselves.

~ LOUISE OTTO

Instead of thinking about where you are, think about where you want to be. It takes twenty years of hard work to become an overnight success.

~ DIANA RANKIN

To the lack of incentive to effort, which is the awful shadow under which we live, may be traced the wreck and ruin of scores of colored youth.

~ MARY CHURCH TERRELL

I believe that you cannot go any further than you can think. I certainly believe if you don't desire a thing, you will never get it.

~ CHARLESZETTA WADDLES

Don't Let Others Prevent You from Achieving Your Goals

When things go wrong, don't go with them.

~ ANON.

You can imprison a man, but not an idea. You can exile a man, but not an idea. You can kill a man, but not an idea.

~ BENAZIR BHUTTO

In my business, you measure your respect by the enemies you make.

〜 THEO E. COLBORN

We need to find the courage to say NO to the things and people that are not serving us if we want to rediscover ourselves and live our lives with authenticity.

〜 BARBARA DE ANGELIS

It never pays to deal with the flyweights of the world. They take far too much pleasure in thwarting you at every turn.

〜 SUE GRAFTON

I am not afraid of the pen, or the scaffold, or the sword. I will tell the truth whenever I please.

〜 MOTHER JONES

Once I decide to do something, I can't have people telling me I can't. If there's a roadblock, you jump over it, walk around it, crawl under it.

〜 KITTY KELLEY

Problems arise in that one has to find a balance between what people need from you and what you need for yourself.

〜 JESSYE NORMAN

If your efforts are sometimes greeted with indifference, don't lose heart. The sun puts on a wonderful show at daybreak, yet most of the people in the audience go on sleeping.

〜 ADA TEIXEIRA

Plan Your Work and Work Your Plan

So long as I believe I have to do certain things, I will just go right ahead. That's how I run my life.

〜 CORAZAN AQUINO

Reappraise the past, reevaluate where we've been, clarify where we are, and predict or anticipate where we are headed.

~ TONI CADE BAMBARA

No matter what the competition is, I try to find a goal that day and better that goal.

~ BONNIE BLAIR

If you really want something you can figure out how to make it happen.

~ CHER

A schedule defends from chaos and whim. It is a net for catching days. It is a scaffolding on which a worker can stand and labor with both hands at sections of time.

~ ANNIE DILLARD

You decide what it is you want to accomplish and then you lay out your plans to get there, and then you just do it. It's pretty straightforward.

~ NANCY DITZ

What does so-called success or failure matter if only you have succeeded in doing the thing you set out to do. The DOING is all that really counts.

~ EVA LE GALLIENNE

Goals are dreams with deadlines.

~ DIANA SCHARF HUNT

Get out of the blocks, run your race, stay relaxed. If you run your race, you'll win. Channel your energy. Focus.

~ CAROL LEWIS

Know what you want to do—then do it. Make straight for your goal and go undefeated in spirit to the end.

~ ERNESTINE SCHUMANN-HEINK

I love the challenge of starting at zero every day and seeing how much I can accomplish.

~ MARTHA STEWART

Enjoy the Effort It Takes to Achieve Your Goal

A good goal is like a strenuous exercise—it makes you stretch.
~ MARY KAY ASH

Manual labor to my father was not only good and decent for its own sake, but as he was given to saying, it straightened out one's thoughts.
~ MARY ELLEN CHASE

It's weak and despicable to go on wanting things and not trying to get them.
~ JOANNA FIELD

It is good to have an end to journey toward, but it is the journey that matters in the end.
~ URSULA K. LE GUIN

Growth is not concerned with itself.
~ MERIDEL LE SUEUR

The self-confidence one builds from achieving difficult things and accomplishing goals is the most beautiful thing of all.
~ MADONNA

If ambition doesn't hurt you, you haven't got it.
~ KATHLEEN NORRIS

Rely on Yourself as the Judge of Your Success

The closer one gets to the top, the more one finds there is no "top."
~ NANCY BARCUS

You can't assume the responsibility for everything you do—or don't do.
~ SIMONE DE BEAUVOIR

There were angry men confronting me and I caught the flashing of defiant eyes, but above me and within me, there was a spirit stronger than them all.

~ ANTOINETTE BROWN BLACKWELL

A woman finds the natural lay of the land almost unconsciously; and not feeling it incumbent on her to be guide and philosopher to any successor, she takes little pains to mark the route by which she is making her ascent.

~ ANTOINETTE BROWN BLACKWELL

No matter what the competition is, I try to find a goal that day and better that goal.

~ BONNIE BLAIR

It doesn't matter what anybody thinks of what I do. The clock doesn't lie.

~ BONNIE BLAIR

Don't take anyone else's definition of success as your own.

~ JACQUELINE BRISKIN

I'll walk where my own nature would be leading; it vexes me to choose another guide.

~ EMILY BRONTË

You can have your titular recognition. I'll take money and power.

~ HELEN GURLEY BROWN

My passions were all gathered together like fingers that made a fist. Drive is considered aggression today; I knew it then as purpose.

~ BETTE DAVIS

In the multitude of middle-aged men who go about their vocations in a daily course determined for them much in the same way as they tie their cravats, there is always a good number who once meant to shape their own deeds and alter the world a little.

~ GEORGE ELIOT

I never really address myself to any image anybody has of me. That's like fighting with ghosts.

~ SALLY FIELD

I was raised to sense what someone wanted me to be and be that kind of person. It took me a long time not to judge myself through someone else's eyes.

~ SALLY FIELD

Remember if people talk behind your back, it only means you're two steps ahead!

~ FANNIE FLAGG

Normal is not something to aspire to, it's something to get away from.

~ JODIE FOSTER

It's a sign of your own worth sometimes if you are hated by the right people.

~ MILES FRANKLIN

I'm always making a comeback but nobody ever tells me where I've been.

~ BILLIE HOLIDAY

Don't compromise yourself. You're all you've got.

~ JANIS JOPLIN

The world may take your reputation from you, but it cannot take your character.

~ EMMA DUNHAM KELLEY

For me it's the challenge—the challenge to try to beat myself or do better than I did in the past. I try to keep in mind not what I have accomplished but what I have to try to accomplish in the future.

~ JACKIE JOYNER-KERSEE

There's a very fine line between a groove and a rut; a fine line between eccentrics and people who are just plain nuts.

~ CHRISTINE LAVIN

Promises that you make to yourself are often like the Japanese plum tree—they bear no fruit.

        ⁓ FRANCES MARION

I can honestly say that I was never affected by the question of the success of an undertaking. If I felt it was the right thing to do, I was for it regardless of the possible outcome.

        ⁓ GOLDA MEIR

I'm not going to let my life revolve around losing weight. I have other things to do.

        ⁓ ROSIE O'DONNELL

What exactly is success? For me it is to be found not in applause, but in the satisfaction of feeling that one is realizing one's ideal.

        ⁓ ANNA PAVLOVA

You cannot do good work if you take your mind off the work to see how the community is taking it.

        ⁓ DOROTHY L. SAYERS

You have to define success in your own way. What maintains your dignity and integrity and what is your life's plan, where do you want to put your efforts. I could be richer and more famous, but I would have to give up things that are of infinitely more value.

        ⁓ DR. LAURA SCHLESSINGER

Our victory is sure to come, and I can endure anything but recreancy to principle.

        ⁓ LUCY STONE

If you just set out to be liked, you would be prepared to compromise on anything at any time, and you would achieve nothing.

        ⁓ MARGARET THATCHER

I will not change just to court popularity.

        ⁓ MARGARET THATCHER

When the shriveled skin of the ordinary is stuffed out with meaning,
it satisfies the senses amazingly.

~ VIRGINIA WOOLF

Work Toward Your Goal Every Day

There are people who put their dreams in a little box and say, "Yes,
I've got dreams, of course, I've got dreams." Then they put the box
away and bring it out once in a while to look in it, and yep, they're
still there. These are great dreams, but they never even get out of the
box. It takes an uncommon amount of guts to put your dreams on
the line, to hold them up and say, "How good or how bad am I?"
That's where courage comes in.

~ ERMA BOMBECK

Life is denied by lack of attention, whether it be to cleaning
windows or trying to write a masterpiece.

~ NADIA BOULANGER

Grudge no expense—yield to no opposition—forget fatigue—till, by the
strength of prayer and sacrifice, the spirit of love shall have overcome.

~ MARIA WESTON CHAPMAN

To look back is to relax one's vigil.

~ BETTE DAVIS

Until I die, I'm going to keep doing. My people need me. They need
somebody that's not taking from them and is giving them something.

~ CLARA MCBRIDE HALE

If you don't wake up with something in your stomach every day that
makes you think, "I want to make this movie," it'll never get made.

~ SHERRY LANSING

When you stop talking, you've lost your customer.

~ ESTEE LAUDER

To tend, unfailingly, unflinchingly, towards a goal, is the secret of success.
~ ANNA PAVLOVA

Be Passionate about Your Goals

The woman who sees both sides of an issue is very likely on a fence or up a tree.
~ ANON.

That they can strengthen through the empowerment of others is essential wisdom often gathered by women.
~ MARY FIELD BELENKY

I feel that one must deliberate then act, must scan every life choice with rational thinking but then base the decision on whether one's heart will be in it.
~ JEAN SHINODA BOLEN

You have to block everything out and be extremely focused and be relaxed and mellow too.
~ JENNIFER CAPRIATI

Since everything is in our heads, we better not lose them.
~ COCO CHANEL

People are subject to moods, to temptations and fears, lethargy and aberration and ignorance, and the staunchest qualities shift under the stresses and strains of daily life.
~ ILKA CHASE

Whoever said, "It's not whether you win or lose that counts," probably lost.
~ MARTINA NAVRATILOVA

I realized a long time ago that a belief which does not spring from a conviction in the emotions is no belief at all.
~ EVELYN SCOTT

Realizing Your Dreams Requires Discipline

To put a tempting face aside when duty demands every faculty is a lesson which takes most men longest to learn.
> GERTRUDE ATHERTON

Give to the world the best you have and the best will come back to you.
> MADELINE BRIDGES

Lack of discipline leads to frustration and self-loathing.
> MARIE CHAPIAN

You must have discipline to have fun.
> JULIA CHILD

Those who set their minds on virtue will do no evil.
> CHINESE PROVERB

What does so-called success or failure matter if only you have succeeded in doing the thing you set out to do. The DOING is all that really counts.
> EVA LE GALLIENNE

Temptations come, as a general rule, when they are sought.
> MARGARET OLIPHANT

A mind which really lays hold of a subject is not easily detached from it.
> IDA TARBELL

Don't Shortchange Yourself by Taking Shortcuts

I don't want to be a passenger in my own life.
> DIANE ACKERMAN

Champions know there are no shortcuts to the top. They climb the mountain one step at a time. They have no use for helicopters!
> JUDI ADLER

You must have discipline to have fun.

~ JULIA CHILD

It is necessary to try to surpass one's self always; this occupation ought to last as long as life.

~ CHRISTINA AUGUSTA, QUEEN OF SWEDEN

Being professional in whatever you do is important. Talent alone is not enough.

~ KATHY IRELAND

Incident piled on incident no more makes life than brick piled on brick makes a house.

~ EDITH RONALD MIRRIELEES

Believe in All of Your Possibilities

The optimism of a healthy mind is indefatigable.

~ MARGERY ALLINGHAM

If you think you can, you can. And if you think you can't, you're right.

~ MARY KAY ASH

I was born to be a remarkable woman; it matters little in what way or how.... I shall be famous or I will die.

~ MARIE BASHKIRTSEFF

You can imprison a man, but not an idea. You can exile a man, but not an idea. You can kill a man, but not an idea.

~ BENAZIR BHUTTO

To be one woman, truly, wholly, is to be all women. Tend one garden and you will birth worlds.

~ KATE BRAVERMAN

Don't be afraid of the space between your dreams and reality. If you can dream it, you can make it so.

~ BELVA DAVIS

You really can change the world if you care enough.

~ MARIAN WRIGHT EDELMAN

We couldn't possibly know where it would lead, but we knew it had to be done.

~ BETTY FRIEDAN

We always attract into our lives whatever we think about most, believe in most strongly, expect on the deepest level, and imagine most vividly.

~ SHAKTI GAWAIN

You can have anything you want if you want it desperately enough. You must want it with an inner exuberance that erupts through the skin and joins the energy that created the world.

~ SHEILA GRAHAM

I never intended to become a run-of-the-mill person.

~ BARBARA JORDAN

Our concern must be to live while we're alive ... to release our inner selves from the spiritual death that comes with living behind a facade designed to conform to external definitions of who and what we are.

~ ELISABETH KUBLER-ROSS

There is only one real sin and that is to persuade oneself that the second best is anything but second best.

~ DORIS LESSING

I hope I shall have ambition until the day I die.

~ CLARE BOOTHE LUCE

I have the same goal I've had ever since I was a little girl. I want to rule the world.

~ MADONNA

Nothing's far when one wants to get there.

~ QUEEN MARIE OF RUMANIA

I don't know much about being a millionaire, but I'll bet I'd be darling at it.

~ DOROTHY PARKER

The one who cares the most wins.... That's how I knew I'd end up with everyone else waving the white flags and not me. That's how I knew I'd be the last person standing when it was all over.... I cared the most.

~ ROSEANNE

Perhaps the best function of parenthood is to teach the young creature to love with safety, so that it may be able to venture unafraid when later emotion comes; the thwarting of the instinct to love is the root of all sorrow and not sex only but divinity itself is insulted when it is repressed. To disapprove, to condemn—the human soul shrivels under barren righteousness.

~ FREYA STARK

I have always wanted to be somebody, but I see now I should have been more specific.

~ LILY TOMLIN

Success is the sweetest revenge.

~ VANESSA WILLIAMS

All my life I've been competing—and competing to win. I came to realize that in this way, this cancer was the toughest competition I had faced yet. I made up my mind that I was going to lick it all the way. I not only wasn't going to let it kill me, I wasn't even going to let it put me on the shelf.

~ BABE DIDRIKSON ZAHARIAS

Visualize Your Final Destination Clearly

Far away in the sunshine are my highest aspirations. I may not reach them, but I can look up and see the beauty, believe in them and try to follow where they lead.

~ LOUISA MAY ALCOTT

Don't leave before the miracle happens!

~ ANON.

Reappraise the past, reevaluate where we've been, clarify where we are, and predict or anticipate where we are headed.

~ TONI CADE BAMBARA

It helped me in the air to keep my small mind contained in earthly human limits, not lost in vertiginous space and elements unknown.

~ DIANA COOPER

I have always been driven by some distant music—a battle hymn no doubt—for I have been at war from the beginning. I've never looked back before. I've never had the time and it has always seemed so dangerous.

~ BETTE DAVIS

What allows us, as human beings, to psychologically survive life on earth, with all of its pain, drama, and challenges, is a sense of purpose and meaning.

~ BARBARA DE ANGELIS

It's but little good you'll go a-watering the last year's crop.

~ GEORGE ELIOT

Living in the past is a dull and lonely business; looking back strains the neck muscles, causes you to bump into people not going your way.

~ EDNA FERBER

Just don't give up trying to do what you really want to do. Where there is love and inspiration, I don't think you can go wrong.

~ ELLA FITZGERALD

I am suffocated and lost when I have not the bright feeling of progression.

~ MARGARET FULLER

I was nervous and confident at the same time, nervous about going out there in front of all of those people, with so much at stake, and confident that I was going to go out there and win.

~ ALTHEA GIBSON

Yes, I have doubted. I have wandered off the path, but I always return. It is intuitive, an intrinsic, built-in sense of direction. I seem always to find my way home.

~ HELEN HAYES

You have to know exactly what you want out of your career. If you want to be a star, you don't bother with other things.

~ MARILYN HORNE

Those who begin many things finish but a few.

~ ITALIAN PROVERB

People don't pay much attention to you when you are second best. I wanted to see what it felt like to be number one.

~ FLORENCE GRIFFITH JOYNER

Before you begin a thing remind yourself that difficulties and delays quite impossible to foresee are ahead.... You can only see one thing clearly, and that is your goal. Form a mental vision of that and cling to it through thick and thin.

~ KATHLEEN NORRIS

Dreams grow holy put in action; work grows fair through starry dreaming. But where each flows on unmingling, both are fruitless and in vain.

~ ADELAIDE PROCTOR

A kitten is chiefly remarkable for rushing about like mad at nothing whatever, and generally stopping before it gets there.

~ AGNES REPPLIER

To pursue yourself is an interesting and absorbing thing to do. Once you have caught the scent of a hidden being, your own hidden being, you won't readily be deflected from the tracking down of it.

~ CYNTHIA PROPPER SETON

Nothing contributes so much to tranquilize the mind as a steady purpose—a point on which the soul may fix its intellectual eye.

~ MARY WOLLSTONECRAFT SHELLY

Trusting Your Better Judgment

If Something Sounds Too Good to Be True, It Probably Is

If you buy cheap meat, when it boils you smell what you have saved.

~ ARABIC PROVERB

Diets, like clothes, should be tailored to you.

~ JOAN RIVERS

Don't Let Others Set Limits for You

I have an almost complete disregard of precedent and a faith in the possibility of something better. It irritates me to be told how things always have been done.... I defy the tyranny of precedent. I cannot afford the luxury of a closed mind. I go for anything new that might improve the past.

~ CLARA BARTON

The door that nobody else will go in at, seems always to swing open widely for me.
~ CLARA BARTON

The Wright brothers flew through the smoke screen of impossibility.
~ DOROTHEA BRANDE

Don't take anyone else's definition of success as your own.
~ JACQUELINE BRISKIN

I don't go by the rule book—I lead from the heart, not the head.
~ DIANA, PRINCESS OF WALES

When she stopped conforming to the conventional picture of femininity she finally began to enjoy being a woman.
~ BETTY FRIEDAN

The history of human growth is at the same time the history of every new idea heralding the approach of a brighter dawn, and the brighter dawn has always been considered illegal, outside of the law.
~ EMMA GOLDMAN

Genius is expansive, irresistible, and irresistibly expansive. If it is in you, no cords can confine it.
~ GAIL HAMILTON

Today's shocks are tomorrow's conventions.
~ CAROLYN HEILBRUN

Decisions, particularly important ones, have always made me sleepy, perhaps because I know that I will have to make them by instinct, and thinking things out is only what other people tell me I should do.
~ LILLIAN HELLMAN

Individuals learn faster than institutions and it is always the dinosaur's brain that is the last to get the new messages.
~ HAZEL HENDERSON

Go ahead and do it. It's much easier to apologize after something's been done than to get permission ahead of time.

~ GRACE MURRAY HOPPER

Once I decide to do something, I can't have people telling me I can't. If there's a roadblock, you jump over it, walk around it, crawl under it.

~ KITTY KELLEY

Confronted by an absolutely infuriating review, it is sometimes helpful for the victim to do a little personal research on the critic. Is there any truth to the rumor that he had no formal education beyond the age of eleven? Was he ever arrested for burglary? I don't know that you will prove anything this way, but it is perfectly harmless and quite soothing.

~ JEAN KERR

I was and I always shall be hampered by what I think other people will say.

~ VIOLETTE LEDUC

Innovators are inevitably controversial.

~ EVA LE GALLIENNE

I'm not going to limit myself just because some people won't accept the fact that I can do something else.

~ DOLLY PARTON

Criticism ... makes very little dent upon me, unless I think there is some real justification and something should be done.

~ ELEANOR ROOSEVELT

It is healthier, in any case, to write for the adults one's children will become than for the children one's "mature" critics often are.

~ ALICE WALKER

I was the kind nobody thought could make it. I had a funny Boston accent. I couldn't pronounce my R's. I wasn't a beauty.

~ BARBARA WALTERS

305

Power is strength and the ability to see yourself through your own
eyes and not through the eyes of another.

~ AGNES WHISTLING ELK

Be Yourself

The expectation of an unpleasantness is more terrible than the thing
itself.

~ MARIE BASHKIRTSEFF

To see a shadow and think it is a tree—that is a pity; but to see a tree
and to think it a shadow can be fatal.

~ PHYLLIS BOTTOME

Success is often achieved by those who don't know that failure is
inevitable.

~ COCO CHANEL

I was always looking outside myself for strength and confidence, but
it comes from within. It is there all the time.

~ ANNA FREUD

All I can do is act according to my deepest instinct, and be whatever
I must be—crazy or ribald or sad or compassionate or loving or
indifferent. That is all anybody can do.

~ KATHERINE HATHAWAY

A person needs at intervals to separate himself from family and
companions and go to new places. He must go without his familiars
in order to be open to influences, to change.

~ KATHERINE HATHAWAY

My recipe for life is not being afraid of myself, afraid of what I think
or of my opinions.

~ EARTHA KITT

You cannot do good work if you take your mind off the work to see how the community is taking it.

~ DOROTHY L. SAYERS

Be content to stand in the light, and let the shadow fall where it will.

~ MARY W. STEWART

Trust Your Intuition

I feel there are two people inside of me—me and my intuition. If I go against her, she'll screw me every time, and if I follow her, we get along quite nicely.

~ KIM BASINGER

You must train your intuition—you must trust the small voice inside you which tells you exactly what to say, what to decide.

~ INGRID BERGMAN

Every advance in social progress removes us more and more from the guidance of instinct, obliging us to depend upon reason for the assurance that our habits are really agreeable to the laws of health.

~ EMILY BLACKWELL

Trust your hunches.... Hunches are usually based on facts filed away just below the conscious level. Warning! Do not confuse your hunches with wishful thinking. This is the road to disaster.

~ DR. JOYCE BROTHERS

Every human being has, like Socrates, an attendant spirit; and wise are they who obey its signals. If it does not always tell us what to do, it always cautions us what not to do.

~ LYDIA MARIA CHILD

Every time you don't follow your inner guidance, you feel a loss of energy, loss of power, a sense of spiritual deadness.

~ SHAKTI GAWAIN

By learning to contact, listen to, and act on our intuition, we can directly connect to the higher power of the universe and allow it to become our guiding force.

~ SHAKTI GAWAIN

We need to let our intuition guide us, and then be willing to follow that guidance directly and fearlessly.

~ SHAKTI GAWAIN

I move on feeling and have learned to distrust those who don't.

~ NIKKI GIOVANNI

Instinct is the nose of the mind.

~ MADAME DE GIRARDIN

Yes, I have doubted. I have wandered off the path, but I always return. It is intuitive, an intrinsic, built-in sense of direction. I seem always to find my way home.

~ HELEN HAYES

Decisions, particularly important ones, have always made me sleepy, perhaps because I know that I will have to make them by instinct, and thinking things out is only what other people tell me I should do.

~ LILLIAN HELLMAN

Advice is what we ask for when we already know the answer but wish we didn't.

~ ERICA JONG

Doubt yourself and you doubt everything you see. Judge yourself and you see judges everywhere. But if you listen to the sound of your own voice, you can rise above doubt and judgment. And you can see forever.

~ NANCY KERRIGAN

I give myself, sometimes, admirable advice, but I am incapable of taking it.

~ LADY MARY WORTLEY MONTAGU

I'm often wrong, but never in doubt.

~ IVY BAKER PRIEST

Instinct is a powerful form of natural energy, perhaps comparable in humans to electricity or even atomic energy in the mechanical world.

~ MARGARET A. RIBBLE

Trusting our intuition often saves us from disaster.

~ ANNE WILSON SCHAEF

Let me listen to me and not them.

~ GERTRUDE STEIN

I go by instinct.... I don't worry about experience.

~ BARBARA STREISAND

To Death I yield, but not to Doubt, who slays before!

~ EDITH M. THOMAS

Trust your gut.

~ BARBARA WALTERS

Once you get rid of the idea that you must please other people before you please yourself, and you begin to follow your own instincts—only then can you be successful. You become more satisfied, and when you are, other people tend to be satisfied with what you do.

~ RAQUEL WELCH

Follow your instincts. That's where true wisdom manifests itself.

~ OPRAH WINFREY

Let Your Values Be Your Guide

The essential conditions of everything you do must be choice, love, passion.

~ NADIA BOULANGER

There is only one history of any importance, and it is the history of what you once believed in, and the history of what you came to believe in.

~ KAY BOYLE

The ability to take pride in your own work is one of the hallmarks of sanity.

~ NIKKI GIOVANNI

The one thing that doesn't abide by majority rule is a person's conscience.

~ HARPER LEE

A friend is one who withholds judgment no matter how long you have his unanswered letter.

~ SOPHIE IRENE LOEB

What one decides to do in crisis depends on one's philosophy of life, and that philosophy cannot be changed by an incident. If one hasn't any philosophy in crises, others make the decision.

~ JEANNETTE RANKIN

There has never been a useful thought or a profound truth that has not found its century and admirers.

~ MADAME DE STAËL

The needle of our conscience is as good a compass as any.

~ RUTH WOLFF

$\mathcal{R}$especting Others

Recognize and Respect Differences

Don't judge any woman until you have walked two moons in her moccasins.

~ AMERICAN INDIAN PROVERB

To know one's self is wisdom, but to know one's neighbor is genius.

~ MINNA ANTRIM

I know that everyone brings to the work his or her own experiences and background and may interpret the piece like a Rorschach, in their own way.

~ IDA APPLEBROOG

There are no little events in life, those we think of no consequence may be full of fate, and it is at our own risk if we neglect the acquaintances and opportunities that seem to be casually offered, and of small importance.

~ AMELIA BARR

The Christian tradition was passed on to me as a great rich mixture, a bouillabaisse of human imagination and wonder brewed from the richness of individual lives.

~ MARY BATESON

Unless one's philosophy is all-inclusive, nothing can be understood.

~ MARY RITTER BEARD

Connected knowers do not measure other people's words by some impersonal standard. Their purpose is not to judge but to understand.

~ MARY FIELD BELENKY

Nature is just enough; but men and women must comprehend and accept her suggestions.

~ ANTOINETTE BROWN BLACKWELL

To live and let live, without clamor for distinction or recognition; to wait on divine love; to write truth first on the tablet of one's own heart—this is the sanity and perfection of living, and my human ideal.

~ MARY BAKER EDDY

The motto should not be: Forgive one another; rather understand one another.

~ EMMA GOLDMAN

Someone has said that it requires less mental effort to condemn than to think.

~ EMMA GOLDMAN

[Tolerance] is the greatest gift of the mind; it requires the same effort of the brain that it takes to balance oneself on a bicycle.

~ HELEN KELLER

Africa has her mysteries, and even a wise man cannot understand them. But a wise man respects them.

~ MIRIAM MAKEBA

We're frightened of what makes us different.

~ ANNE RICE

If you judge people, you have no time to love them.

      ~ MOTHER TERESA

To argue over who is the more noble is nothing more than to dispute whether dirt is better for making bricks or for making mortar.

      ~ TERESA OF AVILA

What women want is what men want. They want respect.

      ~ MARILYN VOS SAVANT

Truth has never been, can never be, contained in any one creed or system.

      ~ MARY AUGUSTA (ARNOLD) WARD

Honesty Connotes Respect

Accurate information is a key part of motivation.

      ~ MARY ANN ALLISON

The best proof of love is trust.

      ~ DR. JOYCE BROTHERS

The best way to get where you want to be is to please those who own the road.

      ~ ELENA CASTEDO-ELLERMAN

The woman who does not choose to love should cut the matter short at once, by holding out no hopes to her suitor.

      ~ MARGUERITE DE VALOIS

Being considerate of others will take you and your children further in life than any college or professional degree.

      ~ MARIAN WRIGHT EDELMAN

Gossip is a sort of smoke that comes from the dirty tobacco-pipes of those who diffuse it; it proves nothing but the bad taste of the smoker.

      ~ GEORGE ELIOT

The scornful nostril and the high head gather not the odors that lie on the track of truth.

~ GEORGE ELIOT

The principle was right there—you couldn't miss it. The more you did for your customers, the more they did for us.

~ DEBBI FIELDS

A gossip's mouth is the devil's postbag.

~ GAELIC PROVERB

In rejecting secrecy I had also rejected the road to cynicism.

~ CATHARINE MARSHALL

When one is frank, one's very presence is a compliment.

~ MARIANNE MOORE

Truth is a rough, honest, helter-skelter terrier, that none like to see brought into their drawing rooms.

~ OUIDA

It's an indulgence to sit in a room and discuss your beliefs as if they were a juicy piece of gossip.

~ AYN RAND

The truth is the kindest thing we can give folks in the end.

~ HARRIET BEECHER STOWE

Expect the Best of Others

Hire the best. Pay them fairly. Communicate frequently. Provide challenges and rewards. Believe in them. Get out of their way and they'll knock your socks off.

~ MARY ANN ALLISON

Treat a horse like a woman and a woman like a horse. And they'll both win for you.

~ ELIZABETH ARDEN

Invest in the human soul. Who knows, it might be a diamond in the rough.

~ MARY MCLEOD BETHUNE

A hero is someone we can admire without apology.

~ KITTY KELLEY

All the goodness, beauty, and perfection of a human being belong to the one who knows how to recognize these qualities.

~ GEORGETTE LEBLANC

A good marriage is at least 80 percent good luck in finding the right person at the right time. The rest is trust.

~ NANETTE NEWMAN

We need our heroes.

~ ELEANOR ROOSEVELT

It is healthier to see the good points of others than to analyze our own bad ones.

~ FRANÇOISE SAGAN

Show Compassion, Not Pity

Power is the ability to do good things for others.

~ BROOKE ASTOR

The deadliest feeling that can be offered to a woman is pity.

~ VICKI BAUM

It is impossible to fulfill the law concerning love for Me, God eternal, apart from the law concerning love for your neighbors.

~ SAINT CATHERINE OF SIENA

Service is the rent we pay for the privilege of living on this earth.
~ SHIRLEY CHISHOLM

Reform is born of need, not pity.
~ REBECCA HARDING DAVIS

Nobody who is somebody looks down on anybody.
~ MARGARET DELAND

I am convinced that any feeling of exaltation because we have people under us should be conquered, for I am sure that if we enjoy being over people, there will be something in our manner which will make them dislike being under us.
~ MARY PARKER FOLLETT

"Honesty" without compassion and understanding is not honesty, but subtle hostility.
~ ROSE N. FRANZBLAU

It's compassion that makes gods of us.
~ DOROTHY GILMAN

Enthusiasm is the divine particle in our composition: with it we are great, generous, and true; without it, we are little, false, and mean.
~ L.E. LANDON

Religion without humanity is a poor human stuff.
~ SOJOURNER TRUTH

The best index to a person's character is (a) how he treats people who can't do him any good, and (b) how he treats people who can't fight back.
~ ABIGAIL VAN BUREN

Theories and goals of education don't matter a whit if you do not consider your students to be human beings.
~ LOU ANN WALKER

Every Individual Is Worthy of Unbiased Regard

I believe every person has the ability to achieve something important, and with that in mind I regard everyone as special.
 ⌒ MARY KAY ASH

The Christian tradition was passed on to me as a great rich mixture, a bouillabaisse of human imagination and wonder brewed from the richness of individual lives.
 ⌒ MARY BATESON

Unless one's philosophy is all-inclusive, nothing can be understood.
 ⌒ MARY RITTER BEARD

The fact that we are human beings is infinitely more important than all the peculiarities that distinguish human beings from one another.
 ⌒ SIMONE DE BEAUVOIR

The sexes in each species of beings ... are always true equivalents— equals but not identicals.
 ⌒ ANTOINETTE BROWN BLACKWELL

To understand another human being you must gain some insight into the conditions which made him what he is.
 ⌒ MARGARET BOURKE-WHITE

Like snowflakes, the human pattern is never cast twice. We are uncommonly and marvelously intricate in thought and action.
 ⌒ ALICE CHILDRESS

Everyone needs to be valued. Everyone has the potential to give something back.
 ⌒ DIANA, PRINCESS OF WALES

Animals are such agreeable friends—they ask no questions, they pass no criticisms.
 ⌒ GEORGE ELIOT

Every human being is trying to say something to others. Trying to cry out I am alive, notice me! Speak to me! Confirm that I am important, that I matter!

~ MARION D. HANKS

Tyranny and anarchy are alike incompatible with freedom, security, and the enjoyment of opportunity.

~ JEANE KIRKPATRICK

All sweeping assertions are erroneous.

~ L.E. LANDON

Because you're not what I would have you be, I blind myself to who, in truth, you are.

~ MADELEINE L'ENGLE

So once I shut down my privilege of disliking anyone I choose and holding myself aloof if I could manage it, greater understanding, growing compassion came to me.

~ CATHARINE MARSHALL

We cannot safely assume that other people's minds work on the same principles as our own. All too often, others with whom we come in contact do not reason as we reason, or do not value the things we value, or are not interested in what interests us.

~ ISABEL BRIGGS MYERS

There is not one big cosmic meaning for all, there is only the meaning we each give to our life, an individual meaning, an individual plot, like an individual novel, a book for each person.

~ ANAÏS NIN

To have one's individuality completely ignored is like being pushed quite out of life. Like being blown out as one blows out a light.

~ EVELYN SCOTT

It's funny how your initial approach to a person can determine your feelings toward them, no matter what facts develop later on.

~ DOROTHY UHNAK

Nobody really knows Indians who cheat them and treat them badly.

~ SARAH WINNEMUCCA

Know When to Speak, When to Listen

Don't give advice unless you're asked.

~ AMY ALCOTT

Waiting is one of the great arts.

~ MARGERY ALLINGHAM

We don't want to push our ideas on to customers, we simply want to make what they want.

~ LAURA ASHLEY

Really listening and suspending one's own judgment is necessary in order to understand other people on their own terms. As we have noted, this is a process that requires trust and builds trust.

~ MARY FIELD BELENKY

Listening, not imitation, may be the sincerest form of flattery.

~ DR. JOYCE BROTHERS

Never fail to know that if you are doing all the talking, you are boring somebody.

~ HELEN GURLEY BROWN

Tact is after all a kind of mind-reading.

~ SARAH ORNE JEWETT

This is the gist of what I know:
Give advice and buy a foe.

~ PHYLLIS MCGINLEY

Listening is not merely not talking, though even that is beyond most of our powers; it means taking a vigorous, human interest in what is being told us.

～ ALICE DEUR MILLER

The passion for setting people right is in itself an afflictive disease.

～ MARIANNE MOORE

It's easier to be a critic than an author.

～ YIDDISH PROVERB

Respect Young and Old Alike

If we have the courage and tenacity of our forebears, who stood firmly like a rock against the lash of slavery, we shall find a way to do for our day what they did for theirs.

～ MARY MCLEOD BETHUNE

Love and respect are the most important aspects of parenting, and of all relationships.

～ JODIE FOSTER

If we can genuinely honor our mother and father, we are not only at peace with ourselves but we can then give birth to our future.

～ SHIRLEY MACLAINE

What we forget as children is that our parents are children, also. The child in them has not been satisfied or met or loved, often.

～ EDNA O'BRIEN

Theories and goals of education don't matter a whit if you do not consider your students to be human beings.

～ LOU ANN WALKER

Give Respect While the Recipient Is Able to Enjoy It

Any mother could perform the jobs of several air-traffic controllers with ease.

~ LISA ALTHER

It isn't easy to be the person who sometimes has to try to preserve your happiness at the expense of your fun.

~ MARGARET CULKIN BANNING

We really have no definition of mother in our law books. Mother was believed to have been so basic that no definition was deemed necessary.

~ JUDGE MARIANNE O. BATTANI

A remembrance can mean nothing to the one remembered; it can only remind the ones left behind how little they did while you were still alive.

~ SANDRA BERNHARD

Like all children I had taken my father for granted. Now that I had lost him, I felt an emptiness that could never be filled.

~ BENAZIR BHUTTO

Any relic of the dead is precious, if they were valued living.

~ EMILY BRONTË

You know, fathers just have a way of putting everything together.

~ ERIKA COSBY

Whenever I try to recall that long-ago first day at school only one memory shines through: my father held my hand.

~ MARCELENE COX

My father ... lived as if he were poured of iron, and loved his family with a vulnerability that was touching.

~ MARI E. EVANS

Mother knows best.

~ EDNA FERBER

To her the name of father was another name for love.

~ FANNY FERN

My dear father! When I remember him, it is always with his arms
open wide to love and comfort me.

~ ISOBEL FIELD

Pray for the dead and fight like hell for the living.

~ MOTHER JONES

I was not close to my father, but he was very special to me.
Whenever I did something as a little girl—learn to swim or act in a
school play, for instance—he was fabulous. There would be this
certain look in his eyes. It made me feel great.

~ DIANE KEATON

According to my method of thinking, and that of many others, not
woman but the mother is the most precious possession of the nation,
so precious that society advances its highest well-being when it
protects the functions of the mother.

~ ELLEN KEY

If we can genuinely honor our mother and father, we are not only at
peace with ourselves but we can then give birth to our future.

~ SHIRLEY MACLAINE

I love eulogies. They are the most moving kind of speech because
they attempt to pluck meaning from the fog, and on short order,
when the emotions are still ragged and raw and susceptible to leaps.

~ PEGGY NOONAN

If you think a complimentary thought about someone, don't just
think it. Dare to compliment people and pass on compliments to
them from others.

~ CATHERINE PONDER

She makes everything possible.

~ HELEN REDDY

The history, the root, the strength of my father is the strength we now rest on.

~ CAROLYN M. RODGERS

My father would pick me up and hold me high in the air. He dominated my life as long as he lived, and was the love of my life for many years after he died.

~ ELEANOR ROOSEVELT

When you're jumping so high for something so far up in the sky, you have to know that there is definitely someone there who can catch you, someone who knows how to catch you and when. Mom is just that way.

~ PICABO STREET

My father got me strong and straight and slim
And I give thanks to him.
My mother bore me glad and sound and sweet,
I kiss her feet.

~ MARGUERITE WILKINSON

Into the father's grave the daughter, sometimes a gray-haired woman, lays away forever the little pet names and memories which to all the rest of the world are but foolishness.

~ CONSTANCE FENIMORE WOOLSON

Respect a Person's Right to Be Themselves

Love thy neighbor as thyself, but choose your neighborhood.

~ LOUISE BEAL

Family jokes, though rightly cursed by strangers, are the bond that keeps most families alive.

~ STELLA BENSON

The secret of a happy marriage is finding the right person. You know they're right if you love to be with them all of the time.

~ JULIA CHILD

Great mischief comes from attempts to steady other people's altars.

~ MARY BAKER EDDY

True patriotism doesn't exclude an understanding of the patriotism of others.

~ QUEEN ELIZABETH II

One person's constant is another person's variable.

~ SUSAN GERHART

The closer I'm bound in love to you, the closer I am to free.

~ INDIGO GIRLS

Freedom works.

~ JEANE KIRKPATRICK

There is an incredible amount of magic and feistiness in black men that nobody has been able to wipe out. But everybody has tried.

~ TONI MORRISON

Boys don't make passes at female smart-asses.

~ LETTY COTTIN POGREBIN

I love different folks.

~ ELEANOR H. PORTER

No one worth possessing can be quite possessed.

~ SARA TEASDALE

Consider Yourself on Equal Footing with Others

It is no good to think that other people are out to serve our interests.

~ IVY COMPTON-BURNETT

The desire to conquer is itself a sort of subjection.
~ GEORGE ELIOT

The only people who would be in government are those who care more about people than they do about power.
~ MILLICENT FENWICK

Leaders can be moral—and they should be moral—without imposing their morality on others.
~ GERALDINE FERRARO

Laws are felt only when the individual comes into conflict with them.
~ SUZANNE LAFOLLETTE

It seems odd that whenever man chooses to play God, God loses.
~ FELICIA LAMPORT

What we forget as children is that our parents are children, also. The child in them has not been satisfied or met or loved, often.
~ EDNA O'BRIEN

Coercion. The unpardonable crime.
~ DOROTHY MILLER RICHARDSON

It is not fair to ask of others what you are not willing to do yourself.
~ ELEANOR ROOSEVELT

Something in me has always been opposed to capital punishment. What right has one group of human beings to take away the life of any other human being?
~ ELEANOR ROOSEVELT

Virtue can only flourish among equals.
~ MARY WOLLSTONECRAFT SHELLEY

As soon as you bring up money, I notice, conversation gets sociological, then political, then moral.
~ JANE SMILEY

Ambition if it feeds at all, does so on the ambition of others.

~ SUSAN SONTAG

You can stand tall without standing on someone. You can be a victor without having victims.

~ HARRIET WOODS

Where the Mind is biggest, the Heart, the Senses, Magnanimity, Charity, Tolerance, Kindliness, and the rest of them scarcely have room to breathe.

~ VIRGINIA WOOLF

Everyone Is Entitled to Their Opinion

When the habitually even-tempered suddenly fly into a passion, that explosion is apt to be more impressive than the outburst of the most violent amongst us.

~ MARGERY ALLINGHAM

There are some people that you cannot change, you must either swallow them whole or leave them alone.

~ MARGOT ASQUITH

Where an opinion is general, it is usually correct.

~ JANE AUSTEN

You've got to ensure that the holders of an opinion, however unpopular, are allowed to put across their points of view.

~ BETTY BOOTHROYD

There is space within sisterhood for likeness and difference, for the subtle differences that challenge and delight; there is space for disappointment—and surprise.

~ CHRISTINE DOWNING

Leaders can be moral—and they should be moral—without imposing their morality on others.

~ GERALDINE FERRARO

It takes a disciplined person to listen to convictions which are different from their own.

~ DOROTHY FULDHEIM

The highest result of education is tolerance.

~ HELEN KELLER

In a society where the rights and potential of women are constrained, no man can be truly free. He may have power, but he will not have freedom.

~ MARY F. ROBINSON

Ambition, old as mankind, the immemorial weakness of the strong.

~ VITA SACKVILLE-WEST

When one clings to the myth of superiority, one must constantly overlook the virtues and abilities of others.

~ ANNE WILSON SCHAEF

We have no more right to put our discordant states of mind into the lives of those around us and rob them of their sunshine and brightness then we have to enter their houses and steal their silverware.

~ JULIA SETON

Be Patient with Others—and Yourself

Patience with others is Love, Patience with self is Hope, Patience with God is Faith.

~ ADEL BESTAVROS

I believe I was impatient with unintelligent people from the moment I was born: a tragedy—for I am myself three-parts a fool.

~ MRS. PATRICK CAMPBELL

We are told that people stay in love because of chemistry, or because they remain intrigued with each other, because of many kindnesses, because of luck.... But part of it has got to be forgiveness and gratefulness.

~ ELLEN GOODMAN

Enthusiasm is the divine particle in our composition: with it we are great, generous, and true; without it, we are little, false, and mean.

~ L.E. LANDON

I am convinced, the longer I live, that life and its blessings are not so unjustly distributed as when we are suffering greatly we are inclined to suppose.

~ MARY TODD LINCOLN

The easiest thing a human being can do is to criticize another human being.

~ LYNN M. LITTLE

Who thinks it just to be judged by a single error?

~ BERYL MARKHAM

I learned that true forgiveness includes total self-acceptance. And out of acceptance wounds are healed and happiness is possible again.

~ CATHARINE MARSHALL

For me it's not possible to forget, and I don't understand people who, when the love is ended, can bury the other person in hatred or oblivion. For me, a man I have loved becomes a kind of brother.

~ JEANNE MOREAU

It is a purely relative matter where one draws the plimsoll-line of condemnation, and ... if you find the whole of humanity falls below it you have simply made a mistake and drawn it too high. And you are probably below it yourself.

~ FRANCES PARTRIDGE

To do exactly as your neighbors do is the only sensible rule.

~ EMILY POST

People genuinely happy in their choices seem less often tempted to force them on other people than those who feel martyred and broken by their lives.

～ JANE RULE

Learn from the Experiences of Others

Speak not against anyone whose burden you have not weighed yourself.
～ MARION ZIMMER BRADLEY

Nothing's easier than believing we understand experiences we've never had.
～ GWEN BRISTOW

No, I don't understand my husband's theory of relativity, but I know my husband, and I know he can be trusted.
～ ELSA EINSTEIN

We all live with the objective of being happy, our lives are all different and yet the same.
～ ANNE FRANK

One can find traces of every life in each life.
～ SUSAN GRIFFIN

Next to genius is the power of feeling where true genius lies.
～ SARAH JOSEPHA HALE

Remember that you are all people and that all people are you.
～ JOY HARJO

One woman understands another.
～ IRISH PROVERB

It's odd that you can get so anesthetized by your own pain or your own problem that you don't quite fully share the hell of someone close to you.

~ LADY BIRD JOHNSON

There is no king who has not had a slave among his ancestors, and no slave who has not had a king among his.

~ HELEN KELLER

A gossip is one who talks to you about others; a bore is one who talks to you about himself; and a brilliant conversationalist is one who talks to you about yourself.

~ LISA KIRK

I'm not afraid of too many things, and I got that invincible kind of attitude from my father.

~ QUEEN LATIFAH

The more I traveled the more I realized that fear makes strangers of people who should be friends.

~ SHIRLEY MACLAINE

There is no hierarchy of values by which one culture has the right to insist on all its own values and deny those of another.

~ MARGARET MEAD

Ideal conversation must be an exchange of thought, and not, as many of those who worry about their shortcomings believe, an eloquent exhibition of wit or oratory.

~ EMILY POST

Networking is an enrichment program, not an entitlement program.

~ SUSAN ROANE

Respect for people is the cornerstone of communication and networking in the nineties.

~ SUSAN ROANE

You always admire what you really don't understand.
～ ELEANOR ROOSEVELT

Women have moved and shaken me, but I have been nourished by men.
～ MAY SARTON

We should not permit tolerance to degenerate into indifference.
～ MARGARET CHASE SMITH

Those are the same stars, and that is the same moon, that look down upon your brothers and sisters, and which they see as they look up to them, though they are ever so far away from us, and each other.
～ SOJOURNER TRUTH

Whatever good I have accomplished as an actress I believe came in direct proportion to my efforts to portray black women who have made positive contributions to my heritage.
～ CICELY TYSON

Everybody in the world ought to be sorry for everybody else. We all have our little private hell.
～ BETTINA VON HUTTON

Our mothers and our grandmothers, some of them: moving to music not yet written.
～ ALICE WALKER

Be Kind in All Encounters

The basic difference between being assertive and being aggressive is how our words and behavior affect the rights and well-being of others.
～ SHARON ANTHONY BOWER

So often the truth is told with hate, and lies are told with love.
～ RITA MAE BROWN

It is impossible to fulfill the law concerning love for Me, God eternal, apart from the law concerning love for your neighbors.

~ SAINT CATHERINE OF SIENA

I think women need kindness more than love. When one human being is kind to another, it's a very deep matter.

~ ALICE CHILDRESS

Life is just a short walk from the cradle to the grave—and it sure behooves us to be kind to one another along the way.

~ ALICE CHILDRESS

I'm a competitive person, but I have never understood people's competitiveness at the expense of their colleagues.

~ GERALDINE FERRARO

You know, we're all going in the same direction, or at least trying to. So we need to live together, get along together, and give each other enough space to be comfortable on that road.

~ LILLIAN GIDEON

Cruelty is the only sin.

~ ELLEN GLASGOW

The demand for equal rights in every vocation of life is just and fair; but, after all, the most vital right is the right to love and be loved.

~ EMMA GOLDMAN

We are told that people stay in love because of chemistry, or because they remain intrigued with each other, because of many kindnesses, because of luck.... But part of it has got to be forgiveness and gratefulness.

~ ELLEN GOODMAN

Welcome is the best cheer.

~ GREEK PROVERB

Live in my heart and pay no rent.

~ IRISH PROVERB

Love is blind to blemishes and fault.

~ IRISH PROVERB

Love conceals ugliness, and hate sees many faults.

~ IRISH PROVERB

It is terrible to destroy a person's picture of himself in the interests of truth or some other abstraction.

~ DORIS LESSING

The easiest thing a human being can do is to criticize another human being.

~ LYNN M. LITTLE

Etiquette—a fancy word for simple kindness.

~ ELSA MAXWELL

Good manners are the techniques of expressing consideration for the feelings of others.

~ ALICE DEUR MILLER

Moments of kindness and reconciliation are worth having, even if the parting has to come sooner or later.

~ ALICE MUNRO

Violence is a symptom of impotence.

~ ANAÏS NIN

Beware of allowing a tactless word, rebuttal, a rejection to obliterate the whole sky.

~ ANAÏS NIN

Your luck is how you treat people.

~ BRIDGET O'DONNELL

There are worse words than cuss words; there are words that hurt.

~ TILLIE OLSEN

Truth is a rough, honest, helter-skelter terrier, that none like to see brought into their drawing rooms.

～ OUIDA

The will to be totally rational is the will to be made out of glass and steel: and to use others as if they were glass and steel.

～ MARGE PIERCY

Manners are a sensitive awareness of the feelings of others. If you have that awareness, you have good manners, no matter what fork you use.

～ EMILY POST

Great opportunities to help others seldom come, but small ones come daily.

～ IVY BAKER PRIEST

Coercion. The unpardonable crime.

～ DOROTHY MILLER RICHARDSON

And hearts have been broken from harsh words spoken
That sorrow can ne'er set right.

～ MARGARET ELIZABETH SANGSTER

That which is horrifying to you don't do to anybody else.

～ DR. LAURA SCHLESSINGER

My feeling is that there is nothing in life but refraining from hurting others, and comforting those that are sad.

～ OLIVE SCHREINER

We can say "Peace on Earth." We can sing about it, preach about it or pray about it, but if we have not internalized the mythology to make it happen inside us, then it will not be.

～ BETTY SHABAZZ

There are chapters in every life which are seldom read and certainly not aloud.

～ CAROL SHIELDS

Politeness is the art of choosing among your thoughts.

~ MADAME DE STAËL

The truth is the kindest thing we can give folks in the end.

~ HARRIET BEECHER STOWE

One filled with joy preaches without preaching.

~ MOTHER TERESA

Religion without humanity is a poor human stuff.

~ SOJOURNER TRUTH

The best index to a person's character is (a) how he treats people who can't do him any good, and (b) how he treats people who can't fight back.

~ ABIGAIL VAN BUREN

A hurtful act is the transference to others of the degradation which we bear in ourselves.

~ SIMONE WEIL

The best way to hold a man is in your arms.

~ MAE WEST

Keep the other person's well-being in mind when you feel an attack of soul-purging truth coming on.

~ BETTY WHITE

Respect Does Not Always Equate with Affection

Pillars are fallen at thy feet
Fanes quiver in the air
A prostrate city is thy seat
And thou alone art there.

~ LYDIA MARIA CHILD

There is little place in the political scheme of things for an
independent, creative personality, for a fighter. Anyone who takes that
role must pay a price.

~ SHIRLEY CHISHOLM

In my business, you measure your respect by the enemies you make.

~ THEO E. COLBORN

On what strange stuff Ambition feeds!

~ ELIZA COOK

True patriotism doesn't exclude an understanding of the patriotism
of others.

~ QUEEN ELIZABETH II

The crocodile doesn't harm the bird that cleans his teeth for him. He
eats the others but not that one.

~ LINDA HOGAN

Personal virtue is a good in itself, but it is not a sufficient means to
an end of good government.

~ JEANE KIRKPATRICK

Whatever people in general do not understand, they are always
prepared to dislike; the incomprehensible is always the obnoxious.

~ L.E. LANDON

$\mathcal{W}$orking Together

The Family Is the Greatest Team of All

Within our family there was no such thing as a person who did not matter. Second cousins thrice removed mattered.

~ SHIRLEY ABBOTT

All the wealth of the world cannot be compared with the happiness of living together happily united.

~ MARGARET D'YOUVILLE

There's a thread that binds all of us together, pull one end of the thread, the strain is felt all down the line.

~ ROSAMOND MARSHALL

Love from one being to another can only be that two solitudes come nearer, recognize and protect and comfort each other.

~ HAN SUYIN

We Must Work in Harmony With Nature

For the American Indian, the ability of all creatures to share in the process of ongoing creation makes all things sacred.

～ PAULA GUNN ALLEN

We are the land. To the best of my understanding, that is the fundamental idea that permeates American Indian life.

～ PAULA GUNN ALLEN

I knew without a glimmer of doubt that all things in the universe were connected by a living truth that would not relent its continuing search for wholeness until every form of life was united.

～ LYNN V. ANDREWS

You know, we're all going in the same direction, or at least trying to. So we need to live together, get along together, and give each other enough space to be comfortable on that road.

～ LILLIAN GIDEON

If we are to survive on this planet, there must be compromises.

～ STORM JAMESON

Be Positive and Pull Together

Cooperation is doing with a smile what you have to do anyway.

～ ANON.

You know, we're all going in the same direction, or at least trying to. So we need to live together, get along together, and give each other enough space to be comfortable on that road.

～ LILLIAN GIDEON

As contagion of sickness makes sickness, contagion of trust can make trust.

～ MARIANNE MOORE

Competition is about passion for perfection, and passion for other people who join in this impossible quest.

         ⁓ MARIAH BURTON NELSON

Happiness is a sunbeam which may pass through a thousand bosoms without losing a particle of its original ray; nay, when it strikes on a kindred heart, like the converged light on a mirror, it reflects itself with redoubled brightness. It is not perfected till it is shared.

         ⁓ JANE PORTER

The tourist may complain of other tourists, but he would be lost without them.

         ⁓ AGNES REPPLIER

If enough people think of a thing and work hard enough at it, I guess it's pretty nearly bound to happen, wind and weather permitting.

         ⁓ LAURA INGALLS WILDER

Don't Be Afraid to Ask for Help

The smartest thing I ever said was "Help me."

         ⁓ ANON.

The healthy, the strong individual, is the one who asks for help when he needs it. Whether he has an abscess on his knee or in his soul.

         ⁓ RONA BARRETT

My only advice is to stay aware, listen carefully and yell for help if you need it.

         ⁓ JUDY BLUME

Get the knack of getting people to help you and also pitch in yourself.

         ⁓ RUTH GORDON

Silence is not certain token
That no secret grief is there;
Sorrow which is never spoken
Is the heaviest load to bear.
～ FRANCES RIDLEY HAVERGAL

Don't do anything that someone else can do for you because there
are only so many things that only you can do.
～ JINGER HEATH

It is true that no one can harm the person who wears armor. But no
one can help him either.
～ KRISTIN HUNTER

Trouble shared is trouble halved.
～ DOROTHY L. SAYERS

We can't help everyone, but everyone can help someone.
～ DR. LORETTA SCOTT

Trouble is part of your life, and if you don't share it, you don't give
the person who loves you a chance to love you enough.
～ DINAH SHORE

Strong Teams Are Composed of Strong Individuals

Ideally, couples need three lives; one for him, one for her, and one
for them together.
～ JACQUELINE BISSET

Follow your interests, get the best available education and training,
set your sights high, be persistent, be flexible, keep your options
open, accept help when offered, and be prepared to help others.
～ MILDRED SPIEWAK DRESSELHAUS

You know, we're all going in the same direction, or at least trying to. So we need to live together, get along together, and give each other enough space to be comfortable on that road.

~ LILLIAN GIDEON

We must remember that one determined person can make a significant difference, and that a small group of determined people can change the course of history.

~ SONIA JOHNSON

There's a thread that binds all of us together, pull one end of the thread, the strain is felt all down the line.

~ ROSAMOND MARSHALL

Whatever my individual desires were to be free, I was not alone. There were others who felt the same way.

~ ROSA PARKS

Most leaders are indispensable, but to produce a major social change, many ordinary people must also be involved.

~ ANNE FIROR SCOTT

Communication is a continual balancing act, juggling the conflicting needs for intimacy and independence. To survive in the world, we have to act in concert with others, but to survive as ourselves, rather than simply as cogs in a wheel, we have to act alone.

~ DEBORAH TANNEN

We'll Triumph If We Stand Together

You've got to be willing to stay committed to someone over the long run, and sometimes it doesn't work out. But often if you become real honest with yourself and honest with each other, and put aside whatever personal hurt and disappointment you have to really understand yourself and your spouse, it can be the most wonderful experience you've ever had.

∼ HILLARY RODHAM CLINTON

A single arrow is easily broken, but not ten in a bundle.

∼ JAPANESE PROVERB

We must stand together; if we don't, there will be no victory for any one of us.

∼ MOTHER JONES

There's a thread that binds all of us together, pull one end of the thread, the strain is felt all down the line.

∼ ROSAMOND MARSHALL

Whatever my individual desires were to be free, I was not alone. There were others who felt the same way.

∼ ROSA PARKS

I've always believed that one woman's success can only help another woman's success.

∼ GLORIA VANDERBILT

Recognize Individual Efforts

Alone we can do so little; together we can do so much.

∼ HELEN KELLER

We all act as hinges—fortuitous links between other people.

∼ PENELOPE LIVELY

There's a thread that binds all of us together, pull one end of the thread, the strain is felt all down the line.

~ ROSAMOND MARSHALL

We seldom stop to think how many people's lives are entwined with our own. It is a form of selfishness to imagine that every individual can operate on his own or can pull out of the general stream and not be missed.

~ IVY BAKER PRIEST

Most leaders are indispensable, but to produce a major social change, many ordinary people must also be involved.

~ ANNE FIROR SCOTT

We Must Give Before We Can Take

Sharing is sometimes more demanding than giving.

~ MARY BATESON

When one hand washes another, both become clean.

~ DUTCH PROVERB

The human heart, at whatever age, opens only to the heart that opens in return.

~ MARIA EDGEWORTH

Compromise, if not the spice of life, is its solidity.

~ PHYLLIS MCGINLEY

The only alternative to war is peace and the only road to peace is negotiations.

~ GOLDA MEIR

My friend and I have built a wall
Between us thick and wide:
The stones of it are laid in scorn
And plastered high with pride.

◡ ELIZABETH CUTTER MORROW

There Is No "I" in "Team"

My whole life, whether it be long or short, shall be devoted to your service and the service of our great imperial family to which we all belong. But I shall not have the strength to carry out this resolution alone unless you join in it with me.

◡ QUEEN ELIZABETH II

Get the knack of getting people to help you and also pitch in yourself.

◡ RUTH GORDON

A person who believes … that there is a whole of which one is a part, and that in being a part one is whole: such a person has no desire whatever, at any time, to play God. Only those who have denied their being yearn to play at it.

◡ URSULA K. LE GUIN

We all act as hinges—fortuitous links between other people.

◡ PENELOPE LIVELY

Unless I am a part of everything I am nothing.

◡ PENELOPE LIVELY

Women Are Unstoppable When They Work Together

For what is done or learned by one class of women becomes, by virtue of their common womanhood, the property of all women.

◡ ELIZABETH BLACKWELL

344

We learn best to listen to our own voices if we are listening at the same time to other women—whose stories, for all our differences, turn out, if we listen well, to be our stories also.

~ BARBARA DEMING

Remember the dignity of your womanhood. Do not appeal, do not beg, do not grovel. Take courage, join hands, stand beside us, fight with us.

~ CHRISTABEL PANKHURST

Today whenever women gather together it is not necessarily nurturing. It is coalition building. And if you feel the strain, you may be doing some good work.

~ BERNICE JOHNSON REAGON

Women's art, though created in solitude, wells up out of community. There is, clearly, both enormous hunger for the work thus being diffused, and an explosion of creative energy, bursting through the coercive choicelessness of the system on whose boundaries we are working.

~ ADRIENNE RICH

A Team Should Commit to a Common Goal

We all have the same dreams.

~ JOAN DIDION

That is always our problem, not how to get control of people, but how all together we can get control of a situation.

~ MARY PARKER FOLLETT

Leader and followers are both following the invisible leader—the common purpose.

~ MARY PARKER FOLLETT

You know, we're all going in the same direction, or at least trying to. So we need to live together, get along together, and give each other enough space to be comfortable on that road.

~ LILLIAN GIDEON

The streams which would otherwise diverge to fertilize a thousand meadows, must be directed into one deep narrow channel before they can turn a mill.

~ ANNA JAMESON

There's a thread that binds all of us together, pull one end of the thread, the strain is felt all down the line.

~ ROSAMOND MARSHALL

I always feel the movement is a sort of mosaic. Each of us puts in one little stone, and then you get a great mosaic at the end.

~ ALICE PAUL

Each Team Member Has Unique Talents

The essential feature of common thought is not that it is held in common but that it has been produced in common ... the core of the social process is not likeness, but the harmonizing of differences through interpenetration.

~ MARY PARKER FOLLETT

The unifying of opposites is the eternal process.

~ MARY PARKER FOLLETT

Imitation is for shirkers, like-mindedness for the comfort lovers, unifying for the creators.

~ MARY PARKER FOLLETT

Unity, not uniformity, must be our aim. We attain unity only through variety. Differences must be integrated, not annihilated, not absorbed.

~ MARY PARKER FOLLETT

What people often mean by getting rid of conflict is getting rid of diversity, and it is of the utmost importance that these should not be considered the same.

~ MARY PARKER FOLLETT

Alone we can do so little; together we can do so much.

~ HELEN KELLER

Pears cannot ripen alone. So we ripened together.

~ MERIDEL LE SUEUR

When one's own problems are unsolvable and all best efforts are frustrated, it is lifesaving to listen to other people's problems.

~ SUZANNE MASSIE

One must either accept some theory or else believe one's own instinct or follow the world's opinion.

~ GERTRUDE STEIN

Make the Most of Both Male and Female Strengths

The unifying of opposites is the eternal process.

~ MARY PARKER FOLLETT

While you don't need a formal written contract before you get married, I think it's important for both partners to spell out what they expect from each other.... There are always plenty of surprises—and lots of give and take—once you're married.

~ MURIEL FOX

Marriage is not a reform school.

~ ANN LANDERS

Now men and women are separate and unequal. We should be hand in hand; in fact, we should have our arms around one another.

~ CLORIS LEACHMAN

Men and women are like right and left hands: it doesn't make sense not to use both.

~ JEANNETTE RANKIN

Collaboration Yields Effective Results

There are three ways of dealing with difference: domination, compromise, and integration. By domination only one side gets what it wants; by compromise neither side gets what it wants; by integration we find a way by which both sides may get what they wish.

⌒ MARY PARKER FOLLETT

Women and men have to fight together to change society—and both will benefit.

⌒ MURIEL FOX

Every time a man unburdens his heart to a stranger he reaffirms the love that unites humanity.

⌒ GERMAINE GREER

I know some good marriages—marriages where both people are just trying to get through their days by helping each other, being good to each other.

⌒ ERICA JONG

Good communication is as stimulating as black coffee, and just as hard to sleep after.

⌒ ANNE MORROW LINDBERGH

Exchange is creation.

⌒ MURIEL RUKEYSER

One must either accept some theory or else believe one's own instinct or follow the world's opinion.

⌒ GERTRUDE STEIN

Cooperation is an intelligent functioning of the concept of laissez faire—a thorough conviction that nobody can get there unless everybody gets there.

⌒ VIRGINIA BURDEN TOWER

*B*roadening Your Horizons

Be Open to All Possibilities

I don't want to get to the end of my life and find that I lived just the length of it. I want to have lived the width of it as well.
～ DIANE ACKERMAN

Finite to fail, but infinite to venture.
～ EMILY DICKINSON

Your world is as big as you make it.
～ GEORGIA DOUGLAS JOHNSON

I always keep myself in a position of being a student.
～ JACKIE JOYNER-KERSEE

When one paints an ideal, one does not need to limit one's imagination.
～ ELLEN KEY

Her curiosity instructed her more than the answers she was given.
～ CLARICE LISPECTOR

I want, by understanding myself, to understand others. I want to be all that I am capable of becoming.

~ KATHERINE MANSFIELD

New things cannot come where there is no room.

~ MARLO MORGAN

I think the key is for women not to set any limits.

~ MARTINA NAVRATILOVA

I think, at a child's birth, if a mother could ask a fairy godmother to endow it with the most useful gift, that gift should be curiosity.

~ ELEANOR ROOSEVELT

On the human chessboard, all moves are possible.

~ MIRIAM SCHIFF

I'll always push the envelope. To me, the ultimate sin in life is to be boring. I don't play it safe.

~ CYBIL SHEPHERD

Success is not a doorway, it's a staircase.

~ DOTTIE WALTERS

Change is the watchword of progression. When we tire of well-worn ways, we seek for new. This restless craving in the souls of men spurs them to climb, and to seek the mountain view.

~ ELLA WHEELER WILCOX

Dullness is a misdemeanor.

~ ETHEL WILSON

Learning Improves Your Existing Skills

To try to be better is to be better.

~ CHARLOTTE CUSHMAN

Follow your interests, get the best available education and training, set your sights high, be persistent, be flexible, keep your options open, accept help when offered, and be prepared to help others.

~ MILDRED SPIEWAK DRESSELHAUS

The effect of having other interests beyond the domestic works well. The more one does and sees and feels, the more one is able to do, and the more genuine may be one's own appreciation of fundamental things like home, and love, and understanding companionship.

~ AMELIA EARHART

If you do things well, do them better. Be daring, be first, be different, be just.

~ ANITA RODDICK

One who wants to know is better than one who already knows.

~ YIDDISH PROVERB

Never Settle

It's not a very big step from contentment to complacency.

~ SIMONE DE BEAUVOIR

The minute you settle for less than you deserve, you get even less than you settled for.

~ MAUREEN DOWD

"Good enough never is" has become the motto of this company.

~ DEBBI FIELDS

One can never consent to creep when one feels an impulse to soar.

~ HELEN KELLER

There is only one real sin and that is to persuade oneself that the second best is anything but second best.

~ DORIS LESSING

Show me a sensible person who likes himself or herself! I know myself too well to like what I see. I know but too well that I'm not what I'd like to be.

~ GOLDA MEIR

If I'd been a housemaid, I'd have been the best in Australia—I couldn't help it. It's got to be perfection for me.

~ NELLIE MELBA

Were there none who were discontented with what they have, the world would never reach anything better.

~ FLORENCE NIGHTINGALE

Self-complacency is fatal to progress.

~ MARGARET ELIZABETH SANGSTER

Woman's discontent increases in exact proportion to her development.

~ ELIZABETH CADY STANTON

Untilled ground, however rich, will bring forth thistles and thorns; so also the mind of man.

~ THÉRÈSE OF LISIEUX

Discontent and disorder were signs of energy and hope, not of despair.

~ C.V. WEDGWOOD

From the discontent of man, the world's best progress springs.

~ ELLA WHEELER WILCOX

Once conform, once do what other people do because they do it, and a lethargy steals over all the finer nerves and faculties of the soul.

~ VIRGINIA WOOLF

You Are Limited Only by Your Dreams

Aerodynamically, the bumblebee shouldn't be able to fly, but the bumble bee doesn't know it so it goes on flying anyway.

~ MARY KAY ASH

The state of the world today demands that women become less modest and dream/plan/act/risk on a larger scale.

~ CHARLOTTE BUNCH

I might have been born in a hovel but I am determined to travel with the wind and the stars.

~ JACQUELINE COCHRAN

The brain is wider than the sky.

~ EMILY DICKINSON

My motto: *sans limites.*

~ ISADORA DUNCAN

If we could only give, just once, the same amount of reflection to what we want to get out of life that we give to the question of what to do with a two weeks' vacation, we would be startled at our false standards and the aimless procession of our busy days.

~ DOROTHY CANFIELD FISHER

So long as we think dugout canoes are the only possibility—all that is real or can be real—we will never see the ship, we will never feel the free wind blow.

~ SONIA JOHNSON

One can never consent to creep when one feels an impulse to soar.

~ HELEN KELLER

Our visions begin with our desires.

~ AUDRE LORDE

A lot of young girls have looked to their career paths and have said they'd like to be chief. There's been a change in the limits people see.

~ WILMA PEARL MANKILLER

[My father] said, Don't grow up to be a woman, and what he meant by that was, a housewife ... without any interests.

~ MARIA GOEPPERT MAYER

Our being is subject to all the chances of life. There are so many things we are capable of, that we could be or do. The potentialities are so great that we never, any of us, are more than one-fourth fulfilled.

~ KATHERINE ANNE PORTER

Every man is free to rise as far as he's able or willing, but the degree to which he thinks determines the degree to which he'll rise.

~ AYN RAND

What else are we gonna live by if not dreams? We need to believe in something. What would really drive us crazy is to believe this reality we run into every day is all there is. If I don't believe that there's a happy ending out there—that will-you-marry-me in the sky—I can't keep working today.

~ JILL ROBINSON

There is a proper balance between not asking enough of oneself and asking or expecting too much.

~ MAY SARTON

Man can only receive what he sees himself receiving.

~ FLORENCE SCOVEL SHINN

Reach high, for stars lie hidden in your soul. Dream deep, for every dream precedes the goal.

~ PAMELA VAULL STARR

People think that at the top there isn't much room. They tend to think of it as an Everest. My message is that there is tons of room at the top.

~ MARGARET THATCHER

I believe that you cannot go any further than you can think. I certainly believe if you don't desire a thing, you will never get it.

~ CHARLESZETTA WADDLES

The possibilities are unlimited as long as you are true to your life's purpose.

~ MARCIA WIEDER

Stay Engaged and Active

They never die, who have the future in them.

~ MERIDEL LE SUEUR

Banality is a terribly likely consequence of the underuse of a good mind.

~ CYNTHIA PROPPER SETON

When you stop learning, stop listening, stop looking and asking questions, always new questions, then it is time to die.

~ LILLIAN SMITH

Catching something is purely a by-product of our fishing. It is the act of fishing that wipes away all grief, lightens all worry, dissolves all fear and anxiety.

~ GLADYS TABER

Untilled ground, however rich, will bring forth thistles and thorns; so also the mind of man.

~ THÉRÈSE OF LISIEUX

Getting bored is not allowed.

~ KAY THOMPSON

I'm tired of playing worn-out depressing ladies in frayed bathrobes. I'm going to get a new hairdo and look terrific and go back to school and even if nobody notices, I'm going to be the most self-fulfilled lady on the block.

~ JOANNE WOODWARD

New Experiences Create New Possibilities

I long to see everything, to know everything, to learn everything!
~ MARIE BASHKIRTSEFF

I always keep myself in a position of being a student.
~ JACKIE JOYNER-KERSEE

We travel to learn; and I have never been in any country where they did not do something better than we do it, think some thoughts better than we think, catch some inspiration from heights above our own.
~ MARIA MITCHELL

If I had to characterize one quality as the genius of feminist thought, culture, and action, it would be the connectivity.
~ ROBIN MORGAN

Intelligence is really a kind of taste: taste in ideas.
~ SUSAN SONTAG

Curiosity is the one thing invincible in Nature.
~ FREYA STARK

Change is the watchword of progression. When we tire of well-worn ways, we seek for new. This restless craving in the souls of men spurs them to climb, and to seek the mountain view.
~ ELLA WHEELER WILCOX

Take a Chance

I never intended to become a run-of-the-mill person.
~ BARBARA JORDAN

Her curiosity instructed her more than the answers she was given.
~ CLARICE LISPECTOR

To change skins, evolve into new cycles, I feel one has to learn to discard. If one changes internally, one should not continue to live with the same objects. They reflect one's mind and psyche of yesterday. I throw away what has no dynamic, living use.

~ ANAÏS NIN

I'll always push the envelope. To me, the ultimate sin in life is to be boring. I don't play it safe.

~ CYBIL SHEPHERD

Do not follow where the path may lead. Go instead where there is no path and leave a trail.

~ MURIEL STRODE

I'm the girl with the unquenchable thirst.

~ ANNE WALDMAN

Always Challenge Yourself

You must learn day by day, year by year, to broaden your horizon. The more things you love, the more you are interested in, the more you enjoy, the more you are indignant about, the more you have left when anything happens.

~ ETHEL BARRYMORE

Follow your interests, get the best available education and training, set your sights high, be persistent, be flexible, keep your options open, accept help when offered, and be prepared to help others.

~ MILDRED SPIEWAK DRESSELHAUS

I used to want the words "She tried" on my tombstone. Now I want "She did it."

~ KATHERINE DUNHAM

People don't pay much attention to you when you are second best. I wanted to see what it felt like to be number one.

~ FLORENCE GRIFFITH JOYNER

Always be smarter than the people who hire you.

~ LENA HORNE

You have to set new goals every day.

~ JULIE KRONE

A lot of young girls have looked to their career paths and have said they'd like to be chief. There's been a change in the limits people see.

~ WILMA PEARL MANKILLER

Were there none who were discontented with what they have, the world would never reach anything better.

~ FLORENCE NIGHTINGALE

Today, if you are not confused, you are not thinking clearly.

~ IRENE PETER

We're half the people, we should be half the Congress.

~ JEANNETTE RANKIN

Until we can understand the assumptions in which we are drenched we cannot know ourselves.

~ ADRIENNE RICH

If you do things well, do them better. Be daring, be first, be different, be just.

~ ANITA RODDICK

You have to erect a fence and say, "Okay, scale this."

~ LINDA RONSTADT

Woman must not accept; she must challenge.

~ MARGARET SANGER

I've always had such high expectations for myself. I'm aware of them, but I can't relax them.

~ MARY DECKER SLANEY

My expectations—which I extended whenever I came close to accomplishing my goals—made it impossible to ever feel satisfied with my successes.

⌒ ELLEN SUE STERN

I always felt that I hadn't achieved what I wanted to achieve. I always felt I could get better. That's the whole incentive.

⌒ VIRGINIA WADE

Don't Worry What Others Think

If I smashed the traditions it was because I knew no traditions.

⌒ MAUDE ADAMS

If one sticks too rigidly to one's principles, one would hardly see anybody.

⌒ AGATHA CHRISTIE

I think the key is for women not to set any limits.

⌒ MARTINA NAVRATILOVA

I've always tried to go a step past wherever people expected me to end up.

⌒ BEVERLY SILLS

The widening of woman's sphere is to improve her lot. Let us do it, and if the world scoff, let it scoff—if it sneer, let it sneer.

⌒ LUCY STONE

I'm tired of playing worn-out depressing ladies in frayed bathrobes. I'm going to get a new hairdo and look terrific and go back to school and even if nobody notices, I'm going to be the most self-fulfilled lady on the block.

⌒ JOANNE WOODWARD

Stay Alert for Opportunities to Grow

I think the inner person is the most important.... I would like to see an invention that keeps the mind alert. That's what is important.
~ JULIA CHILD

The road was new to me, as roads always are, going back.
~ SARAH ORNE JEWETT

I always keep myself in a position of being a student.
~ JACKIE JOYNER-KERSEE

To change skins, evolve into new cycles, I feel one has to learn to discard. If one changes internally, one should not continue to live with the same objects. They reflect one's mind and psyche of yesterday. I throw away what has no dynamic, living use.
~ ANAÏS NIN

Curiosity is the one thing invincible in Nature.
~ FREYA STARK

Change is the watchword of progression. When we tire of well-worn ways, we seek for new. This restless craving in the souls of men spurs them to climb, and to seek the mountain view.
~ ELLA WHEELER WILCOX

A person should live if only for curiosity's sake.
~ YIDDISH PROVERB

Surprise Yourself

True genius doesn't fulfill expectations, it shatters them.
~ ARLENE CROCE

Yesterday I dared to struggle. Today I dare to win.
~ BERNADETTE DEVLIN

When one paints an ideal, one does not need to limit one's imagination.

~ ELLEN KEY

Her curiosity instructed her more than the answers she was given.

~ CLARICE LISPECTOR

I am willing to put myself through anything; temporary pain or discomfort means nothing to me as long as I can see that the experience will take me to a new level. I am interested in the unknown, and the only path to the unknown is through breaking barriers, an often painful process.

~ DIANA NYAD

Use All Your Senses to Experience Life

We live on the leash of our senses.

~ DIANE ACKERMAN

We travel to learn; and I have never been in any country where they did not do something better than we do it, think some thoughts better than we think, catch some inspiration from heights above our own.

~ MARIA MITCHELL

Reading makes immigrants of us all. It takes us away from home, but more important, it finds homes for us everywhere.

~ HAZEL ROCHMAN

I'm the girl with the unquenchable thirst.

~ ANNE WALDMAN

Work Hard at Your New Interests

I used to want the words "She tried" on my tombstone. Now I want "She did it."
~ KATHERINE DUNHAM

"Good enough never is" has become the motto of this company.
~ DEBBI FIELDS

You have set yourself a difficult task, but you will succeed if you persevere.
~ HELEN KELLER

You have to set new goals every day.
~ JULIE KRONE

If I'd been a housemaid, I'd have been the best in Australia—I couldn't help it. It's got to be perfection for me.
~ NELLIE MELBA

"How does one become a butterfly?" she asked pensively. "You must want to fly so much that you are willing to give up being a caterpillar."
~ TRINA PAULUS

Self-complacency is fatal to progress.
~ MARGARET ELIZABETH SANGSTER

If you want to stand out, don't be different, be outstanding.
~ MEREDITH WEST

Once conform, once do what other people do because they do it, and a lethargy steals over all the finer nerves and faculties of the soul.
~ VIRGINIA WOOLF

It's not enough to just swing at the ball. You've got to loosen your girdle and really let it fly.
~ BABE DIDRIKSON ZAHARIAS

$\mathcal{I}$nfluencing Others

Empower People to Solve Problems Their Own Way

I know that everyone brings to the work his or her own experiences and background and may interpret the piece like a Rorschach, in their own way.

~ IDA APPLEBROOG

People will support that which they help to create.

~ MARY KAY ASH

Those who trust us educate us.

~ GEORGE ELIOT

The manager cannot share his power with division superintendent or foreman or workman, but he can give them opportunities for developing their power.

~ MARY PARKER FOLLETT

Coercive power is the curse of the universe; coactive power, the enrichment and advancement of every human soul.

~ MARY PARKER FOLLETT

There is nothing better than the encouragement of a good friend.

~ KATHERINE HATHAWAY

Nothing fruitful ever comes when plants are forced to flower in the wrong season.

~ BETTE BAO LORD

The best direction is the least possible direction.

~ JOAN MANLEY

Hold up to him his better self, his real self that can dare and do and win out..... People radiate what is in their minds and in their hearts.

~ ELEANOR H. PORTER

Coercion. The unpardonable crime.

~ DOROTHY MILLER RICHARDSON

People who make some other person part of their job are dangerous.

~ DOROTHY L. SAYERS

In my experience, there is only one motivation, and that is desire. No reasons or principle contain it or stand against it.

~ JANE SMILEY

Diplomacy is the art of letting someone have your way.

~ DANIELE VARE

Remember, the bread you meet each day is still rising. Don't scare the dough.

~ MACRINA WIEDERKEHR

Punishment Is an Ineffective Way to Shape Behavior

No punishment has ever possessed enough power of deterrence to prevent the commission of crimes. On the contrary, whatever the punishment, once a specific crime has appeared for the first time, its reappearance is more likely than its initial emergence could ever have been.

◠ HANNAH ARENDT

Fear is not a good teacher. The lessons of fear are quickly forgotten.

◠ MARY BATESON

A sneer is like a flame; it may occasionally be curative because it cauterizes, but it leaves a bitter scar.

◠ MARGARET DELAND

What insult is so keen or so keenly felt, as the polite insult which it is impossible to resent?

◠ JULIA KAVANAGH

Beware of trying to accomplish anything by force.

◠ ANGELA MERICI

You will accomplish more by kind words and a courteous manner than by anger or sharp rebuke, which should never be used except in necessity.

◠ ANGELA MERICI

People who fight fire with fire usually end up with ashes.

◠ ABIGAIL VAN BUREN

Positive Reinforcement Is the Key to Motivation

If you're good to your staff when things are going well, they'll rally when times go bad.

~ MARY KAY ASH

There are two things that people want more than sex and money—recognition and praise.

~ MARY KAY ASH

We treat our people like royalty. If you honor and serve the people who work for you, they will honor and serve you.

~ MARY KAY ASH

Everyone has an invisible sign hanging from their neck saying, "Make me feel important." Never forget this message when working with people.

~ MARY KAY ASH

Sandwich every bit of criticism between two heavy layers of praise.

~ MARY KAY ASH

To sing is to love and affirm, to fly and soar, to coast into the hearts of the people who listen, to tell them that life is to live, that love is there, that nothing is a promise, but that beauty exists, and must be hunted for and found.

~ JOAN BAEZ

O lovely Sisters! is it true
That they are all inspired by you,
And write by inward magic charm'd,
And high enthusiasm warm'd?

~ JOANNA BAILLIE

Words of affection, howso'er express'd,
The latest spoken still are deem'd the best.

~ JOANNA BAILLIE

Praise is the only gift for which people are really grateful.

~ LADY MARGUERITE BLESSINGTON

Kind words smooth all the "Paths o' Life"
And smiles make burdens light,
And uncomplainin' friends can make
A daytime out o' night.

~ CARRIE JACOBS BOND

I praise loudly; I blame softly.

~ CATHERINE II

The test of being a good host is how well the departing guest likes
himself.

~ MARCELENE COX

Love makes the wildest spirit tame, and the tamest spirit wild.

~ ALEXIS DELP

Praise the young and they will make progress.

~ IRISH PROVERB

Words are less needful to sorrow than to joy.

~ HELEN HUNT JACKSON

A gossip is one who talks to you about others; a bore is one who
talks to you about himself; and a brilliant conversationalist is one
who talks to you about yourself.

~ LISA KIRK

There isn't much that tastes better than praise from those who are
wise and capable.

~ SELMA LAGERLÖF

What you praise you increase.

~ CATHERINE PONDER

What men and women need is encouragement.... Instead of always
harping on a man's faults, tell him of his virtues. Try to pull him out
of his rut of bad habits.

~ ELEANOR H. PORTER

You take people as far as they will go, not as far as you would like them to go.

~ JEANNETTE RANKIN

I believe in using words, not fists.

~ SUSAN SARANDON

To hear how special and wonderful we are is endlessly enthralling.

~ GAIL SHEEHY

There is nothing stronger in the world than gentleness.

~ HAN SUYIN

A fly does not mind dying in coconut cream.

~ SWAHILI PROVERB

To feel valued, to know, even if only once in a while, that you can do a job well is an absolutely marvelous feeling.

~ BARBARA WALTERS

Drive the horse with oats, not with curses and oaths.

~ YIDDISH PROVERB

Remember That People Look to You for Guidance

The speed of the leader is the speed of the gang.

~ MARY KAY ASH

Your wits make others witty.

~ CATHERINE THE GREAT

Most people are not for or against anything; the first object of getting people together is to make them respond somehow, to overcome inertia.

~ MARY PARKER FOLLETT

Good humor, like the jaundice, makes every one of its own complexion.
~ ELIZABETH INCHBALD

The pitcher cries for water to carry and a person for work that is real.
~ MARGE PIERCY

No leader can be too far ahead of his followers.
~ ELEANOR ROOSEVELT

The success of your presentation will be judged not by the knowledge you send but by what the listener receives.
~ LILY WALTERS

Focus on Strengths, Not Weaknesses

It is easier to influence strong than weak characters in life.
~ MARGOT ASQUITH

It is better to arm and strengthen your hero, than to disarm and enfeeble your foe.
~ ANNE BRONTË

Once a woman has forgiven a man, she must not reheat his sins for breakfast.
~ MARLENE DIETRICH

Some people change their ways when they see the light, others when they feel the heat.
~ CAROLINE SCHOEDER

There is only one answer to destructiveness and that is creativity.
~ SYLVIA ASHTON WARNER

Avoid Criticism and Comparison

There are words which sever hearts more than sharp swords; there are words the point of which sting the heart through the course of a whole life.

~ FREDERIKA BREMER

I don't give advice. I can't tell anybody what to do. Instead I say this is what we know about this problem at this time. And here are the consequences of these actions.

~ DR. JOYCE BROTHERS

An ass may bray a good while before he shakes the stars down.

~ GEORGE ELIOT

Wear a smile and have friends; wear a scowl and have wrinkles.

~ GEORGE ELIOT

Those who are lifting the world upward and onward are those who encourage more than criticize.

~ ELIZABETH HARRISON

No pear falls into a shut mouth.

~ ITALIAN PROVERB

Once a human being has arrived on this earth, communication is the largest single factor determining what kinds of relationships he makes with others and what happens to him in the world about him.

~ VIRGINIA SATIR

Nagging is the repetition of unpalatable truths.

~ BARONESS EDITH SUMMERSKILL

I would prefer a thousand times to receive reproofs than to give them to others.

~ THÉRÈSE OF LISIEUX

Orthodox criticism ... is a murderer of talent. And because the most modest and sensitive people are the most talented, having the most imagination and sympathy, these are the first ones to get killed off.

~ BRENDA UELAND

Influencing Others Is a Great Challenge and Great Blessing

Housework is a breeze. Cooking is a pleasant diversion. Putting up a retaining wall is a lark. But teaching is like climbing a mountain.

~ FAWN M. BRODIE

Blessed influence of one truly loving soul on another!

~ GEORGE ELIOT

Once you wake up thought in a man, you can never put it to sleep again.

~ ZORA NEALE HURSTON

The true secret of giving advice is, after you have honestly given it, to be perfectly indifferent whether it is taken or not and never persist in trying to set people right.

~ HANNAH WHITALL SMITH

Truth, like surgery, may hurt, but it cures.

~ HAN SUYIN

The only people in the world who can change things are those who can sell ideas.

~ LOIS WYSE

Encourage Others to Speak Openly

No blame should attach to telling the truth.
~ ANITA BROOKNER

The human heart, at whatever age, opens only to the heart that opens in return.
~ MARIA EDGEWORTH

Most people would rather be seen through than not seen at all.
~ ADA LEVERSON

When we are listened to, it creates us, makes us unfold and expand. Ideas actually begin to grow within us and come to life.
~ BRENDA UELAND

There was a definite process by which one made people into friends, and it involved talking to them and listening to them for hours at a time.
~ REBECCA WEST

Be Kind, Genuine, and Giving

Praise out of season, or tactlessly bestowed, can freeze the heart as much as blame.
~ PEARL S. BUCK

I'm not a competitive person, and I think women like me because they don't think I'm competitive, just nice.
~ BARBARA BUSH

The best way to get where you want to be is to please those who own the road.
~ ELENA CASTEDO-ELLERMAN

A bit of fragrance always clings to the hand that gives you roses.
~ CHINESE PROVERB

As perfume to the flower, so is kindness to speech.

~ KATHERINE FRANCKE

To be told we are loved is not enough. We must feel loved.

~ LAUREN HUTTON

Now and then one sees a face which has kept its smile pure and undefiled. Such a smile transfigures; such a smile, if the artful but know it, is the greatest weapon a face can have.

~ HELEN HUNT JACKSON

No one has it who isn't capable of genuinely liking others, at least at the actual moment of meeting and speaking. Charm is always genuine; it may be superficial but it isn't fake.

~ P.D. JAMES

If you can learn from hard knocks, you can also learn from soft touches.

~ CAROLYN KENMORE

I'm convinced that it's energy and humor. The two of them combined equal charm.

~ JUDITH KRANTZ

It's never what you say, but how you make it sound sincere.

~ MARYA MANNES

We must give alms. Charity wins souls and draws them to virtue.

~ ANGELA MERICI

Time's passage through the memory is like molten glass that can be opaque or crystallize at any given moment at will: a thousand days are melted into one conversation, one glance, one hurt, and one hurt can be shattered and sprinkled over a thousand.

~ GLORIA NAYLOR

Scratch a lover, and find a foe.

~ DOROTHY PARKER

A kind word is like a spring day.

⁓ RUSSIAN PROVERB

I really do believe I can accomplish a great deal with a big grin. I know some people find that disconcerting, but that doesn't matter.

⁓ BEVERLY SILLS

Charm is a cunning self-forgetfulness.

⁓ CHRISTINA STEAD

Kind words can be short and easy to speak, but their echoes are truly endless.

⁓ MOTHER TERESA

Charm is the measure of attraction's power
To chain the fleeting fancy of the hour.

⁓ LOUISA THOMAS

The courteous learn their virtue from the discourteous.

⁓ TURKISH PROVERB

Delicate humor is the crowning virtue of the saints.

⁓ EVELYN UNDERHILL

Brevity may be the soul of wit, but not when someone's saying "I love you."

⁓ JUDITH VIORST

Don't confuse being stimulating with being blunt.

⁓ BARBARA WALTERS

Focus on What Matters Most

Make happy those who are near, and those who are far will come.

⁓ CHINESE PROVERB

A man would prefer to come home to an unmade bed and a happy woman than to a neatly made bed and an angry woman.

~ MARLENE DIETRICH

Who gives bread to other's dogs is often barked at by her own.

~ ITALIAN PROVERB

We Get Back What We Give

We make our own criminals, and their crimes are congruent with the national culture we all share. It has been said that a people get the kind of political leadership they deserve. I think they also get the kinds of crime and criminals they themselves bring into being.

~ MARGARET MEAD

They say, "You can't give a smile away; it always comes back." The same is true of a kind word or a conversation starter. What goes around, comes around.

~ SUSAN ROANE

Revolve your world around the customer and more customers will revolve around you.

~ HEATHER WILLIAMS

Charm is the ability to make someone else think that both of you are pretty wonderful.

~ KATHLEEN WINSOR

Be Truthful

Nagging is the repetition of unpalatable truths.

~ BARONESS EDITH SUMMERSKILL

Truth, like surgery, may hurt, but it cures.

~ HAN SUYIN

375

A fly does not mind dying in coconut cream.

~ SWAHILI PROVERB

The best mind-altering drug is truth.

~ LILY TOMLIN

Don't confuse being stimulating with being blunt.

~ BARBARA WALTERS

Nobody likes having salt rubbed into their wounds, even if it is the salt of the earth.

~ REBECCA WEST

The mode of delivering a truth makes, for the most part, as much impression on the mind of the listener as the truth itself.

~ FRANCES WRIGHT

THREE

Achieving Your Goals

Seizing Opportunities

Every Day Brings Another Chance to Make a Difference

Happiness consists of living each day as if it were the first day of
your honeymoon and the last day of your vacation.

~ ANON.

With every rising of the sun, think of your life as just begun.

~ ANON.

Be glad today. Tomorrow may bring tears.
Be brave today. The darkest night will pass.
And golden rays will usher in the dawn.

~ SARAH KNOWLES BOLTON

He alone is great
Who by a life heroic conquers fate.

~ SARAH KNOWLES BOLTON

It is brave to be involved.

~ GWENDOLYN BROOKS

Every day I live I am more convinced that the waste of life lies in the love we have not given, the powers we have not used, the selfish prudence that will risk nothing and which, shirking pain, misses happiness as well.

~ MARY CHOLMONDELEY

It is never too late to be what you might have been.

~ GEORGE ELIOT

How lovely to think that no one need wait a moment, we can start now, start slowly changing the world!

~ ANNE FRANK

You had better live your best and act your best and think your best today; for today is the sure preparation for tomorrow and all the other tomorrows that follow.

~ HARRIET MARTINEAU

A human being has no discernable character until he acts.

~ CONSTANTINE NASH AND VIRGINIA OAKLEY

One's feelings waste themselves in words; they ought all to be distilled into action ... which brings results.

~ FLORENCE NIGHTINGALE

When you make a world tolerable for yourself, you make a world tolerable for others.

~ ANAÏS NIN

Find a need and fill it.

~ RUTH STAFFORD PEALE

Begin doing what you want to do now. We are not living in eternity. We have only this moment, sparkling like a star in our hand—and melting like a snowflake. Let us use it before it is too late.

~ MARIE BEYON RAY

For it isn't enough to talk about peace. One must believe in it. And it isn't enough to believe in it. One must work at it.

~ ELEANOR ROOSEVELT

What you don't do can be a destructive force.

~ ELEANOR ROOSEVELT

My private measure of success is daily. If this were to be the last day of my life would I be content with it? To live in a harmonious balance of commitments and pleasures is what I strive for.

~ JANE RULE

You don't need endless time and perfect conditions. Do it now. Do it today. Do it for twenty minutes and watch your heart start beating.

~ BARBARA SHER

Any ritual is an opportunity for transformation.

~ STARHAWK

Some Opportunities Require More Effort Than Others

The door of opportunity won't open unless you do some pushing.

~ ANON.

It's so hard when I have to, and so easy when I want to.

~ SONDRA ANICE BARNES

I wish I could tell you that the Children's Television Workshop and Sesame Street were thanks to my genius, but it really was a lucky break.

~ JOAN GANZ COONEY

Probably any successful career has X number of breaks in it, and maybe the difference between successful people and those who aren't superachievers is taking advantage of those breaks.

~ JOAN GANZ COONEY

You create your opportunities by asking for them.
~ PATTY HANSEN

I will not be just a tourist in the world of images, just watching images passing by which I cannot live in, make love to, possess as permanent sources of joy and ecstasy.
~ ANAÏS NIN

Slaying the dragon of delay is no sport for the short-winded.
~ SANDRA DAY O'CONNOR

You may be disappointed if you fail, but you are doomed if you don't try.
~ BEVERLY SILLS

Trust Your Instincts

I'm the foe of moderation, the champion of excess. If I may lift a line from a die-hard whose identity is lost in the shuffle, "I'd rather be strongly wrong than weakly right."
~ TALLULAH BANKHEAD

Conviction without experiences makes for harshness.
~ FLANNERY O'CONNOR

Without fanaticism we cannot accomplish anything.
~ EVA PERÓN

To have character is to be big enough to take life on.
~ MARY CAROLINE RICHARDS

The trouble is that not enough people have come together with the firm determination to live the things which they say they believe.
~ ELEANOR ROOSEVELT

The defense force inside of us wants us to be cautious, to stay away from anything as intense as a new kind of action. Its job is to protect us, and it categorically avoids anything resembling danger. But it's often wrong.

~ BARBARA SHER

If I am not for myself, who will be for me? If I am not for others, who am I for? And if not now, when?

~ TALMUD

Commitment leads to action. Action brings your dream closer.

~ MARCIA WIEDER

Positive Change Begins with One Small Step

It is a very dangerous thing to have an idea that you will not practice.

~ PHYLLIS BOTTOME

It is never too late to be what you might have been.

~ GEORGE ELIOT

One's feelings waste themselves in words; they ought all to be distilled into action ... which brings results.

~ FLORENCE NIGHTINGALE

All you have to do is look straight and see the road, and when you see it, don't sit looking at it—walk.

~ AYN RAND

Let no one be deluded that a knowledge of the path can substitute for putting one foot in front of the other.

~ MARY CAROLINE RICHARDS

What you don't do can be a destructive force.

~ ELEANOR ROOSEVELT

"Now" is the operative word. Everything you put in your way is just a method of putting off the hour when you could actually be doing your dream.

~ BARBARA SHER

You don't need endless time and perfect conditions. Do it now. Do it today. Do it for twenty minutes and watch your heart start beating.

~ BARBARA SHER

No matter how big or soft or warm your bed is, you still have to get out of it.

~ GRACE SLICK

Enthusiasm signifies God in us.

~ MADAME DE STAËL

To choose is also to begin.

~ STARHAWK

Procrastination usually results in sorrowful regret. Today's duties put off until tomorrow give us a double burden to bear; the best way is to do them in their proper time.

~ IDA SCOTT TAYLOR

Being stuck is a position few of us like. We want something new but cannot let go of the old—old ideas, beliefs, habits, even thoughts. We are out of contact with our own genius. Sometimes we know we are stuck; sometimes we don't. In both cases we have to do something.

~ INGA TEEKENS

Commitment leads to action. Action brings your dream closer.

~ MARCIA WIEDER

The Smallest Opportunity May Yield the Greatest Reward

Never put off until tomorrow what you can do today, because if you
enjoy it today, you can do it again, tomorrow.

~ ANON.

There are no little events in life, those we think of no consequence
may be full of fate, and it is at our own risk if we neglect the
acquaintances and opportunities that seem to be casually offered, and
of small importance.

~ AMELIA BARR

I am a woman who understands the necessity of an impulse whose
goal or origin still lie beyond me.

~ OLGA BROUMAS

There are half hours that dilate to the importance of centuries.

~ MARY CATHERWOOD

I wish I could tell you that the Children's Television Workshop and
Sesame Street were thanks to my genius, but it really was a lucky break.

~ JOAN GANZ COONEY

Love the moment and the energy of the moment will spread beyond
all boundaries.

~ CORITA KENT

Great opportunities to help others seldom come, but small ones
surround us daily.

~ SALLY KOCH

Economy is the thief of time.

~ ETHEL WATTS MUMFORD

What you don't do can be a destructive force.

~ ELEANOR ROOSEVELT

Any ritual is an opportunity for transformation.

～ STARHAWK

You Can Make Your Own Breaks

To wait for someone else, or to expect someone else to make my life richer, or fuller, or more satisfying, puts me in a constant state of suspension.

～ KATHLEEN TIERNEY ANDRUS

To have character is to be big enough to take life on.

～ MARY CAROLINE RICHARDS

Doing is a quantum leap from imagining.

～ BARBARA SHER

You don't need endless time and perfect conditions. Do it now. Do it today. Do it for twenty minutes and watch your heart start beating.

～ BARBARA SHER

You can't build a reputation on what you intend to do.

～ LIZ SMITH

To choose is also to begin.

～ STARHAWK

Time is the sea in which men grow, are born, or die.

～ FREYA STARK

Commitment leads to action. Action brings your dream closer.

～ MARCIA WIEDER

Luck is a matter of preparation meeting opportunity.

～ OPRAH WINFREY

Greet the Day Expecting Only Good

Youth is, after all, just a moment, but it is the moment, the spark that you always carry in your heart.

~ RAISA M. GORBACHEV

Act, and God will act.

~ JOAN OF ARC

If you're going to be able to look back on something and laugh about it, you might as well laugh about it now.

~ MARIE OSMOND

All that is really necessary for survival of the fittest, it seems, is an interest in life, good, bad, or peculiar.

~ GRACE PALEY

The only man who makes no mistakes is the man who never does anything.

~ ELEANOR ROOSEVELT

The defense force inside of us wants us to be cautious, to stay away from anything as intense as a new kind of action. Its job is to protect us, and it categorically avoids anything resembling danger. But it's often wrong.

~ BARBARA SHER

You learn to build your roads on today, because tomorrow's ground is too uncertain for plans, and futures have a way of falling down in mid-flight.

~ VERONICA SHOFFSTAL

Look at everything as though you were seeing it for the first time or the last time. Then your time on earth will be filled with glory.

~ BETTY SMITH

Don't Be Afraid—Get Busy Living!

I am one of those people who can't help getting a kick out of life—
even when it's a kick in the teeth.
~ POLLY ADLER

Forget the past and live the present hour.
~ SARAH KNOWLES BOLTON

When shall we live if not now?
~ M. F. K. FISHER

Don't be afraid your life will end; be afraid it will never begin.
~ GRACE HANSEN

Life is to be lived. If you have to support yourself, you had bloody
well better find some way that is going to be interesting. And you
don't do that by sitting around wondering about yourself.
~ KATHARINE HEPBURN

I realize that if I wait until I am no longer afraid to act, write, speak,
be, I'll be sending messages on a ouija board, cryptic complaints from
the other side.
~ AUDRE LORDE

To have character is to be big enough to take life on.
~ MARY CAROLINE RICHARDS

The only man who makes no mistakes is the man who never does
anything.
~ ELEANOR ROOSEVELT

Thinking about swimming isn't much like actually getting in the
water. Actually getting in the water can take your breath away.
~ BARBARA SHER

You don't need endless time and perfect conditions. Do it now. Do it
today. Do it for twenty minutes and watch your heart start beating.
~ BARBARA SHER

"Now" is the operative word. Everything you put in your way is just a method of putting off the hour when you could actually be doing your dream.

～ BARBARA SHER

You learn to build your roads on today, because tomorrow's ground is too uncertain for plans, and futures have a way of falling down in mid-flight.

～ VERONICA SHOFFSTAL

Dance to the tune that is played.

～ SPANISH PROVERB

Time is the sea in which men grow, are born, or die.

～ FREYA STARK

I expect some new phases of life this summer, and shall try to get the honey from each moment.

～ LUCY STONE

Do not wait for ideal circumstances, nor the best opportunities; they will never come.

～ JANET ERSKINE STUART

Today's egg is better than tomorrow's hen.

～ TURKISH PROVERB

Learn to drink the cup of life as it comes.

～ AGNES TURNBULL

Do It Now

Time cannot be expanded, accumulated, mortgaged, hastened, or retarded.

～ ANON.

A day is a span of time no one is wealthy enough to waste.

～ ANON.

Now is the only time we own; give, love, toil with a will.
And place no faith in tomorrow, for the clock may then be still.

~ ANON.

The most effective way to do it, is to do it.

~ TONI CADE BAMBARA

The secret of getting ahead is getting started.

~ SALLY BERGER

I don't wait for moods. You accomplish nothing if you do that. Your mind must know it has got to get down to earth.

~ PEARL S. BUCK

The sad truth is that opportunity doesn't knock twice. You can put things off until tomorrow, but tomorrow may never come. Where will you be a few years down the line? Will it be everything you dreamed of? We seal our fate with the choices we take, but don't give a second thought to the chances we take.

~ GLORIA ESTEFAN

My evil genius Procrastination has whispered me to tarry 'til a more convenient season.

~ MARY TODD LINCOLN

I realize that if I wait until I am no longer afraid to act, write, speak, be, I'll be sending messages on a ouija board, cryptic complaints from the other side.

~ AUDRE LORDE

Begin doing what you want to do now. We are not living in eternity. We have only this moment, sparkling like a star in our hand—and melting like a snowflake. Let us use it before it is too late.

~ MARIE BEYON RAY

"Now" is the operative word. Everything you put in your way is just a method of putting off the hour when you could actually be doing your dream.

~ BARBARA SHER

Doing is a quantum leap from imagining.

~ BARBARA SHER

You don't need endless time and perfect conditions. Do it now. Do it today. Do it for twenty minutes and watch your heart start beating.

~ BARBARA SHER

Procrastination usually results in sorrowful regret. Today's duties put off until tomorrow give us a double burden to bear; the best way is to do them in their proper time.

~ IDA SCOTT TAYLOR

To think too long about doing a thing often becomes its undoing.

~ EVA YOUNG

Make the First Move

He who walks in another's tracks leaves no footprints.

~ JOAN L. BRANNON

Now, go take on the day!

~ DR. LAURA SCHLESSINGER

Anything worth doing is worth doing too soon.

~ BARBARA SHER

The bitterest tears shed over graves are for words left unsaid and deeds left undone.

~ HARRIET BEECHER STOWE

If I am not for myself, who will be for me? If I am not for others, who am I for? And if not now, when?

~ TALMUD

And all that you are sorry for is what you haven't done.

~ MARGARET WIDDEMER

Commitment leads to action. Action brings your dream closer.

~ MARCIA WIEDER

Don't Wait—Tomorrow May Be Too Late

You don't get to choose how you're going to die. Or when. You can only decide how you're going to live.

~ JOAN BAEZ

Let me tell thee, time is a very precious gift of God; so precious that He only gives it to us moment by moment. He would not have thee waste it.

~ AMELIA BARR

Change your life today. Don't gamble on the future, act now, without delay.

~ SIMONE DE BEAUVOIR

Time isn't a commodity, something you pass around like cake. Time is the substance of life. When anyone asks you to give your time, they're really asking for a chunk of your life.

~ ANTOINETTE BOSCO

Silences have a climax, when you have got to speak.

~ ELIZABETH BOWEN

I was happy to have children.... I wanted my body, as well as my mind and spirit, to succeed, to reach an appropriate glory.

~ GWENDOLYN BROOKS

The span of life is waning fast
Beware, unthinking youth, beware!
Thy soul's eternity depends
Upon the records moments bear.

~ ELIZA COOK

Yesterday is ashes; tomorrow wood. Only today does the fire burn brightly.

~ ESKIMO PROVERB

I tell myself that God gave my children many gifts—spirit, beauty, intelligence, the capacity to make friends and to inspire respect.... There was only one gift he held back—length of life.

~ ROSE KENNEDY

I realize that if I wait until I am no longer afraid to act, write, speak, be, I'll be sending messages on a ouija board, cryptic complaints from the other side.

~ AUDRE LORDE

Begin doing what you want to do now. We are not living in eternity. We have only this moment, sparkling like a star in our hand—and melting like a snowflake. Let us use it before it is too late.

~ MARIE BEYON RAY

Can anything be sadder than work unfinished? Yes; work never begun.

~ CHRISTINA GEORGINA ROSSETTI

Anything worth doing is worth doing too soon.

~ BARBARA SHER

"Now" is the operative word. Everything you put in your way is just a method of putting off the hour when you could actually be doing your dream.

~ BARBARA SHER

You don't need endless time and perfect conditions. Do it now. Do it today. Do it for twenty minutes and watch your heart start beating.

~ BARBARA SHER

To think too long about doing a thing often becomes its undoing.

~ EVA YOUNG

Be Aware, Pay Attention, and Always Look for Opportunities

Opportunities are everywhere.
~ LUCY BENINGTON

The gods cannot help those who do not seize opportunities.
~ CHINESE PROVERB

Probably any successful career has X number of breaks in it, and maybe the difference between successful people and those who aren't super-achievers is taking advantage of those breaks.
~ JOAN GANZ COONEY

Opportunities are often things you haven't noticed the first time around.
~ CATHERINE DENEUVE

Luck is largely a matter of paying attention.
~ SUSAN M. DODD

Look for opportunity. You can't wait for it to knock on the door.... You might not be home.
~ JINGER HEATH

If written directions alone would suffice, libraries wouldn't need to have the rest of the universities attached.
~ JUDITH MARTIN (MISS MANNERS)

I have always been waiting for something better—sometimes to see the best I had snatched from me.
~ DOROTHY REED MENDENHALL

If you want greater prosperity in your life, start forming a vacuum to receive it.
~ CATHERINE PONDER

Just breathing isn't living!
~ ELEANOR H. PORTER

You can kill time or kill yourself, it comes to the same thing in the end.

~ ELSA TRIOLET

Today's egg is better than tomorrow's hen.

~ TURKISH PROVERB

He who hesitates is last.

~ MAE WEST

Stay Busy and Engaged

Millions long for immortality who do not know what to do with themselves on a rainy Sunday afternoon.

~ SUSAN ERTZ

You create your opportunities by asking for them.

~ PATTY HANSEN

You had better live your best and act your best and think your best today; for today is the sure preparation for tomorrow and all the other tomorrows that follow.

~ HARRIET MARTINEAU

The cure for boredom is curiosity. There is no cure for curiosity.

~ ELLEN PARR

Don't Ignore Daily Tasks While Waiting For Your Big Break

I have a simple philosophy. Fill what's empty. Empty what's full. And scratch where it itches.
～ ALICE ROOSEVELT LONGWORTH

You had better live your best and act your best and think your best today; for today is the sure preparation for tomorrow and all the other tomorrows that follow.
～ HARRIET MARTINEAU

You can learn new things at any time in your life if you're willing to be a beginner. If you actually learn to like being a beginner, the whole world opens up to you.
～ BARBARA SHER

Dance to the tune that is played.
～ SPANISH PROVERB

Do not wait for ideal circumstances, nor the best opportunities; they will never come.
～ JANET ERSKINE STUART

Procrastination usually results in sorrowful regret. Today's duties put off until tomorrow give us a double burden to bear; the best way is to do them in their proper time.
～ IDA SCOTT TAYLOR

Some Opportunities Come Once in a Lifetime

Action is the antidote to despair.
～ JOAN BAEZ

You can't make soufflé rise twice.
～ ALICE ROOSEVELT LONGWORTH

Begin doing what you want to do now. We are not living in eternity. We have only this moment, sparkling like a star in our hand—and melting like a snowflake. Let us use it before it is too late.

~ MARIE BEYON RAY

To think too long about doing a thing often becomes its undoing.

~ EVA YOUNG

He who hesitates is last.

~ MAE WEST

Making Your Own Luck

Be Optimistic and Expect the Best

Good luck needs no explanation.
~ SHIRLEY TEMPLE BLACK

Most of life is choices, and the rest is pure dumb luck.
~ MARIAN ERICKSON

Faith is not belief. Belief is passive. Faith is active.
~ EDITH HAMILTON

Every thought we think is creating our future.
~ LOUISE L. HAY

Anyone who has gumption knows what it is, and anyone who hasn't can never know what it is.
~ L.M. MONTGOMERY

Today is a new day. You will get out of it just what you put into it.
~ MARY PICKFORD

Life is like a mirror. Smile at it and it smiles back at you.

~ PEACE PILGRIM

Miracles occur naturally as expressions of love. The real miracle is the love that inspires them. In this sense everything that comes from love is a miracle.

~ MARIANNE WILLIAMSON

Self-Discipline Can Prevent "Bad Luck"

Combine common sense and the Golden Rule, and you will have very little bad luck.

~ ANON.

Today, well lived, will prepare me for both the pleasure and the pain of tomorrow.

~ ANON.

The less I behave like Whistler's mother the night before, the more I look like her the morning after.

~ TALLULAH BANKHEAD

Of course, fortune has its part in human affairs, but conduct is really much more important.

~ JEANNE DETOURBEY

It is not our circumstances that create our discontent or contentment. It is us.

~ VIVIAN GREENE

The doors we open and close each day decide the lives we live.

~ FLORA WHITTEMORE

Hard Work Makes Its Own Luck

The wise don't expect to find life worth living; they make it that way.
~ ANON.

There is no such thing as making the miracle happen spontaneously and on the spot. You've got to work.
~ MARTINA ARROYO

I don't know anything about luck. I've never banked on it, and I'm afraid of people who do. Luck to me is something else; hard work and realizing what is opportunity and what isn't.
~ LUCILLE BALL

I don't believe in luck. We make our own good fortune.
~ DR. JOYCE BROTHERS

Luck is not chance, it's toil: fortune's expensive smile is earned.
~ EMILY DICKINSON

You have to learn the rules of the game. And then you have to play better than anyone else.
~ DIANNE FEINSTEIN

The one important thing I've learned over the years is the difference between taking one's work seriously and taking one's self seriously. The first is imperative and the second is disastrous.
~ MARGOT FONTEYN

The more you invest in a marriage, the more valuable it becomes.
~ AMY GRANT

Love doesn't just sit there, like a stone, it has to be made, like bread; remade all the time, made new.
~ URSULA K. LE GUIN

Some people go through life trying to find out what the world holds for them only to find out too late that it's what they bring to the world that really counts.

⟶ L.M. MONTGOMERY

Today is a new day. You will get out of it just what you put into it.

⟶ MARY PICKFORD

Pennies do not come from heaven—they have to be earned here on earth.

⟶ MARGARET THATCHER

Nothing falls from heaven.

⟶ YIDDISH PROVERB

Don't Rely on Luck to Take the Place of Hard Work

Depend on the rabbit's foot if you must, but it didn't work for the rabbit!

⟶ ANON.

Foolish indeed are those who trust to fortune.

⟶ LADY MURASAKI

The worst cynicism: a belief in luck.

⟶ JOYCE CAROL OATES

Hope for a miracle, but don't depend on one.

⟶ TALMUD

If You're Lucky Enough to Have a Gift, Make the Most of It

Talent isn't genius and no amount of energy can make it so. I want to be great, or nothing. I won't be a commonplace dauber, so I don't intend to try any more.

~ LOUISA MAY ALCOTT

Genius is the gold in the mine; talent is the miner that works and brings it out.

~ LADY MARGUERITE BLESSINGTON

It is one thing to be gifted and quite another thing to be worthy of one's own gift.

~ NADIA BOULANGER

Talent on its own sat gracefully only on the very young. After a certain age it was what you did with it that counted.

~ LIZA CODY

I was born lucky, and I have lived lucky. What I had was used. What I still have is being used. Lucky.

~ KATHARINE HEPBURN

Wishing Won't Make It So—Take Action If You Want Results

If a woman wants her dreams to come true, she must wake up.

~ ANON.

Justice is a concept. Muscle is the reality.

~ LINDA BLANDFORD

All that is necessary to break the spell of inertia and frustration is this: act as if it were impossible to fail. That is the talisman, the formula, the command of right-about-face that turns us from failure toward success.

~ DOROTHEA BRANDE

No one has a right to sit down and feel hopeless. There's too much work to do.

~ DOROTHY DAY

Self-pity is a death that has no resurrection, a sinkhole from which no rescuing hand can drag you because you have chosen to sink.

~ ELIZABETH ELLIOT

Don't wait for your "ship to come in," and feel angry and cheated when it doesn't. Get going with something small.

~ IRENE KASSORLA

Foolish indeed are those who trust to fortune.

~ LADY MURASAKI

Never grow a wishbone, daughter, where a backbone ought to be.

~ CLEMENTINE PADDLEFORD

Don't sit down and wait for the opportunities to come; you have to get up and make them.

~ MADAME C.J. WALKER

Make Your Own Breaks

Inspiration never arrived when you were searching for it.

~ LISA ALTHER

Luck serves ... as rationalization for every people that is not master of its own destiny.

~ HANNAH ARENDT

This world is run with far too tight a rein for luck to interfere. Fortune sells her wares; she never gives them. In some form or other, we pay for her favors; or we go empty away.

~ AMELIA BARR

Luck enters into every contingency. You are a fool if you forget it— and a greater fool if you count upon it.

~ PHYLLIS BOTTOME

Fate is not an eagle, it creeps like a rat.

~ ELIZABETH BOWEN

All good fortune is a gift of the gods, and ... you don't win the favor of the ancient gods by being good, but by being bold.

~ ANITA BROOKNER

Drama is very important in life: You have to come on with a bang. You never want to go out with a whimper.

~ JULIA CHILD

Superiority to fate is difficult to gain, 'tis not conferred of any, but possible to earn.

~ EMILY DICKINSON

Luck is largely a matter of paying attention.

~ SUSAN M. DODD

The woman who can create her own job is the one who will win fame and fortune.

~ AMELIA EARHART

You are no more exempt from time's inexorable passing than Macbeth. Whether time is your friend or foe depends on how you use it

~ PATRICIA FRIPP

You have to take it as it happens, but you should try to make it happen the way you want to take it.

~ GERMAN PROVERB

To get it right, be born with luck or else make it.
~ RUTH GORDON

It is not our circumstances that create our discontent or
contentment. It is us.
~ VIVIAN GREENE

Life is a narrative that you have a hand in writing.
~ HENRIETTE ANNE KLAUSER

Life is what we make it; always has been, always will be.
~ GRANDMA MOSES

God forgives those who invent what they need.
~ AYN RAND

Those that are afraid of bad luck will never know good.
~ RUSSIAN PROVERB

*W*orking Hard

Hard Work Is the Basis of Every Great Achievement

I am enjoying to a full that period of reflection which is the happiest conclusion to a life of action.

~ WILLA CATHER

If your dream is a big dream, and if you want your life to work on the high level that you say you do, there's no way around doing the work it takes to get you there.

~ JOYCE CHAPMAN

Hard work has made it easy. That is my secret. That is why I win.

~ NADIA COMANECI

The only thing that separates successful people from the ones who aren't is the willingness to work very, very hard.

~ HELEN GURLEY BROWN

You can have unbelievable intelligence, you can have connections, you can have opportunities fall out of the sky. But in the end, hard work is the true, enduring characteristic of successful people.

~ MARSHA EVANS

Opportunities are usually disguised as hard work, so most people don't recognize them.

~ ANN LANDERS

Winning the [Nobel] prize wasn't half as exciting as doing the work itself.

~ MARIA GOEPPERT MAYER

Passion is never enough; neither is skill.

~ TONI MORRISON

Success depends in a very large measure upon individual initiative and exertion, and cannot be achieved except by a dint of hard work.

~ ANNA PAVLOVA

It's not the having, it's the getting.

~ ELIZABETH TAYLOR

We Persevere through Hard Work

As it turns out, social scientists have established only one fact about single women's mental health: employment improves it.

~ SUSAN FALUDI

The only causes of regret are laziness, outbursts of temper, hurting others, prejudice, jealousy, and envy.

~ GERMAINE GREER

Nobody ever drowned in his own sweat.

~ ANN LANDERS

If there is no wind, row.

⟶ LATIN PROVERB

There are no hopeless situations; there are only men who have grown hopeless about them.

⟶ CLARE BOOTHE LUCE

The strength of the drive determines the force required to suppress it.

⟶ MARY JANE SHERFEY

If you don't toil, you won't eat.

⟶ YIDDISH PROVERB

With Hard Work, We Can Achieve Miracles

There are two kinds of talents, man-made talent and God-given talent. With man-made talent you have to work very hard. With God-given talent, you just touch it up once in a while.

⟶ PEARL BAILEY

The sport I love has taken me around the world and shown me many things.

⟶ BONNIE BLAIR

I realized that with hard work, the world was your oyster. You could do anything you wanted to do. I learned that at a young age.

⟶ CHRIS EVERT

When we do the best that we can, we never know what miracle is wrought in our life, or in the life of another.

⟶ HELEN KELLER

Dedication to one's work in the world is the only possible sanctification. Religion in all its forms is dedication to Someone Else's work, not yours.

⟶ CYNTHIA OZICK

There are no shortcuts to any place worth going.

~ BEVERLY SILLS

I like to deliver more than I promise instead of the other way around.

~ DOROTHY UHNAK

Nothing comes easy.

~ YIDDISH PROVERB

Hard Work Is Its Own Reward

Work! Thank God for the swing of it, for the clamoring, hammering, ring of it.

~ ANON.

In the spring, at the end of the day, you should smell like dirt.

~ MARGARET ATWOOD

If you want something done, ask a busy person to do it. The more things you do, the more you can do.

~ LUCILLE BALL

With the power of conviction, there is no sacrifice.

~ PAT BENATAR

I believe you are your work. Don't trade the stuff of your life, time, for nothing more than dollars. That's a rotten bargain.

~ RITA MAE BROWN

When you're following your energy and doing what you want all the time, the distinction between work and play dissolves.

~ SHAKTI GAWAIN

Work is the thing that stays. Work is the thing that sees us through.

~ ELLEN GILCHRIST

Energy is the power that drives every human being. It is not lost by exertion but maintained by it, for it is a faculty of the psyche.

∿ GERMAINE GREER

It is not hard work that is dreary; it is superficial work.

∿ EDITH HAMILTON

As for me, prizes mean nothing. My prize is my work.

∿ KATHARINE HEPBURN

There can be no substitute for work, neither affection nor physical well-being can replace it.

∿ MARIA MONTESSORI

Work is its own cure. You have to like it better than being loved.

∿ MARGE PIERCY

Work ... has always been my favorite form of recreation.

∿ ANNA HOWARD SHAW

A job is not a career. I think I started out with a job. It turned into a career and changed my life.

∿ BARBARA WALTERS

The only genius that's worth anything is the genius for hard work.

∿ KATHLEEN WINSOR

Whoever looks for easy work goes to bed very tired.

∿ YIDDISH PROVERB

Work Hard, but Remember to Play, Too

A family that plays together, stays together.

∿ ANON.

Busy work brings after ease;
Ease brings sport and sport brings rest;
For young and old, of all degrees,
The mingled lot is best.

~ JOANNA BAILLIE

Work, alternated with needful rest, is the salvation of man or woman.

~ ANTOINETTE BROWN BLACKWELL

There is a time for work. And a time for love. That leaves no other time.

~ COCO CHANEL

Neither woman nor man lives by work, or love, alone.... The human
self defines itself and grows through love AND work: All psychology
before and after Freud boils down to that.

~ BETTY FRIEDAN

Maintain a good balance. A personal life adds dimensions to your
professional life and vice versa. It helps nurture creativity through a
deeper understanding of yourself.

~ KATHY IRELAND

When action grows unprofitable, gather information; when
information grows unprofitable, sleep.

~ URSULA K. LE GUIN

For the happiest life, days should be rigorously planned, nights left
open to chance.

~ MIGNON MCLAUGHLIN

Work is the province of cattle.

~ DOROTHY PARKER

Each day, and the living of it, has to be a conscious creation in which
discipline and order are relieved with some play and pure foolishness.

~ MAY SARTON

The only sin passion can commit is to be joyless.

~ DOROTHY L. SAYERS

Sometimes You May Have to Work Twice as Hard

What it comes down to is that anybody can win with the best horse. What makes you good is if you can take the second or third best horse and win.

~ VICKY ARAGON

Beauty can't amuse you, but brainwork—reading, writing, thinking—can.

~ HELEN GURLEY BROWN

Every woman is a human being—one cannot repeat that too often— and a human being must have occupation if he or she is not to become a nuisance to the world.

~ DOROTHY L. SAYERS

A continued atmosphere of hectic passion is very trying if you haven't got any of your own.

~ DOROTHY L. SAYERS

Hard Work Is a Great Tonic

Happiness is often the result of being too busy to be miserable.

~ ANON.

I must have something to engross my thoughts, some object in life which will fill this vacuum and prevent this sad wearing away of the heart.

~ ELIZABETH BLACKWELL

Acting can work a peculiar magic on the actor... It can cure you (at least for the length of a performance) of a whole variety of ailments. Migraine headaches, miserable colds or toothaches will suddenly disappear as you're up there going through your paces.

~ BARBARA HARRIS

No thoroughly occupied man was ever yet very miserable.

~ LETITIA LANDON

I believe in hard work. It keeps the wrinkles out of the mind and spirit.

∾ HELENA RUBINSTEIN

Work With All the Courage of Your Convictions

The worth of every conviction consists precisely in the steadfastness in which it is held.

∾ JANE ADDAMS

The happiest excitement in life is to be convinced that one is fighting for all one is worth on behalf of some clearly seen and deeply felt good.

∾ RUTH BENEDICT

When I stand before God at the end of my life, I would hope that I would not have a single bit of talent left, and could say, "I used everything you gave me."

∾ ERMA BOMBECK

We fought hard. We gave it our best. We did what was right and we made a difference.

∾ GERALDINE FERRARO

The real nature of an ethic is that it does not become an ethic unless and until it goes into action.

∾ MARGARET HALSEY

One's lifework, I have learned, grows with the working and the living. Do it as if your life depended on it, and first thing you know, you'll have made a life out of it. A good life, too.

∾ THERESA HELBURN

Work is a world apart from jobs. Work is the way you occupy your mind and hand and eye and whole body when they're informed by your imagination.

∾ ALICE KOLLER

Happiness consists in the full employment of our faculties in some pursuit.

~ HARRIET MARTINEAU

A faint endeavor ends in a sure defeat.

~ HANNAH MOORE

I believe in my work and in the joy of it. You have to be with the work and the work has to be with you. It absorbs you totally and you absorb it totally.

~ LOUISE NEVELSON

What we make is more important than what we are, particularly if making is our profession.

~ DOROTHY L. SAYERS

Cooking is like love. It should be entered into with abandon or not at all.

~ HARRIET VAN HORNE

Work Hard at Every Task, No Matter How Small

Whatever the job you are asked to do at whatever level, do a good job because your reputation is your resume.

~ MADELEINE ALBRIGHT

Perfection consists not in doing extraordinary things, but in doing ordinary things extraordinarily well.

~ ANGELIQUE ARNAULD

When it comes to getting things done, we need fewer architects and more bricklayers.

~ COLLEEN C. BARRETT

I long to accomplish a great and noble task, but it is my chief duty to accomplish small tasks as if they were great and noble.

~ HELEN KELLER

We can do no great things—only small things with great love.

~ MOTHER TERESA

It's easy to work for somebody else; all you have to do is show up.

~ RITA WARFORD

Life Is Hard Work—Enjoy the Challenge

In life as in the dance: Grace glides on blistered feet.

~ ALICE ABRAMS

People should tell their children what life is all about—it's about work.

~ LAUREN BACALL

Marriage ain't easy but nothing that's worth much ever is.

~ LILLIAN CARTER

It is a rare and difficult attainment to grow old gracefully and happily.

~ LYDIA MARIA CHILD

You've got to sing like you don't need the money. You've got to love like you'll never get hurt. You've got to dance like there's nobody watching. You've got to come from the heart, if you want it to work.

~ SUSANNA CLARK

I slept, and dreamed that life was Beauty;
I woke, and found that life was Duty.

~ ELLEN STURGIS HOOPER

Work in some form or other is the appointed lot of all.

~ ANNA JAMESON

The sentimentalist ages far more quickly than the person who loves his work and enjoys new challenges.

~ LILLIE LANGTRY

The only way to enjoy anything in this life is to earn it first.

~ GINGER ROGERS

Only by pursuing the extremes in one's nature, with all its contradictions, appetites, aversions, rages, can one hope to understand a little … oh, I admit only a very little … of what life is about.

~ FRANÇOISE SAGAN

The First Step Is the Hardest—And Most Important

Success comes before work only in the dictionary.

~ ANON.

A person who has not done one half his day's work by ten o' clock, runs a chance of leaving the other half undone.

~ EMILY BRONTË

There is clearly much left to be done, and whatever else we are going to do, we had better get on with it.

~ ROSALYNN CARTER

Wisdom is harder to do than it is to know.

~ YULA MOSES

You Inspire Others by Your Example

I care. I care a lot. I think of "Cosmopolitan" all day, and I run scared. So it's a combination of fright, caring, and anxiety.

~ HELEN GURLEY BROWN

The secret of joy in work is contained in one word—excellence. To know how to do something well is to enjoy it.

~ PEARL S. BUCK

I have worked all my life, wanted to work all my life, needed to work all my life.

~ LIZ CARPENTER

Excellence encourages one about life generally; it shows the spiritual wealth of the world.

~ GEORGE ELIOT

I'm afraid of being lazy and complacent. I'm afraid of taking myself too seriously.

~ BARBARA HERSHEY

Whether we call it a job or a career, work is more than just something we do. It is a part of who we are.

~ ANITA HILL

There is no other solution to man's progress but the day's honest work, the day's honest decisions, the day's generous utterances, and the day's good deed.

~ CLARE BOOTHE LUCE

Busy people are never busybodies.

~ ETHEL WATTS MUMFORD

It's not so much how busy you are, but why you are busy. The bee is praised. The mosquito is swatted.

~ MARY O'CONNOR

Go to the ant, thou sluggard, learn to live, and by her busy ways, reform thy own.

~ ELIZABETH SMART

Integrate what you believe into every single area of your life. Take your heart to work and ask the most and best of everybody else.

~ MERYL STREEP

Success is having a flair for the thing that you are doing, knowing that is not enough, that you have got to have hard work and a sense of purpose.

⁓ MARGARET THATCHER

Look at a day when you are supremely satisfied at the end. It's not a day when you lounge around doing nothing; it's when you've had everything to do, and you've done it.

⁓ MARGARET THATCHER

The devil tempts all, but the idle tempt the devil.

⁓ TURKISH PROVERB

It's true that heroes are inspiring, but mustn't they also do some rescuing if they are to be worthy of their name? Would Wonder Woman matter if she only sent commiserating telegrams to the distressed?

⁓ JEANETTE WINTERSON

Work in the Service of Others Can Be Very Rewarding

When people go to work, they shouldn't have to leave their hearts at home.

⁓ BETTY BENDER

It is not how many years we live, but rather what we do with them.

⁓ EVANGELINE CORY BOOTH

Service is the rent we pay for the privilege of living on this earth.

⁓ SHIRLEY CHISHOLM

Love grows by service.

⁓ CHARLOTTE P. GILMAN

What a man sows, that shall he and his relations reap.

⁓ CLARISSA GRAVES

Duties are what make life most worth living. Lacking them, you are not necessary to anyone.

~ MARLENE DIETRICH

The measure of a life, after all, is not its duration, but its donation.

~ CORRIE TEN BOOM

Our work brings people face to face with love.

~ MOTHER TERESA

We can do no great things—only small things with great love.

~ MOTHER TERESA

Those who love a cause are those who love the life which has to be led in order to serve it.

~ SIMONE WEIL

Work Can Be All-Consuming

Work is a substitute "religious" experience for many workaholics.

~ MARY DALY

I like to laugh, but on the court, it is my work. I try to smile, but it is so difficult. I concentrate on the ball, not on my face.

~ STEFFI GRAF

Workaholics are energized rather than enervated by their work—their energy paradoxically expands as it is expended.

~ MARILYN MACHLOWITZ

Be Thankful You Have Work to Do

When I can no longer create anything, I'll be done for.
~ COCO CHANEL

If you're in a good profession, it's hard to get bored, because you're never finished—there will always be work you haven't done.
~ JULIA CHILD

Work means so many things! So many! Among other things, work also means freedom.... Without it even the miracle of love is only a cruel deception.
~ ELEANORA DUSE

The years seem to rush by now, and I think of death as a fast approaching end of a journey—double and treble reason for loving as well as working while it is day.
~ GEORGE ELIOT

I don't think that work ever really destroyed anybody. I think that lack of work destroys them a hell of a lot more.
~ KATHARINE HEPBURN

I am fierce for work. Without work I am nothing.
~ WINIFRED HOLTBY

For the last third of life there remains only work. It alone is always stimulating, rejuvenating, exciting and satisfying.
~ KATHE KOLLWITZ

Study as if you were going to live forever; live as if you were going to die tomorrow.
~ MARIA MITCHELL

Sticking With It

Things Worth Having Are Worth Fighting For

The worth of every conviction consists precisely in the steadfastness in which it is held.

~ JANE ADDAMS

A chicken doesn't stop scratching just because worms are scarce.

~ GRANDMA AXIOM

Gift, like genius, I often think only means an infinite capacity for taking pains.

~ JANE ELLICE HOPKINS

It is easier to demolish a house than to build one.

~ IRISH PROVERB

Excellence in any pursuit is the late, ripe fruit of toil.

~ W.M.L. JAY

A soul occupied with great ideas performs small duties.

~ HARRIET MARTINEAU

I can honestly say that I was never affected by the question of the success of an undertaking. If I felt it was the right thing to do, I was for it regardless of the possible outcome.

~ GOLDA MEIR

But the fruit that can fall without shaking indeed is too mellow for me.

~ LADY MARY WORTLEY MONTAGU

What we want is never simple.

~ LINDA PASTAN

Stay up and really burn the midnight oil. There are no compromises.

~ LEONTYNE PRICE

You must do the thing you think you cannot do.

~ ELEANOR ROOSEVELT

I could not, at any age, be content to take my place by the fireside and simply look on. Life was meant to be lived. Curiosity must be kept alive. One must never, for whatever reason, turn his back on life.

~ ELEANOR ROOSEVELT

We Can Overcome All Opposition

As you go along your road in life, you will, if you aim high enough, also meet resistance.... But no matter how tough the opposition may seem, have courage still—and persevere.

~ MADELEINE ALBRIGHT

Let my name stand among those who are willing to bear ridicule and reproach for the truth's sake, and so earn some right to rejoice when the victory is won.

~ LOUISA MAY ALCOTT

Life is not easy for any of us. But what of that? We must have perseverance and above all confidence in ourselves. We must believe that we are gifted for something, and that this thing, at whatever cost, must be attained.

⌐ MARIE CURIE

Until I die, I'm going to keep doing. My people need me. They need somebody that's not taking from them and is giving them something.

⌐ CLARA MCBRIDE HALE

I know some good marriages—marriages where both people are just trying to get through their days by helping each other, being good to each other.

⌐ ERICA JONG

Getting ahead in a difficult profession requires avid faith in yourself. You must be able to sustain yourself against staggering blows. There is no code of conduct to help beginners. That is why some people with mediocre talent, but with great inner drive, go much further than people with vastly superior talent.

⌐ SOPHIA LOREN

The wonderful thing about saints is that they were human. They lost their tempers, got hungry, scolded God, were egotistical or impatient in their turns, made mistakes and regretted them. Still they went on doggedly blundering toward heaven.

⌐ PHYLLIS MCGINLEY

A successful marriage requires falling in love many times, always with the same person.

⌐ MIGNON MCLAUGHLIN

Don't ask me to give in to this body of mine. I can't afford it. Between me and my body there must be a struggle until death.

⌐ SAINT MARGARET OF CORTONA

Being human, we should bear all we can.

⌐ NORMA MEACOCK

Remember that the Devil doesn't sleep, but seeks our ruin in a thousand different ways.

~ ANGELA MERICI

Down you mongrel, Death! Back into your kennel!

~ EDNA ST. VINCENT MILLAY

What one has to do usually can be done.

~ ELEANOR ROOSEVELT

When you get into a tight place and everything goes against you, till it seems as though you could not hang on a minute longer, never give up then, for that is just the place and time that the tide will turn.

~ HARRIET BEECHER STOWE

You may have to fight a battle more than once to win it.

~ MARGARET THATCHER

Our way is not soft grass, it's a mountain path with lots of rocks. But it goes upwards, forward, toward the sun.

~ DR. RUTH WESTHEIMER

If you can't go over, go under.

~ YIDDISH PROVERB

Don't Quit Until the Task is Finished

There are two parts to the creative endeavor: making something, then disseminating it.

~ JANE ALEXANDER

A winner never quits, and a quitter never wins.

~ ANON.

Live with no time out.

~ SIMONE DE BEAUVOIR

Only yield when you must, never "give up the ship," but fight on to the last "with a stiff upper lip!"

~ PHOEBE CARY

Never go to bed mad. Stay up and fight.

~ PHYLLIS DILLER

There is no point at which you can say, "Well, I'm successful now. I might as well take a nap."

~ CARRIE FISHER

I try. I am trying. I was trying. I will try. I shall in the meantime try. I sometimes have tried. I shall still by that time be trying.

~ DIANE GLANCY

I am a stranger to half measures.

~ MARITA GOLDEN

I can remember walking as a child. It was not customary to say you were fatigued. It was customary to complete the goal of the expedition.

~ KATHARINE HEPBURN

New links must be forged as old ones rust.

~ JANE HOWARD

Hope begins in the dark, the stubborn hope that if you just show up and try to do the right thing, the dawn will come. You wait and watch and work: you don't give up.

~ ANNE LAMOTT

Hard times ain't quit and we ain't quit.

~ MERIDEL LE SUEUR

Hope says to us constantly, "go on, go on," and leads us to the grave.

~ FRANCOISE D'AUBIGNE DE MAINTENON

When you put your hand to the plow, you can't put it down until you get to the end of the row.

~ ALICE PAUL

The world is round and the place which may seem like the end may also be only the beginning.
～ IVY BAKER PRIEST

The art of writing is the art of applying the seat of the pants to the seat of the chair.
～ MARY HEATON VORSE

Never think you've seen the last of anything.
～ EUDORA WELTY

No question is ever settled until it is settled right.
～ ELLA WHEELER WILCOX

Out of the strain of the Doing,
Into the peace of the Done.
～ JULIA LOUISE WOODRUFF

Failure is Not an Option

I wrote for twelve years and collected 250 rejection slips before getting any fiction published, so I guess outside reinforcement isn't all that important to me.
～ LISA ALTHER

Entrepreneurs average 3.8 failures before final success. What sets the successful ones apart is their amazing persistence. There are a lot of people out there with good and marketable ideas, but pure entrepreneurial types almost never accept defeat.
～ LISA M. AMOS

Perseverance is failing nineteen times and succeeding the twentieth.
～ JULIE ANDREWS

Don't be discouraged. It's often the last key in the bunch that opens the lock.
～ ANON.

When life knocks you to your knees, and it will, why, get up! If it
knocks you to your knees again, as it will, well, isn't that the best
position from which to pray?

~ ETHEL BARRYMORE

When we know what we want to prove, we go out and find our
facts. They are always there.

~ PEARL S. BUCK

Don't get hung up on a snag in the stream, my dear. Snags are not so
dangerous—it's the debris that clings to them that makes the trouble.
Pull yourself loose and go on.

~ ANNE SHANNON MONROE

It's not worthy of human beings to give up.

~ ALVA REIMER MYRDAL

If I see a door comin' my way, I'm knockin' it down. And if I can't
knock down the door, I'm sliding through the window.

~ ROSIE PEREZ

It takes far less courage to kill yourself than it takes to make yourself
wake up one more time.

~ JUDITH ROSSNER

Life is obstinate and clings closest where it is most hated.

~ MARY WOLLSTONECRAFT SHELLEY

There is something in me—I just can't stand to admit defeat.

~ BEVERLY SILLS

Keep breathing.

~ SOPHIE TUCKER

There was no such thing as defeat if you didn't accept it.

~ FAY WELDON

Every question has an answer.

~ YIDDISH PROVERB

Hard Work Is Its Own Reward

Some people regard discipline as a chore. For me, it is a kind of order that sets me free to fly.

~ JULIE ANDREWS

Success is measured by the willingness to keep trying.

~ ANON.

Success is a great healer.

~ GERTRUDE ATHERTON

The victory of success is half done when one gains the habit of work.

~ SARAH KNOWLES BOLTON

Life leaps like a geyser for those who drill through the rock of inertia.

~ ALEXIS CARREL

You must have discipline to have fun.

~ JULIA CHILD

Excellence is not an act but a habit. The things you do the most are the things you will do the best.

~ MARVA COLLINS

To be somebody you must last.

~ RUTH GORDON

The only thing that happens overnight is recognition. Not talent.

~ CAROL HANEY

If you rest, you rust.

~ HELEN HAYES

Without discipline, there's no life at all.

~ KATHARINE HEPBURN

I don't think success is harmful, as so many people say. Rather I believe it indispensible to talent: if for nothing else than to increase the talent.
~ JEANNE MOREAU

Success is like a liberation, or the first phrase of a love story.
~ JEANNE MOREAU

Happiness is not a station you arrive at, but a manner of traveling.
~ MARGARET LEE RUNBECK

The journey is my home.
~ MURIEL RUKEYSER

Do your duty until it becomes your joy.
~ MARIE VON EBNER-ESCHENBACH

Persistence Pays When All Else Fails

Persistence is the master virtue. Without it, there is no other.
~ ANON.

The race is not always to the swift, but to those who keep on running.
~ ANON.

As long as one keeps searching, the answers come.
~ JOAN BAEZ

The unendurable is the beginning of the curve of joy.
~ DJUNA BARNES

Where I am today has everything to do with the years I spent hanging on to a career by my fingernails.
~ BARBARA ARONSTEIN BLACK

There never was night that had no morn.
~ DINAH MARIA MULOCK CRAIK

Genius at first is little more than a great capacity for receiving discipline.
~ GEORGE ELIOT

All the sugar was in the bottom of the cup.
~ JULIA WARD HOWE

If the cat sits long enough at the hole, she will catch the mouse.
~ IRISH PROVERB

Who longest waits most surely wins.
~ HELEN HUNT JACKSON

We can do anything we want to do if we stick to it long enough.
~ HELEN KELLER

Think of a fine painter attempting to capture an inner vision, beginning with one corner of the canvas, painting what he thinks should be there, not quite pulling it off, covering it over with white paint, and trying again, each time finding out what his painting isn't, until he finally finds out what it is. And when you finally do find out what one corner of your vision is, you're off and running.
~ ANNE LAMOTT

If you don't quit, and don't cheat, and don't run home when trouble arrives, you can only win.
~ SHELLEY LONG

When you get into a tight place and everything goes against you, till it seems as though you could not hang on a minute longer, never give up then, for that is just the place and time that the tide will turn.
~ HARRIET BEECHER STOWE

Learn to self-conquest, persevere thus for a time, and you will perceive very clearly the advantage which you gain from it.
~ TERESA OF AVILA

Patient endurance attends to all things.
~ TERESA OF AVILA

Whether it was work, marriage, or family, I've always been a late
bloomer.

~ SIGOURNEY WEAVER

Keep Your Mind on Your Goals

The future is a great land.

~ ANON.

This will be triumph! This will be happiness! Yea, that very thing,
happiness, which I have been pursuing all my life, and have never yet
overtaken.

~ JOANNA BAILLIE

Old habits are strong and jealous.

~ DOROTHEA BRANDE

It is necessary to try to surpass one's self always; this occupation
ought to last as long as life.

~ CHRISTINA AUGUSTA, QUEEN OF SWEDEN

Trouble, like the hill ahead, straightens out when you advance upon it.

~ MARCELENE COX

We can never go back again, that much is certain. The past is still too
close to us. The things we have tried to forget and put behind us
would stir again, and that sense of fear, of furtive unrest … might in
some manner unforeseen become a living companion, as it had before.

~ DAPHNE DU MAURIER

Once I decide to do something, I can't have people telling me I can't.
If there's a roadblock, you jump over it, walk around it, crawl under it.

~ KITTY KELLEY

Part of being a champ is acting like a champ. You have to learn how to win and not run away when you lose. Everyone has bad stretches and real successes.

～ NANCY KERRIGAN

Life is one long struggle to disinter oneself, to keep one's head above the accumulations, the ever deepening layers of objects ... which attempt to cover one over, steadily, almost irresistibly, like falling snow.

～ ROSE MACAULAY

No star is ever lost we once have seen,
We always may be what we might have been.

～ ADELAIDE PROCTOR

Eternity ... think of it when you are hard pushed.

～ ELIZABETH ANN SETON

Every great work, every big accomplishment, has been brought into manifestation through holding to the vision, and often just before the big achievement, comes apparent failure and discouragement.

～ FLORENCE SCOVEL SHINN

Lifting as they climb, onward and upward they go, struggling and striving and hoping that the buds and blossoms of their desires may burst into glorious fruition ere long.

～ MARY CHURCH TERRELL

Relationships Take Work

Absence does not make the heart grow fonder, but it sure heats up the blood.

～ ELIZABETH ASHLEY

A successful marriage requires falling in love many times, always with the same person.

～ MIGNON MCLAUGHLIN

Love, like a chicken salad or restaurant hash, must be taken with blind faith or it loses its flavor.

~ HELEN ROWLAND

Remain True to Your Principles

At present, our country needs women's idealism and determination, perhaps more in politics than anywhere else.

~ SHIRLEY CHISHOLM

Vows made in storms are forgotten in calms.

~ ENGLISH PROVERB

Our desire must be like a slow and stately ship, sailing across endless oceans, never in search of safe anchorage. Then suddenly, unexpectedly, it will find mooring for a moment.

~ ETTY HILLESUM

The day of the storm is not the time for thatching your roof.

~ IRISH PROVERB

I will write of him who fights and vanquishes his sins, who struggles on through weary years against himself ... and wins.

~ CAROLINE BEGELOW LEROW

He who, having lost one ideal, refuses to give his heart and soul to another and nobler, is like a man who declines to build a house on rock because the wind and rain ruined his house on the sand.

~ CONSTANCE NADEN

Morality, like physical cleanliness, is not acquired once and for all: it can only be kept and renewed by a habit of constant watchfulness and discipline.

~ VICTORIA OCAMPO

You have to accept whatever comes and the only important thing is that you meet it with the best you have to give.

~ ELEANOR ROOSEVELT

Not all things are blest, but the seeds of all things are blest.

~ MURIEL RUKEYSER

It's in the preparation—in those dreary pedestrian virtues they taught you in seventh grade and you didn't believe. It's making the extra call and caring a lot.

~ DIANE SAWYER

People with good intentions never give up!

~ JANE SMILEY

Although none of the rules for becoming alive is valid, it is healthy to keep on formulating them.

~ SUSAN SONTAG

Don't Look Back

We can never go back again, that much is certain. The past is still too close to us. The things we have tried to forget and put behind us would stir again, and that sense of fear, of furtive unrest ... might in some manner unforeseen become a living companion, as it had before.

~ DAPHNE DU MAURIER

Disillusion is a natural stage that follows the holding of an illusion.

~ SUSAN SHAUGHNESSY

Attention to Detail Is Key

Life is denied by lack of attention, whether it be to cleaning windows or trying to write a masterpiece.

~ NADIA BOULANGER

Habit is not mere subjugation, it is a tender tie; when one remembers habit it seems to have been happiness.

~ ELIZABETH BOWEN

Trifles make perfection, but perfection is no trifle.

~ ITALIAN PROVERB

It is with enterprises as with striking fire; we do not meet with success except with reiterated efforts, and often at the instant when we despaired of success.

~ FRANCOISE D'AUBIGNE DE MAINTENON

Morality, like physical cleanliness, is not acquired once and for all: it can only be kept and renewed by a habit of constant watchfulness and discipline.

~ VICTORIA OCAMPO

I've learned ruthless concentration. I can write under any circumstances ... street noises, loud talk, music, you name it.

~ SYLVIA PORTER

It helps, I think, to consider ourselves on a very long journey: the main thing is to keep to the faith, to endure, to help each other when we stumble or tire, to weep and press on.

~ MARY CAROLINE RICHARDS

When you get to the end of your rope, tie a knot in it and hang on.

~ ELEANOR ROOSEVELT

The great thing, and the hard thing, is to stick to things when you have outlived the first interest, and not yet got the second, which comes with a sort of mastery.

~ JANET ERSKINE STUART

In Hollywood, all marriages are happy. It's trying to live together afterwards that causes problems.

~ SHELLEY WINTERS

Learning From Mistakes

Avoid Making the Same Mistake Twice

There is nothing wrong with making mistakes. Just don't respond
with encores.

～ ANON.

When you're stuck in a spiral, to change all aspects of the spin you
need only to change one thing,

～ CHRISTINA BALDWIN

There is no reason to repeat bad history.

～ ELEANOR HOLMES NORTON

Do not be afraid of mistakes, providing you do not make the same
one twice.

～ ELEANOR ROOSEVELT

I try to extract something positive from [every] situation, even if it's
just learning not to make the same mistake twice.

～ CLAUDIA SCHIFFER

No doing without some ruing.

~ SIGRID UNDSET

Everyone Makes Mistakes—They're a Fact of Life

Life is not life unless you make mistakes.

~ JOAN COLLINS

Mistakes are part of the dues one pays for a full life.

~ SOPHIA LOREN

Flops are a part of life's menu and I've never been a girl to miss out on any of the courses.

~ ROSALIND RUSSELL

Be aware that young people have to be able to make their own mistakes and that times change.

~ GINA SHAPIRA

Mistakes are the usual bridge between inexperience and wisdom.

~ PHYLLIS THEROUS

Learn from Mistakes, and Take Correction in Stride

Sometimes what you want to do has to fail so you won't.

~ MARGUERITTE HARMON BRO

An error gracefully acknowledged is a victory won.

~ CAROLINE L. GASCOIGNE

There is no wisdom equal to that which comes after the event.

~ GERALDINE JEWSBURY

I think success has no rules, but you can learn a great deal from failure.

~ JEAN KERR

There are no mistakes, no coincidences. All events are blessings given to us to learn from.

~ ELISABETH KUBLER-ROSS

We will be victorious if we have not forgotten how to learn.

~ ROSA LUXEMBURG

It is very easy to forgive others their mistakes. It takes more grit and gumption to forgive them for having witnessed your own.

~ JESSAMYN WEST

Progress Is a Matter of Trial and Error

People fail forward to success.

~ MARY KAY ASH

Apparent failure may hold in its rough shell the germs of a success that will blossom in time, and bear fruit throughout eternity.

~ FRANCES ELLEN WATKINS HARPER

If you have made mistakes, even serious mistakes, there is always another chance for you.

~ MARY PICKFORD

A new idea is rarely born like Venus attended by graces. More commonly it's modeled of baling wire and acne. More commonly it wheezes and tips over.

~ MARGE PIERCY

A series of failures may culminate in the best possible result.

~ GISELA RICHTER

The only man who makes no mistakes is the man who never does anything.

～ ELEANOR ROOSEVELT

No honest work of man or woman "fails"; it feeds the sum of all human action.

～ MICHELENE WANDOR

Successes Are Remembered More Readily Than Mistakes

I was born to be a remarkable woman; it matters little in what way or how.... I shall be famous or I will die.

～ MARIE BASHKIRTSEFF

Some of the biggest failures I ever had were successes.

～ PEARL S. BUCK

There is a glory
In a great mistake.

～ NATHALIA CRANE

Success is a public affair. Failure is a private funeral.

～ ROSALIND RUSSELL

Enjoy the successes that you have, and don't be too hard on yourself when you don't do well. Too many times we beat up on ourselves. Just relax and enjoy it.

～ PATTY SHEEHAN

Mistakes Are Opportunities to Grow

Trouble brings experience, and experience brings wisdom.
~ ANON.

Good judgment comes from experience, and experience comes from poor judgment.
~ ANON.

If I had to live my life again, I'd make the same mistakes, only sooner.
~ TALLULAH BANKHEAD

Show me a person who has never made a mistake and I'll show you somebody who has never achieved much.
~ JOAN COLLINS

Experience is how life catches up with us and teaches us to love and forgive each other.
~ JUDY COLLINS

Failure is just another way to learn how to do something right.
~ MARIAN WRIGHT EDELMAN

It is not easy, but you have to be willing to make mistakes. And the earlier you make those mistakes, the better.
~ JANE CAHILL PFEIFFER

Never Fail to Try for Fear of Making a Mistake

The error of the past is the success of the future. A mistake is evidence that someone tried to do something.
~ ANON.

The person interested in success has to learn to view failure as a healthy, inevitable part of the process of getting to the top.
~ DR. JOYCE BROTHERS

Failure after long perseverance is much grander than never to have a striving good enough to be called a failure.

~ GEORGE ELIOT

The sight of a cage is only frightening to the bird that has once been caught.

~ RACHEL FIELD

Your success depends on your ability to dream and follow through on those dreams.

~ JINGER HEATH

Keep trying. Take care of the small circle around you. When you have succeeded with them, then move outwards, one small step at a time.

~ AUDREY HEPBURN

It takes as much courage to have tried and failed as it does to have tried and succeeded.

~ ANNE MORROW LINDBERGH

Take chances, make mistakes. That's how you grow. Pain nourishes your courage. You have to fail in order to practice being brave.

~ MARY TYLER MOORE

It is better to be young in your failures than old in your successes.

~ FLANNERY O'CONNOR

There might be false starts and do-overs. You are entitled to experiment before you find your calling.

~ JANE PAULEY

Fear nothing, for every renewed effort raises all former failures into lessons, all sins into experience.

~ KATHERINE TINGLEY

Life is the only real counselor. Wisdom unfiltered through personal experience does not become a part of the moral tissue.

~ EDITH WHARTON

Learn to Laugh at Your Mistakes

I am one of those people who can't help getting a kick out of life—even when it's a kick in the teeth.

~ POLLY ADLER

When we begin to take our failures nonseriously, it means we are ceasing to be afraid of them. It is of immense importance to learn to laugh at ourselves.

~ KATHERINE MANSFIELD

Don't Dwell on Past Mistakes

Your past is always going to be the way it was. Stop trying to change it.

~ ANON.

Here's to the past. Thank God it's past!

~ ANON.

There is a way to look at the past. Don't hide from it. It will not catch you if you don't repeat it.

~ PEARL BAILEY

One loses many laughs by not laughing at oneself.

~ SARA JEANNETTE DUNCAN

Forget your mistakes, but remember what they taught you.

~ DOROTHY GALYEAN

Supposing you have tried and failed again and again. You may have a fresh start any moment you choose, for this thing that we call "failure" is not the falling down, but the staying down.

~ MARY PICKFORD

Failure is a disappointment but not defeat.

~ JEANNE ROBERTSON

Memories are the key not to the past, but to the future.

~ CORRIE TEN BOOM

Believe in Yourself, Even If Others Believe You Are Mistaken

To look backward for a while is to refresh the eye, to restore it, and to render it more fit for its prime function of looking forward.

~ MARGARET FAIRLESS BARBER

The past is finished. There is nothing to be gained by going over it. Whatever it gave us in the experiences it brought us was something we had to know.

~ REBECCA BEARD

A peacefulness follows any decision, even the wrong one.

~ RITA MAE BROWN

I had already learned from more than a decade of political life that I was going to be criticized no matter what I did, so I might as well be criticized for something I wanted to do.

~ ROSALYNN CARTER

Better a false belief than no belief at all.

~ GEORGE ELIOT

The only failure a man ought to fear is failure in cleaving to the purpose he sees to be best.

~ GEORGE ELIOT

A mistake is simply another way of doing things.

~ KATHERINE GRAHAM

If any good results to a man from believing a lie, it certainly comes from the honesty of his belief.

~ MARGARET COLLIER GRAHAM

You don't always win your battles, but it's good to know you fought.

~ MARJORIE HOLMES

I'm often wrong, but never in doubt.

~ IVY BAKER PRIEST

The entire history of science is a progression of exploded fallacies.

~ AYN RAND

I believe in recovery, and I believe that as a role model I have the responsibility to let young people know that you can make a mistake and come back from it.

~ ANN RICHARDS

The sheer rebelliousness in giving ourselves permission to fail frees a childlike awareness and clarity.... When we give ourselves permission to fail, we at the same time give ourselves permission to excel.

~ ELOISE RISTAD

The follies which a man regrets most in his life are those which he didn't commit when he had the opportunity.

~ HELEN ROWLAND

Disillusion is a natural stage that follows the holding of an illusion.

~ SUSAN SHAUGHNESSY

$\mathcal{O}$vercoming Worries

Don't Waste Your Time Fretting about the Past

Forgetting is the cost of living cheerfully.
$\sim$ ZOË AKINS

Of course I realized there was a measure of danger. Obviously I faced the possibility of not returning when I first considered going. Once faced and settled there really wasn't any good reason to refer to it again.
$\sim$ AMELIA EARHART

The past cannot be changed. The future is yet in your power.
$\sim$ MARY PICKFORD

Expect Good Things to Happen for You

Most people go through life dreading they'll have a traumatic experience.
~ DIANE ARBUS

When fear seizes, change what you are doing. You are doing something wrong.
~ JEAN CRAIGHEAD GEORGE

You will find a joy in overcoming obstacles.
~ HELEN KELLER

Everybody knows if you are too careful you are so occupied in being careful that you are sure to stumble over something.
~ GERTRUDE STEIN

Some Things Are Out of Your Control

Events that are predestined require but little management. They manage themselves. They slip into place while we sleep, and suddenly we are aware that the thing we fear to attempt, is already accomplished.
~ AMELIA BARR

If it is your time, love will track you down like a cruise missile.
~ LYNDA BARRY

O golden Silence, bid our souls be still, and on the foolish fretting of our care lay thy soft touch of healing unaware!
~ JULIA DORR

Stress is basically a disconnection from the earth, a forgetting of the breath. Stress is an ignorant state. It believes that everything is an emergency. Nothing is that important. Just lie down.
~ NATALIE GOLDBERG

When you learn not to want things so badly, life comes to you.
~ JESSICA LANGE

No day is so bad it can't be fixed with a nap.
~ CARRIE SNOW

Have Faith That You Will Overcome Adversity

Worries are the most stubborn habits in the world. Even after a poor man has won a huge lottery prize, he will still for months wake up in the night with a start, worrying about food and rent.
~ VICKI BAUM

Faith is the virtue of the storm, just as happiness is the virtue of the sunshine.
~ RUTH BENEDICT

Although the world is full of suffering, it is also full of the overcoming of it.
~ HELEN KELLER

It is a peaceful thing to be one succeeding.
~ GERTRUDE STEIN

Don't Let Worry Keep You from Taking Action

We must act in spite of fear, not because of it.
~ ANON.

Go ahead and do it. It's much easier to apologize after something's been done than to get permission ahead of time.
~ GRACE MURRAY HOPPER

Great self-destruction follows upon unfounded fear.
~ URSULA K. LE GUIN

Worry is like racing the engine of an automobile without letting in the clutch.

~ CORRIE TEN BOOM

Energy Wasted on Worry Can't Be Used to Make Progress

Worry is a complete cycle of inefficient thought revolving around a pivotal fear.

~ ANON.

Worry a little bit every day and in a lifetime you will lose a couple of years. If something is wrong, fix it if you can. But train yourself not to worry. Worry never fixes anything.

~ MARY HEMINGWAY

If things happen all the time you are never nervous. It is when they are not happening that you are nervous.

~ GERTRUDE STEIN

Worry is like a rocking chair—it keeps you moving but doesn't get you anywhere.

~ CORRIE TEN BOOM

Don't Worry about Growing Older

To live is so startling it leaves little time for anything else.

~ MARLENE DIETRICH

Death does not frighten me, but dying obscurely and above all uselessly does.

~ ISABELLE EBERHARDT

Don't be afraid your life will end; be afraid it will never begin.

~ GRACE HANSEN

Stop worrying about the potholes in the road and celebrate the journey!

~ BARBARA HOFFMAN

A man ninety years old was asked to what he attributed his longevity. "I reckon," he said, with a twinkle in his eye, "it's because most nights I went to bed and slept when I should have sat up and worried."

~ DOROTHEA KENT

I postpone death by living, by suffering, by error, by risking, by giving, by losing.

~ ANAÏS NIN

You're as Brave as You Make Others Believe You Are

Everyone thought I was bold and fearless and even arrogant, but inside I was always quaking.

~ KATHARINE HEPBURN

Fear is a sign—usually a sign that I'm doing something right.

~ ERICA JONG

Fear is the single strongest motivating force in our lives.... The more frightened you become, the better your chances of achieving success.

~ LOIS KOREY

This morning I threw up at a board meeting. I was sure the cat was out of the bag, but no one seemed to think anything about it; apparently it's quite common for people to throw up at board meetings.

~ JANE WAGNER

Worry less about what other people think about you, and more about what you think about them.

~ FAY WELDON

Learn to Know What's Worth Your Concern

FEAR: False Evidence Appearing Real.

~ ANON.

Mountains appear more lofty the nearer they are approached, but great men resemble them not in this particular.

~ LADY MARGUERITE BLESSINGTON

Worry is as useless as a handle on a snowball.

~ MITZI CHANDLER

Fear is created not by the world around us, but in the mind, by what we think is going to happen.

~ ELIZABETH GAWAIN

Stress is basically a disconnection from the earth, a forgetting of the breath. Stress is an ignorant state. It believes that everything is an emergency. Nothing is that important. Just lie down.

~ NATALIE GOLDBERG

You just have to learn not to care about the dusty mites under the beds.

~ MARGARET MEAD

Any concern too small to be turned into a prayer is too small to be made into a burden.

~ CORRIE TEN BOOM

It is far harder to kill a phantom than a reality.

~ VIRGINIA WOOLF

A lion doesn't fear a fly.

~ YIDDISH PROVERB

Focus on Today—Don't Worry about Tomorrow

You can't start worrying about what's going to happen. You get spastic enough worrying about what's happening now.

      ~ LAUREN BACALL

The really frightening thing about middle age is that you know you'll grow out of it!

      ~ DORIS DAY

A request not to worry … is perhaps the least soothing message capable of human utterance.

      ~ MIGNON G. EBERHART

Worry is like a rocking chair—it gives you something to do, but doesn't get you anywhere.

      ~ DOROTHY GALYEAN

That fear of missing out on things makes you miss out on everything.

      ~ ETTY HILLESUM

We have to fight them daily, like fleas, those many small worries about the morrow, for they sap our energies.

      ~ ETTY HILLESUM

T'ain't worthwhile to wear a day all out before it comes.

      ~ SARAH ORNE JEWETT

A worried man could borrow a lot of trouble with practically no collateral.

      ~ HELEN NIELSEN

It ain't no use putting up your umbrella till it rains!

      ~ ALICE CALDWELL RICE

Those who foresee the future and recognize it as tragic are often seized upon by a madness which forced them to commit the very acts which make it certain that what they dread will happen.

      ~ REBECCA WEST

Accepting Uncertainty as a Part of Life

No One Knows What the Day Will Bring

With each sunrise, we start anew.

~ ANON.

To expect life to be tailored to your specifications is to invite trouble.

~ ANON.

Experience has no textbooks nor proxies. She demands that her pupils answer to her roll-call personally.

~ MINNA ANTRIM

You can't start worrying about what's going to happen. You get spastic enough worrying about what's happening now.

~ LAUREN BACALL

Time is a dressmaker specializing in alterations.

~ FAITH BALDWIN

All decisions are made on insufficient evidence.

~ RITA MAE BROWN

For good and evil, man is a free creative spirit. This produces the
very queer world we live in, a world in continuous creation and
therefore continuous change and insecurity.

~ JOYCE CARY

It's quite possible to leave your home for a walk in the early
morning air and return a different person—beguiled, enchanted.

~ MARY CHASE

Living is a form of not being sure, not knowing what next, or how.
The moment you know how, you begin to die a little. The artist
never entirely knows. We guess. We may be wrong, but we take leap
after leap in the dark.

~ AGNES DE MILLE

Not knowing when the dawn will come, I open every door.

~ EMILY DICKINSON

Everything passes; everything wears out; everything breaks.

~ FRENCH PROVERB

Life is not orderly. No matter how we try to make life so, right in the
middle of it we die, lose a leg, fall in love, drop a jar of applesauce.

~ NATALIE GOLDBERG

Time has told me less than I need to know.

~ GWEN HARWOOD

Truly nothing is to be expected but the unexpected.

~ ALICE JAMES

The only thing that makes life possible is permanent, intolerable
uncertainty, not knowing what comes next.

~ URSULA K. LE GUIN

Nothing, perhaps, is strange, once you have accepted life itself, the great strange business which includes all lesser strangeness.
～ ROSE MACAULAY

None of us knows what the next change is going to be, what unexpected opportunity is just around the corner, waiting a few months or a few years to change all the tenor of our lives.
～ KATHLEEN NORRIS

The shortest period of time lies between the minute you put some money away for a rainy day and the unexpected arrival of rain.
～ JANE BRYANT QUINN

I wanted a perfect ending. Now I've learned, the hard way, that some poems don't rhyme, and some stories don't have a clear beginning, middle, and end. Life is about not knowing, having to change, taking the moment and making the best of it without knowing what's going to happen next.
～ GILDA RADNER

Where will I be five years from now? I delight in not knowing.
～ MARLO THOMAS

We live in an epoch in which the solid ground of our preconceived ideas shakes daily under our certain feet.
～ BARBARA WARD

I said here's the river I want to flow on, here's the direction I want to go, and put my boat in. I was ready for the river to take unexpected turns and present obstacles.
～ NANCY WOODHULL

Always Give Your Best, Even When You're Uncertain

Life is my college. May I graduate well, and earn some honors!
～ LOUISA MAY ALCOTT

It's a simple formula: do your best and somebody might like it.
~ DOROTHY BAKER

The decision to speak out is the vocation and lifelong peril by which the intellectual must live.
~ KAY BOYLE

Exceptional talent does not always win its reward unless favoured by exceptional circumstances.
~ MARY ELIZABETH BRADDON

There is no security, no assurance that because we wrote something good two months ago, we will do it again. Actually, every time we begin, we wonder how we ever did it before.
~ NATALIE GOLDBERG

For me life is a challenge. And it will be a challenge if I live to be a hundred or if I get to be a trillionaire.
~ BEAH RICHARDS

There Are No Guarantees in Love or Life

Love involves a peculiar unfathomable combination of understanding and misunderstanding.
~ DIANE ARBUS

The power to love what is purely abstract is given to few.
~ MARGOT ASQUITH

The sweetest joy, the wildest woe is love.
~ PEARL BAILEY

Real love is a pilgrimage. It happens when there is no strategy, but it is very rare because most people are strategists.
~ ANITA BROOKNER

Accept that all of us can be hurt, that all of us can—and surely will at times—fail. Other vulnerabilities, like being embarrassed or risking love, can be terrifying, too.
~ DR. JOYCE BROTHERS

Every time I think that I'm getting old, and gradually going to the grave, something else happens.
~ LILLIAN CARTER

The pain of love is the pain of being alive. It is a perpetual wound.
~ MAUREEN DUFFY

There is no way to take the danger out of human relationships.
~ BARBARA GRIZZUTI HARRISON

When something has been perfect, there is a tendency to try hard to repeat it.
~ EDNA O'BRIEN

Impermanence is the very essence of joy—the drop of bitterness that enables one to perceive the sweet.
~ MYRTLE REED

No one from the beginning of time has had security.
~ ELEANOR ROOSEVELT

Life is uncertain. Eat dessert first.
~ ERNESTINE ULMER

There's no insurance against death and poverty.
~ YIDDISH PROVERB

Try to Relax and Enjoy the Ride

Variety is the soul of pleasure.
~ APHRA BEHN

I have had more than half a century of such happiness. A great deal of worry and sorrow, too, but never a worry or a sorrow that was not offset by a purple iris, a lark, a bluebird, or a dewy morning glory.

～ MARY MCLEOD BETHUNE

It has never been, and never will be easy work! But the road that is built in hope is more pleasant to the traveler than the road built in despair, even though they both lead to the same destination.

～ MARION ZIMMER BRADLEY

When nothing is sure, everything is possible.

～ MARGARET DRABBLE

Most of life is choices, and the rest is pure dumb luck.

～ MARIAN ERICKSON

The most beautiful thing is inevitability of events, and the most ugly thing is trying to resist inevitability.

～ KATHERINE HATHAWAY

If we can recognize that change and uncertainty are basic principles, we can greet the future and the transformation we are undergoing with the understanding that we do not know enough to be pessimistic.

～ HAZEL HENDERSON

There will be something—anguish or elation—that is peculiar to this day alone. I rise from sleep and say: hail to the morning! come down to me, my beautiful unknown.

～ JESSICA POWERS

"The world is a wheel always turning," philosophized Mrs. Pelz. "Those who were high go down low, and those who've been low go up higher."

～ ANZIA YEZIERSKA

Uncharted Paths May Lead to Great Discoveries

I've learned that you'll never be disappointed if you always keep an eye on uncharted territory, where you'll be challenged and growing and having fun.

～ KIRSTIE ALLEY

Once you start asking questions, innocence is gone.

～ MARY ASTOR

The sad truth is that opportunity doesn't knock twice. You can put things off until tomorrow but tomorrow may never come. Where will you be a few years down the line? Will it be everything you dreamed of? We seal our fate with the choices we take, but don't give a second thought to the chances we take.

～ GLORIA ESTEFAN

Whenever you take a step forward, you are bound to disturb something.

～ INDIRA GANDHI

Isn't it splendid to think of all the things there are to find out about? It just makes me feel glad to be alive—it's such an interesting world. It wouldn't be half so interesting if we knew all about everything, would it? There'd be no scope for imagination then, would there?

～ L.M. MONTGOMERY

You May Not Like the End Result, But You Can Try Again

The two hardest things to handle in life are failure and success.

～ ANON.

It's astonishing in this world how things don't turn out at all the way you expect them to.

～ AGATHA CHRISTIE

Nature can seem cruel, but she balances her books.

~ ALISON LURIE

A finished person is a boring person.

~ ANNA QUINDLEN

Don't Be Afraid to Try

Fear is an emotion indispensable for survival.

~ HANNAH ARENDT

Anything I've ever done that ultimately was worthwhile ... initially scared me to death.

~ BETTY BENDER

You will suffer and you will have hurt. You will have joy and you will have peace.

~ ALISON CHEEK

No great deed is done by falterers who ask for certainty.

~ GEORGE ELIOT

It is vain to say human beings ought to be satisfied with tranquility: they must have action; and they will have it if they cannot find it.

~ GEORGE ELIOT

The sad truth is that opportunity doesn't knock twice. You can put things off until tomorrow but tomorrow may never come. Where will you be a few years down the line? Will it be everything you dreamed of? We seal our fate with the choices we take, but don't give a second thought to the chances we take.

~ GLORIA ESTEFAN

No rose without a thorn.

~ FRENCH PROVERB

There is a spirit and a need and a man at the beginning of every great human advance. Every one of these must be right for that particular moment of history, or nothing happens.

    ~ CORETTA SCOTT KING

Courage can't see around corners, but goes around them anyway.

    ~ MIGNON MCLAUGHLIN

Before you begin a thing remind yourself that difficulties and delays quite impossible to foresee are ahead.... You can only see one thing clearly, and that is your goal. Form a mental vision of that and cling to it through thick and thin.

    ~ KATHLEEN NORRIS

Freedom is not for the timid.

    ~ VIJAYA LAKSHMI PANDIT

The most ominous of fallacies: the belief that things can be kept static by inaction.

    ~ FREYA STARK

Be Flexible and Open to Possibilities

Fluidity and discontinuity are central to the reality in which we live.

    ~ MARY BATESON

One person's constant is another person's variable.

    ~ SUSAN GERHART

The world is quite right. It does not have to be consistent.

    ~ CHARLOTTE P. GILLMAN

Happiness is something that comes into our lives through doors we don't even remember leaving open.

    ~ ROSE WILDER LANE

Happiness Can Be Elusive

Results are what you expect; consequences are what you get.

~ ANON.

The trouble is not that we are never happy—it is that happiness is so episodical.

~ RUTH BENEDICT

Happiness is not a horse; you cannot harness it.

~ CHINESE PROVERB

*F*inding And Showing Courage

Tackle a Difficult Situation and the Next One May Seem Easier

The spirit of man is an inward flame; a lamp the world blows upon but never puts out.

~ MARGOT ASQUITH

As you get older, you find that often the wheat, disentangling itself from the chaff, comes out to meet you.

~ GWENDOLYN BROOKS

The soul should always stand ajar, ready to welcome the ecstatic experience.

~ EMILY DICKINSON

Courage is very important. Like a muscle, it is strengthened by use.

~ RUTH GORDON

Fear is a sign—usually a sign that I'm doing something right.

~ ERICA JONG

Fear is the single strongest motivating force in our lives.... The more frightened you become, the better your chances of achieving success.

~ LOIS KOREY

I became more courageous by doing the very things I needed to be courageous for—first, a little, and badly. Then, bit by bit, more and better. Being avidly—sometimes annoyingly—curious and persistent about discovering how others were doing what I wanted to do.

~ AUDRE LORDE

Courage is the ladder on which all the other virtues mount.

~ CLARE BOOTHE LUCE

I realized that if what we call human nature can be changed, then absolutely anything is possible. And from that moment, my life changed.

~ SHIRLEY MACLAINE

I am optimistic and confident in all that I do. I affirm only the best for myself and others. I am the creator of my life and my world. I meet daily challenges gracefully and with complete confidence. I fill my mind with positive, nurturing, and healing thoughts.

~ ALICE POTTER

I believe that anyone can conquer fear by doing the things he fears to do, provided he keeps doing them until he gets a record of successful experiences behind him.

~ ELEANOR ROOSEVELT

A woman's life can really be a succession of lives, each revolving around some emotionally compelling situation or challenge, and each marked off by some intense experience.

~ WALLIS SIMPSON, DUCHESS OF WINDSOR

Fear nothing, for every renewed effort raises all former failures into lessons, all sins into experience.

~ KATHERINE TINGLEY

A lion doesn't fear a fly.

~ YIDDISH PROVERB

If You Believe You Are Brave, Others Will Believe It, Too

There are some women who seem to be born without fear, just as there are people who are born without the ability to feel pain.... Providence appears to protect such women, maybe out of astonishment.

～ MARGARET ATWOOD

Any coward can fight a battle when he's sure of winning; but give me the man who has pluck to fight when he's sure of losing. That's my way, sir; and there are many victories worse than defeat.

～ GEORGE ELIOT

I think laughter may be a form of courage.... As humans we sometimes stand tall and look into the sun and laugh, and I think we are never more brave than when we do that.

～ LINDA ELLERBEE

I was nervous and confident at the same time, nervous about going out there in front of all of those people, with so much at stake, and confident that I was going to go out there and win.

～ ALTHEA GIBSON

It is best to act with confidence, no matter how little right you have to it.

～ LILLIAN HELLMAN

Grab the broom of anger and drive off the beast of fear.

～ ZORA NEALE HURSTON

I am not afraid.... I was born to do this.

～ JOAN OF ARC

Become so wrapped up in something that you forget to be afraid.

～ LADY BIRD JOHNSON

I have accepted fear as a part of my life—specifically the fear of change.... I have gone ahead despite the pounding in the heart that says: turn back.

～ ERICA JONG

To keep our faces toward change, and behave like free spirits in the presence of fate, is strength undefeatable.

~ HELEN KELLER

Being "brave" means doing or facing something frightening.... Being "fearless" means being without fear.

~ PENELOPE LEACH

I am deliberate and afraid of nothing.

~ AUDRE LORDE

If you are brave too often, people will come to expect it of you.

~ MIGNON MCLAUGHLIN

There ain't nothing from the outside can lick any of us.

~ MARGARET MITCHELL

There were always in me, two women at least, one woman desperate and bewildered, who felt she was drowning and another who would leap into a scene, as upon a stage, conceal her true emotions because they were weaknesses, helplessness, despair, and present to the world only a smile, an eagerness, curiosity, enthusiasm, interest.

~ ANAÏS NIN

I am optimistic and confident in all that I do. I affirm only the best for myself and others. I am the creator of my life and my world. I meet daily challenges gracefully and with complete confidence. I fill my mind with positive, nurturing, and healing thoughts.

~ ALICE POTTER

I'm not afraid of too many things, and I got that invincible kind of attitude from my father.

~ QUEEN LATIFAH

Kill the snake of doubt in your soul, crush the worms of fear in your heart, and mountains will move out of your way.

~ KATE SEREDY

The best protection any woman can have … is courage.

~ ELIZABETH CADY STANTON

Know That You Are Not Alone

Human beings need to belong to a tradition and equally need to know about the world in which they find themselves.

~ PAULA GUNN ALLEN

Fear knocked at the door. Faith answered. And lo, no one was there.

~ ANON.

There are some women who seem to be born without fear, just as there are people who are born without the ability to feel pain.... Providence appears to protect such women, maybe out of astonishment.

~ MARGARET ATWOOD

Courage is fear that has said its prayers.

~ DOROTHY BERNARD

Heroic deeds, to use whatever dower
Heaven has bestowed, to test our utmost power.

~ SARAH KNOWLES BOLTON

I think laughter may be a form of courage … as humans we sometimes stand tall and look into the sun and laugh, and I think we are never more brave than when we do that.

~ LINDA ELLERBEE

When life's problems seem overwhelming, look around and see what other people are coping with. You may consider yourself fortunate.

~ ANN LANDERS

Let us not fear the hidden. Or each other.

~ MURIEL RUKEYSER

Faith is the only known cure for fear.

~ LENA K. SADLER

Considering how dangerous everything is, nothing is really very frightening.

~ GERTRUDE STEIN

Life is to life in such a way that we are not afraid to die.

~ TERESA OF AVILA

Being Frightened and Overcoming Fear Helps You Grow

It is not in the still calm of life, or the repose of a pacific station, that great characters are formed ... great necessities call out great virtues.

~ ABIGAIL ADAMS

What I emphasize is for people to make choices based not on fear, but on what really gives them a sense of fulfillment.

~ PAULINE ROSE CHANCE

I wanted to be scared again.... I wanted to feel unsure again. That's the only way I learn, the only way I feel challenged.

~ CONNIE CHUNG

Fear is a sign—usually a sign that I'm doing something right.

~ ERICA JONG

A champion is afraid of losing. Everyone else is afraid of winning.

~ BILLIE JEAN KING

Life shrinks or expands in proportion to one's courage.

~ ANAÏS NIN

In order to feel anything, you need strength.

~ ANNA MARIA ORTESE

You gain strength, courage, and confidence by every experience in which you really stop to look fear in the face.

～ ELEANOR ROOSEVELT

Once You Have Developed Courage, It Is Yours for Life

Courage! I have shown it for years; think you I shall lose it at the moment when my sufferings are to end?

～ MARIE ANTOINETTE

I like the man who faces what he must,
With steps triumphant and a heart of cheer;
Who fights the daily battle without fear.

～ SARAH KNOWLES BOLTON

It isn't for the moment you are stuck that you need courage, but for the long uphill climb back to sanity and faith and security.

～ ANNE MORROW LINDBERGH

I survived my childhood by birthing many separate identities to stand in for one another in times of great stress and fear.

～ ROSEANNE

Your Courage Can Help Others to Be Brave

What after all has maintained the human race on this old globe, despite all the calamities of nature and all the tragic failings of mankind, if not the faith in new possibilities and the courage to advocate them?

～ JANE ADDAMS

Courage is what it takes to stand up and speak; courage is also what it takes to sit down and listen.

～ ANON.

It is brave to be involved.

~ GWENDOLYN BROOKS

To know how to say what others only know how to think is what
makes men poets or sages; and to dare to say what others only dare
to think makes men martyrs or reformers—or both.

~ ELIZABETH CHARLES

Courage to be is the key to revelatory power of the feminist revolution.

~ MARY DALY

The only failure a man ought to fear is failure in cleaving to the
purpose he sees to be best.

~ GEORGE ELIOT

Fear of success can also be tied into the idea that success means
someone else's loss. Some people are unconsciously guilty because
they believe their victories are coming at the expense of another.

~ JOAN C. HARVEY

I am not afraid.... I was born to do this.

~ JOAN OF ARC

To keep our faces toward change, and behave like free spirits in the
presence of fate, is strength undefeatable.

~ HELEN KELLER

My recipe for life is not being afraid of myself, afraid of what I think
or of my opinions.

~ EARTHA KITT

People living deeply have no fear of death.

~ ANAÏS NIN

Remember the dignity of your womanhood. Do not appeal, do not beg,
do not grovel. Take courage, join hands, stand beside us, fight with us.

~ CHRISTABEL PANKHURST

A brave man is seldom unkind.

~ PRETTY-SHIELD, CROW MEDICINE WOMAN

Every problem in your life goes away in front of a bull because this problem, the bull, is bigger than all other problems. Of course, I have fear, but it is fear that I will fail the responsibility I have taken on in front of all those people—not fear of the bull.

~ CRISTINA SANCHEZ

Truth is the only safe ground to stand upon.

~ ELIZABETH CADY STANTON

I never wanted to be a hero, but on the other hand I am not anxious to cultivate cowardice.

~ GERTRUDE STEIN

I am not afraid of a fight; I have to do my duty, come what may.

~ THÉRÈSE OF LISIEUX

In true courage there is always an element of choice, of an ethical choice, and of anguish, and also of action and deed. There is always a flame of spirit in it, a vision of some necessity higher than oneself.

~ BRENDA UELAND

It May Be Difficult to Be Courageous, But It's Worth the Effort

I am one of those people who can't help getting a kick out of life— even when it's a kick in the teeth.

~ POLLY ADLER

The brave man is not he who feels no fear,
For that were stupid and irrational;
But he, whose noble soul its fear subdues,
And barely dares the danger nature shrinks from.

~ JOANNA BAILLIE

It takes a lot of courage to show your dreams to someone else.

~ ERMA BOMBECK

Courage is the price that life exacts for granting peace.

~ AMELIA EARHART

Don't be afraid of hard work.

~ MARIAN WRIGHT EDELMAN

What we have most to fear is failure of the heart.

~ SONIA JOHNSON

Real courage is when you know you're licked before you begin, but you begin anyway and see it through no matter what.

~ HARPER LEE

Courage and clemency are equal virtues.

~ MARY DELARIVIÈRE MANLEY

If one is willing to do a thing he is afraid to do, he does not have to … face a situation fearlessly, and [if] there is no situation to face; it falls away of its own weight.

~ FLORENCE SCOVEL SHINN

Fear less, hope more; east less, chew more; whine less, breathe more; talk less, say more; love more, and all good things will be yours.

~ SWEDISH PROVERB

I have a lot of things to prove to myself. One is that I can live my life fearlessly.

~ OPRAH WINFREY

A Little Fear Can Be a Good Thing

I wanted to be scared again.... I wanted to feel unsure again. That's the only way I learn, the only way I feel challenged.

 ~ CONNIE CHUNG

Fear is a question: What are you afraid of, and why? Just as the seed of health is an illness, because illness contains information, our fears are a treasure house of self-knowledge if we explore them.

 ~ MARILYN FERGUSON

A champion is afraid of losing. Everyone else is afraid of winning.

 ~ BILLIE JEAN KING

You can't underestimate the power of fear.

 ~ PATRICIA NIXON

Don't Be Afraid of the Past

Comedy is tragedy plus time.

 ~ CAROL BURNETT

Courage is as often the outcome of despair as of hope; in the one case we have nothing to lose, in the other everything to gain.

 ~ DIANE DE POTTIERS

Only when we are no longer afraid do we begin to live.

 ~ DOROTHY THOMPSON

Fear nothing, for every renewed effort raises all former failures into lessons, all sins into experience.

 ~ KATHERINE TINGLEY

It takes great courage to break with one's past history and stand alone.

 ~ MARION WOODMAN

Don't Allow Fear to Immobilize You

Hope is the anchor of the soul, the stimulus to action, and the incentive to achievement.

~ ANON.

Introversion, at least if extreme, is a sign of mental and spiritual immaturity.

~ PEARL S. BUCK

Fear is the fire that melts Icarian wings.

~ FLORENCE EARLE COATES

Old age is no place for sissies.

~ BETTE DAVIS

Courage is as often the outcome of despair as of hope; in the one case we have nothing to lose, in the other everything to gain.

~ DIANE DE POTTIERS

Being old isn't for sissies.

~ MILLICENT FENWICK

There seemed to be endless obstacles—it seemed that the root cause of them all was fear.

~ JOANNA FIELD

Fear is created not by the world around us, but in the mind, by what we think is going to happen.

~ ELIZABETH GAWAIN

Many women miss their greatest chance of happiness through a want of courage in a decisive moment.

~ WINIFRED GORDON

All we are asked to bear we can bear. That is the law of the spiritual life. The only hindrance to the working of this law, as of all benign laws, is fear.

~ ELIZABETH GOUDGE

I have not ceased being fearful, but I have ceased to let fear control me.
～ ERICA JONG

Fear is the single strongest motivating force in our lives.… The more frightened you become, the better your chances of achieving success.
～ LOIS KOREY

It takes as much courage to have tried and failed as it does to have tried and succeeded.
～ ANNE MORROW LINDBERGH

The only courage that matters is the kind that gets you from one moment to the next.
～ MIGNON MCLAUGHLIN

How very little can be done under the spirit of fear.
～ FLORENCE NIGHTINGALE

Fear is one thing. To let fear grab you and swing you around by the tail is another.
～ KATHERINE PATERSON

However confused the scene of our life appears, however torn we may be who now do face that scene, it can be faced, and we can go on to be whole.
～ MURIEL RUKEYSER

The most destructive element in the human mind is fear. Fear creates aggressiveness; aggressiveness engenders hostility; hostility engenders fear—a disastrous circle.
～ DOROTHY THOMPSON

There are those who have discovered that fear is death in life, and have willingly risked physical death and loss of all that is considered valuable in order to live in freedom.
～ VIRGINIA BURDEN TOWER

Fear is faith that it won't work out.
～ SISTER MARY TRICKY

We are always afraid to start something that we want to make very good, true, and serious.

~ BRENDA UELAND

Women have to summon up courage to fulfill dormant dreams.

~ ALICE WALKER

I think that wherever your journey takes you, there are new gods waiting there, with divine patience—and laughter.

~ SUSAN M. WATKINS

Talent is helpful in writing, but guts are absolutely necessary.

~ JESSAMYN WEST

Use Your Fears and Challenges to Expand Your Mind

The habits of a vigorous mind are formed in contending with difficulties.

~ ABIGAIL ADAMS

The trouble with most people is that they think with their hopes or fears or wishes rather than with their minds.

~ NANCY ASTOR

I wanted to be scared again.... I wanted to feel unsure again. That's the only way I learn, the only way I feel challenged.

~ CONNIE CHUNG

Fear is a question: What are you afraid of, and why? Just as the seed of health is an illness, because illness contains information, our fears are a treasure house of self-knowledge if we explore them.

~ MARILYN FERGUSON

Courage is very important. Like a muscle, it is strengthened by use.

~ RUTH GORDON

I have lived my life according to this principle: If I'm afraid of it, then I must do it.

~ ERICA JONG

There is nothing in the universe that I fear, but that I shall not know all my duty or fail to do it.

~ MARY LYON

You gain strength, courage, and confidence by every experience in which you really stop to look fear in the face.

~ ELEANOR ROOSEVELT

I am never afraid of what I know.

~ ANNA SEWELL

A woman's life can really be a succession of lives, each revolving around some emotionally compelling situation or challenge, and each marked off by some intense experience.

~ WALLIS SIMPSON, DUCHESS OF WINDSOR

Many think they have a kind heart who only have weak nerves.

~ MARIE VON EBNER-ESCHENBACH

Love is what we are born with. Fear is what we learn.

~ MARIANNE WILLIAMSON

Make Your Own Way

What after all has maintained the human race on this old globe, despite all the calamities of nature and all the tragic failings of mankind, if not the faith in new possibilities and the courage to advocate them?

~ JANE ADDAMS

Courage is what it takes to stand up and speak; courage is also what it takes to sit down and listen.

~ ANON.

476

If you have enough fantasies, you're ready, in the event that something happens.

>　SHEILA BALLANTYNE

Never forget that life can only be nobly inspired and rightly lived if you take it bravely and gallantly, as a splendid adventure in which you are setting out into an unknown country, to meet many a joy, to find many a comrade, to win and lose many a battle.

>　ANNIE BESANT

Courage is the power to let go of the familiar.

>　MARY BRYANT

Catch courage.

>　CAROLYN HEILBRUN

Everyone has a talent. What is rare is the courage to nurture it in solitude and to follow the talent to the dark places where it leads.

>　ERICA JONG

I have accepted fear as a part of my life—specifically the fear of change.... I have gone ahead despite the pounding in the heart that says: turn back.

>　ERICA JONG

It takes courage to lead a life. Any life.

>　ERICA JONG

There is plenty of courage among us for the abstract, but not for the concrete.

>　HELEN KELLER

The fearful are caught as often as the bold.

>　HELEN KELLER

My imagination makes me human and makes me a fool; it gives me all the world and exiles me from it.

>　URSULA K. LE GUIN

Courage can't see around corners, but goes around them anyway.
~ MIGNON MCLAUGHLIN

To create one's own world in any of the arts takes courage.
~ GEORGIA O'KEEFE

When you have decided what you believe, what you feel must be
done, have the courage to stand alone and be counted.
~ ELEANOR ROOSEVELT

I have met brave women who are exploring the outer edge of
human possibility, with no history to guide them, and with a courage
to make themselves vulnerable that I find moving beyond words.
~ GLORIA STEINEM

There are those who have discovered that fear is death in life, and
have willingly risked physical death and loss of all that is considered
valuable in order to live in freedom.
~ VIRGINIA BURDEN TOWER

Think like a queen. A queen is not afraid to fail. Failure is another
steppingstone to greatness.
~ OPRAH WINFREY

*A*djusting to Change

Change Must Have Purpose to Be Truly Useful

Women must think strategically about creating ongoing pressure for change.

~ MARY BAKER

There may be ways in which we can work for change. We don't have to do dramatic things or devote our entire lives to it. We can lead normal lives but at the same time try hard not to be bystanders.

~ HELEN BAMBER

Life is change. Growth is optional. Choose wisely.

~ KAREN KAISER CLARK

The challenges of change are always hard. It is important that we begin to unpack those challenges that confront this nation and realize that we each have a role that requires us to change and become more responsible for shaping our own future.

~ HILLARY RODHAM CLINTON

Change is an easy panacea. It takes character to stay in one place and by happy there.

~ ELIZABETH CLARKE DUNN

They were so strong in their beliefs that there came a time when it hardly mattered what exactly those beliefs were; they all fused into a single stubbornness.

~ LOUISE ERDRICH

All change is not growth, as all movement is not forward.

~ ELLEN GLASGOW

The mind of the most logical thinker goes so easily from one point to another that it is not hard to mistake motion for progress.

~ MARGARET COLLIER GRAHAM

Our fathers valued change for the sake of its results; we value it in the act.

~ ALICE MEYNELL

Fear of Change is Fear of Life Itself

Life is measured by the rapidity of change, the succession of influences that modify the being.

~ GEORGE ELIOT

You don't have to be afraid of change. You don't have to worry about what's being taken away. Just look to see what's been added.

~ JACKIE GREER

It's the most unhappy people who most fear change.

~ MIGNON MCLAUGHLIN

Freedom to Change Is One of Life's Great Gifts

Change is the constant, the signal for rebirth, the egg of the phoenix.

~ CHRISTINA BALDWIN

Life is measured by the rapidity of change, the succession of influences that modify the being.

~ GEORGE ELIOT

Everyday life confronts us with new problems to be solved which force us to adjust our old programs accordingly.

~ DR. ANN FARADAY

No one can persuade another to change. Each of us guards a gate of change that can only be opened from the inside. We cannot open the gate of another, either by argument or emotional appeal.

~ MARILYN FERGUSON

Change occurs when one becomes what she is, not when she tries to become what she is not.

~ RUTH P. FREEDMAN

There is no good reason why we should not develop and change until the last day we live.

~ KAREN HORNEY

Happiness, to some, is elation; to others it is mere stagnation.

~ AMY LOWELL

It's the most unhappy people who most fear change.

~ MIGNON MCLAUGHLIN

The moment of change is the only poem.

~ ADRIENNE RICH

Changes are not only possible and predictable, but to deny them is to be an accomplice to one's own unnecessary vegetation.

~ GAIL SHEEHY

I have found that sitting in a place where you have never sat before can be inspiring.

~ DODIE SMITH

If we cannot do what we will, we must will what we can.

~ YIDDISH PROVERB

Flexibility and Change Are Necessary for Growth

You must change in order to survive.

~ PEARL BAILEY

True revolutions ... restore more than they destroy.

~ LOUISE BOGAN

People change and forget to tell each other.

~ LILLIAN HELLMAN

Individuals learn faster than institutions and it is always the dinosaur's brain that is the last to get the new messages.

~ HAZEL HENDERSON

We measure success and depth by length and time, but it is possible to have a deep relationship that doesn't always stay the same.

~ BARBARA HERSHEY

We're just getting started. We're just beginning to meet what will be the future—we've got the Model T.

~ GRACE MURRAY HOPPER

Continuity gives us roots; change gives us branches, letting us stretch and grow and reach new heights.

~ PAULINE R. KEZER

Nothing should be permanent except struggle with the dark side within ourselves.

~ SHIRLEY MACLAINE

A change of heart is the essence of all other change, and it has brought about me a reeducation of the mind.

      ∿ EMMELINE PETHICK-LAWRENCE

Things good in themselves ... perfectly valid in the integrity of their origins, become fetters if they cannot alter.

      ∿ FREYA STARK

Look at Change as an Opportunity

I've learned that you'll never be disappointed if you always keep an eye on uncharted territory, where you'll be challenged and growing and having fun.

      ∿ KIRSTIE ALLEY

One of the dreariest spots on life's road is the point of conviction that nothing will ever again happen to you.

      ∿ FAITH BALDWIN

Those interested in perpetuating present conditions are always in tears about the marvelous past that is about to disappear, without having so much as a smile for the young future.

      ∿ SIMONE DE BEAUVOIR

Variety is the soul of pleasure.

      ∿ APHRA BEHN

You don't have to be afraid of change. You don't have to worry about what's being taken away. Just look to see what's been added.

      ∿ JACKIE GREER

The most amazing thing about little children ... was their fantastic adaptability.

      ∿ KRISTIN HUNTER

To keep our faces toward change, and behave like free spirits in the presence of fate, is strength undefeatable.

~ HELEN KELLER

It's the most unhappy people who most fear change.

~ MIGNON MCLAUGHLIN

Let a man turn to his own childhood—no further—if he will renew his sense of remoteness, and of the mystery of change.

~ ALICE MEYNELL

Change Is Inevitable—Make the Best of It and Move On

Mourning is not forgetting.... It is an undoing. Every minute tie has to be untied and something permanent and valuable recovered and assimilated from the dust.

~ MARGERY ALLINGHAM

All love shifts and changes. I don't know if you can be wholeheartedly in love all the time.

~ JULIE ANDREWS

With renunciation life begins.

~ AMELIA BARR

It is never any good dwelling on goodbyes. It is not the being together that it prolongs, it is the parting.

~ ELIZABETH ASQUITH BIBESCO

Nothing fails like success; nothing is so defeated as yesterday's triumphant cause.

~ PHYLLIS MCGINLEY

Someday change will be accepted as life itself.

~ SHIRLEY MACLAINE

Let nothing disturb thee,
Let nothing affright thee,
All things are passing,
God changeth never.

~ TERESA OF AVILA

Nothing succeeds like failure.

~ REBECCA WEST

The things we fear most in organizations—fluctuations, disturbances, imbalances—are the primary sources of creativity.

~ MARGARET J. WHEATLEY

Awkward Changes Give Way to Important Growth

Every new truth begins in a shocking heresy.

~ MARGARET DELAND

When you have a baby, you set off an explosion in your marriage, and when the dust settles, your marriage is different from what it was. Not better, necessarily; not worse, necessarily; but different.

~ NORA EPHRON

Today's shocks are tomorrow's conventions.

~ CAROLYN HEILBRUN

Birth is violent, whether it be the birth of a child or the birth of an idea.

~ MARIANNE WILLIAMSON

Any truth creates a scandal.

~ MARGUERITE YOURCENAR

$\mathcal{G}$rowing from Adversity

Life's Challenges Make You Stronger

The habits of a vigorous mind are formed in contending with difficulties.

~ ABIGAIL ADAMS

In life as in the dance: Grace glides on blistered feet.

~ ALICE ABRAMS

I think there is this about the great troubles—they teach us the art of cheerfulness; whereas the small ones cultivate the industry of discontent.

~ MARY ADAMS

Time engraves our faces with all the tears we have not shed.

~ NATALIE CLIFFORD BARNEY

When something bad happens to me, I think I'm able to deal with it in a pretty good way. That makes me lucky. Some people fall apart at the first little thing that happens.

~ CHRISTIE BRINKLEY

I have always grown from my problems and challenges, from the things that didn't work out. That's when I've really learned.

~ CAROL BURNETT

Suffering raises up those souls that are truly great; it is only small souls that are made mean-spirited by it.

~ ALEXANDRA DAVID-NÉEL

A wounded deer leaps highest.

~ EMILY DICKINSON

To live is to suffer, to survive is to find some meaning in the suffering.

~ ROBERTA FLACK

Experience may be hard but we claim its gifts because they are real, even though our feet bleed on its stones.

~ MARY PARKER FOLLETT

At every step the child should be allowed to meet the real experience of life; the thorns should never be plucked from his roses.

~ ELLEN KEY

I think my biggest achievement is that after going through a rather difficult time, I consider myself comparatively sane. I'm proud of that.

~ JACQUELINE KENNEDY ONASSIS

It is the north wind that lashes men into Vikings; it is the soft, luscious south wind which lulls them into lotus dreams.

~ OUIDA

Difficulties, opposition, criticism—these things are meant to be overcome, and there is a special joy in facing them and in coming out on top. It is only when there is nothing but praise that life loses its charm and I begin to wonder what I should do about it.

~ VIJAYA LAKSHMI PANDIT

They sicken of calm, who know the storm.

~ DOROTHY PARKER

Troubles cured you salty as a country ham, smoky to the taste, thick-skinned and tender inside.

~ MARGE PIERCY

What was hard to bear is sweet to remember.

~ PORTUGESE PROVERB

And I think that's important, to know how the water's gone over the dam before you start to describe it. It helps to have been over the dam yourself.

~ E. ANNIE PROULX

Every time you meet a situation, though you think at the time it is an impossibility and you go through the torture of the damned, once you have met it and lived through it, you find that forever after you are freer than you were before.

~ ELEANOR ROOSEVELT

Women are like tea bags; put them in hot water and they get stronger.

~ ELEANOR ROOSEVELT

Without the burden of afflictions it is impossible to reach the height of grace. The gift of grace increases as the struggles increase.

~ SAINT ROSE OF LIMA

To be tested is good. The challenged life may be the best therapist.

~ GAIL SHEEHY

The secret of a leader lies in the tests he has faced over the whole course of his life and the habit of action he develops in meeting those tests.

~ GAIL SHEEHY

It constantly happens that the Lord permits a soul to fall so that it may grow humbler.

~ TERESA OF AVILA

Challenges make you discover things about yourself that you never really knew. They're what make the instrument stretch, what make you go beyond the norm.

~ CICELY TYSON

Things Worth Having May Come at a Cost

It is not in the still calm of life, or the repose of a pacific station, that great characters are formed ... great necessities call out great virtues.

~ ABIGAIL ADAMS

I have always fought for ideas—until I learned that it isn't ideas but grief, struggle, and flashes of vision which enlighten.

~ MARGARET ANDERSON

Pleasure is not pleasant unless it cost dear.

~ ANON.

Experience is a good teacher, but she sends in terrific bills.

~ MINNA ANTRIM

I have had more than half a century of such happiness. A great deal of worry and sorrow, too, but never a worry or a sorrow that was not offset by a purple iris, a lark, a bluebird, or a dewy morning glory.

~ MARY MCLEOD BETHUNE

In order to have great happiness, you have to have great pain and unhappiness—otherwise how would you know when you're happy?

~ LESLIE CARON

A gem cannot be polished without friction, nor a person perfected without trials.

~ CHINESE PROVERB

There is little place in the political scheme of things for an independent, creative personality, for a fighter. Anyone who takes that role must pay a price.

~ SHIRLEY CHISHOLM

The thing that makes you exceptional, if you are at all, is inevitably that which must also make you lonely.

~ LORRAINE HANSBURY

Comfort is not known if poverty does not come before it.

~ IRISH PROVERB

Flowers grow out of dark moments.

~ CORITA KENT

There is no victory without pain.

~ LOLITA LEBRON

People who are born even-tempered, placid and untroubled—secure from violent passions or temptations to evil—those who have never needed to struggle all night with the angel to emerge lame but victorious at dawn, never become great saints.

~ EVA LE GALLIENNE

It is somehow reassuring to discover that the word "travel" is derived from "travail," denoting the pains of childbirth.

~ JESSICA MITFORD

Those who don't know how to weep with their whole heart don't know how to laugh either.

~ GOLDA MEIR

Excellence costs a great deal.

~ MAY SARTON

If you want a place in the sun, you've got to put up with a few blisters.

~ ABIGAIL VAN BUREN

He who serves God with what costs him nothing, will do very little service, you may depend on it.

~ SUSAN WARNER

Failure Teaches Us How to Succeed

Three failures denotes uncommon strength. A weakling had not enough grit to fail thrice.

~ MINNA ANTRIM

I have always grown from my problems and challenges, from the things that didn't work out. That's when I've really learned.

~ CAROL BURNETT

This struggle of people against their conditions, this is where you find the meaning in life.

~ ROSE CHERNIN

A gem cannot be polished without friction, nor a person perfected without trials.

~ CHINESE PROVERB

I have learned in the great University of Hard Knocks a philosophy that no woman who has had an easy life ever acquires. I have learned to live each day as it comes, and not to borrow trouble by dreading tomorrow. It is the dark menace of the future that makes cowards of us.

~ DOROTHY DIX

If I win several tournaments in a row, I get so confident I'm in a cloud. A loss gets me eager again.

~ CHRIS EVERT

It is only after an unknown number of unrecorded labors, after a host of noble hearts have succumbed in discouragement, convinced that their cause is lost; it is only then that cause triumphs.

~ MADAME GUIZOT

Happiness is to take up the struggle in the midst of the raging storm, not to pluck the lute in the moonlight or recite poetry among the blossoms.

⌒ DING LING

Until you've lost your reputation, you never realize what a burden it was or what freedom really is.

⌒ MARGARET MITCHELL

If ambition doesn't hurt you, you haven't got it.

⌒ KATHLEEN NORRIS

I think my biggest achievement is that after going through a rather difficult time, I consider myself comparatively sane. I'm proud of that.

⌒ JACQUELINE KENNEDY ONASSIS

The secret of a leader lies in the tests he has faced over the whole course of his life and the habit of action he develops in meeting those tests.

⌒ GAIL SHEEHY

When You Hit Bottom, There's Nowhere to Go but Up

The unendurable is the beginning of the curve of joy.

⌒ DJUNA BARNES

I have had more than half a century of such happiness. A great deal of worry and sorrow, too, but never a worry or a sorrow that was not offset by a purple iris, a lark, a bluebird, or a dewy morning glory.

⌒ MARY MCLEOD BETHUNE

The thought that we are enduring the unendurable is one of the things that keeps us going.

⌒ MOLLY HASKELL

I have been in sorrow's kitchen and licked out all the pots. Then I have stood on the peaky mountain wrapped in rainbows, with a harp and sword in my hands.

~ ZORA NEALE HURSTON

There is often in people to whom "the worst" has happened an almost transcendent freedom, for they have faced "the worst" and survived it.

~ CAROL PEARSON

And I think that's important, to know how the water's gone over the dam before you start to describe it. It helps to have been over the dam yourself.

~ E. ANNIE PROULX

A blustering night, a fair day follows.

~ SPANISH PROVERB

In my end is my beginning.

~ MARY STUART

The sun shines brighter after a shower.

~ YIDDISH PROVERB

Through Adversity, We Learn How Strong We Can Be

My unreality is chiefly this: I have never felt much like a human being. It's a splendid feeling.

~ MARGARET ANDERSON

A diamond is a chunk of coal that made good under pressure.

~ ANON.

If you haven't had at least a slight poetic crack in the heart, you have been cheated by nature.

~ PHYLLIS BATTELLE

When something bad happens to me, I think I'm able to deal with it in a pretty good way. That makes me lucky. Some people fall apart at the first little thing that happens.

　～ CHRISTIE BRINKLEY

True knowledge comes only through suffering.

　～ ELIZABETH BARRETT BROWNING

Suffering raises up those souls that are truly great; it is only small souls that are made mean-spirited by it.

　～ ALEXANDRA DAVID-NÉEL

He disposes Doom who hath suffered him.

　～ EMILY DICKINSON

Prosperity provideth, but adversity proveth friends.

　～ QUEEN ELIZABETH I

Suffering has always been with us, does it really matter in what form it comes? All that matters is how we bear it and how we fit it into our lives.

　～ ETTY HILLESUM

At every step the child should be allowed to meet the real experience of life; the thorns should never be plucked from his roses.

　～ ELLEN KEY

You can't be brave if you've only had wonderful things happen to you.

　～ MARY TYLER MOORE

In all things preserve integrity; and the consciousness of thine own uprightness will alleviate the toil of business, soften the hardness of ill-success and disappointments, and give thee an humble confidence before God, when the ingratitude of man, or the iniquity of the times may rob thee of other rewards.

　～ BARBARA PALEY

Difficulties, opposition, criticism—these things are meant to be overcome, and there is a special joy in facing them and in coming out on top. It is only when there is nothing but praise that life loses its charm and I begin to wonder what I should do about it.

⌒ VIJAYA LAKSHMI PANDIT

Troubles cured you salty as a country ham, smoky to the taste, thick-skinned and tender inside.

⌒ MARGE PIERCY

Every time you meet a situation, though you think at the time it is an impossibility and you go through the torture of the damned, once you have met it and lived through it, you find that forever after you are freer than you were before.

⌒ ELEANOR ROOSEVELT

Women are like tea bags; put them in hot water and they get stronger.

⌒ ELEANOR ROOSEVELT

Without the burden of afflictions it is impossible to reach the height of grace. The gift of grace increases as the struggles increase.

⌒ SAINT ROSE OF LIMA

However confused the scene of our life appears, however torn we may be who now do face that scene, it can be faced, and we can go on to be whole.

⌒ MURIEL RUKEYSER

Hot water is my native element. I was in it as a baby, and I have never seemed to get out of it ever since.

⌒ DAME EDITH SITWELL

If you have to be careful because of oppression and censorship, this pressure produces diamonds.

⌒ TATYANA TOLSTAYA

We say: mad with joy. We should say: wise with grief.

⌒ MARGUERITE YOURCENAR

Be Thankful for Your Trials and All They Teach You

If you have been sunned through and through like an apricot on a wall from your earliest days, you are oversensitive to any withdrawal of heat.
~ MARGOT ASQUITH

Everybody's heart is open, you know, when they have recently escaped from severe pain, or are recovering the blessing of health.
~ JANE AUSTEN

Time engraves our faces with all the tears we have not shed.
~ NATALIE CLIFFORD BARNEY

A major advantage of age is learning to accept people without passing judgment.
~ LIZ CARPENTER

There are some things you learn best in calm, and some in storm.
~ WILLA CATHER

I think these difficult times have helped me to understand better than before how infinitely rich and beautiful life is in every way that so many things that one goes around worrying about are of no importance whatsoever.
~ ISAK DINESEN

Character cannot be developed in ease and quiet. Only through experience of trial and suffering can the soul be strengthened, ambition inspired, and success achieved.
~ HELEN KELLER

Birds sing after a storm; why shouldn't people feel as free to delight in whatever remains to them?
~ ROSE KENNEDY

Delicious tears! The heart's own dew.
~ L.E. LANDON

Everything in life that we really accept undergoes a change. So suffering must become love. That is the mystery.
~ KATHERINE MANSFIELD

In a way, winter is the real spring, the time when the inner things happen, the resurge of nature.
~ EDNA O'BRIEN

The secret of a leader lies in the tests he has faced over the whole course of his life and the habit of action he develops in meeting those tests.
~ GAIL SHEEHY

Those who have suffered understand suffering and therefore extend their hand.
~ PATTI SMITH

By becoming more unhappy, we sometimes learn how to be less so.
~ ANNE-SOPHIE SWETCHINE

The saints rejoiced at injuries and persecutions, because in forgiving them they had something to present to God when they prayed to Him.
~ TERESA OF AVILA

Challenges make you discover things about yourself that you never really knew. They're what make the instrument stretch, what make you go beyond the norm.
~ CICELY TYSON

Oh, the blues ain't nothing but a good woman feeling bad.
~ GEORGIA WHITE

Like soap for the body so are tears for the soul.
~ YIDDISH PROVERB

Your Heart and Soul Are Stronger Than You Know

A broken heart is what makes life so wonderful five years later, when you see the guy in an elevator and he is fat and smoking a cigar and saying "long-time-no-see." If he hadn't broken your heart, you couldn't have that glorious feeling of relief!

～ PHYLLIS BATTELLE

I am not soft. It is better to be hard, so that you can know what to do.

～ PEARL S. BUCK

It is only the women whose eyes have been washed clear with tears who get the broad vision that makes them little sisters to all the world.

～ DOROTHY DIX

When you can't remember why you're hurt, that's when you're healed. When you have to work real hard to re-create the pain, and you can't quite get there, that's when you're better.

～ JANE FONDA

People are like stained-glass windows. They sparkle and shine when the sun is out, but when the darkness sets in, their true beauty is revealed only if there is a light from within.

～ ELISABETH KUBLER-ROSS

I think hearts are very much like glasses—if they do not break with the first ring, they usually last a considerable time.

～ L.E. LANDON

A good cry lightens the heart.

～ YIDDISH PROVERB

Today's Adversity May Bring Tomorrow's Opportunity

If we had no winter, the spring would not be so pleasant; if we did not sometimes taste of adversity, prosperity would not be so welcome.

~ ANNE BRADSTREET

As you get older, you find that often the wheat, disentangling itself from the chaff, comes out to meet you.

~ GWENDOLYN BROOKS

There is little place in the political scheme of things for an independent, creative personality, for a fighter. Anyone who takes that role must pay a price.

~ SHIRLEY CHISHOLM

You don't develop courage by being happy in your relationships everyday. You develop it by surviving difficult times and challenging adversity.

~ BARBARA DE ANGELIS

Sorrow has its reward. It never leaves us where it found us.

~ MARY BAKER EDDY

The most valuable gift I ever received was the gift of insecurity my father left us. My mother's love might not have prepared me for life the way my father's departure did. He forced us out on the road, where we had to earn our bread.

~ LILLIAN GISH

Your first big trouble can be a bonanza if you live through it. Get through the first trouble, and you'll probably make it through the next one.

~ RUTH GORDON

I thank God for my handicaps for, through them, I have found myself, my work, and my God.

~ HELEN KELLER

Being disabled gave me an immense advantage. People are kinder to you. It puts you on a different level than if you go into a situation whole and secure.

~ DOROTHEA LANGE

Often God has to shut a door in our face, so that He can subsequently open the door through which He wants us to go.

~ CATHARINE MARSHALL

Not being beautiful was the true blessing.... Not being beautiful forced me to develop my inner resources. The pretty girl has a handicap to overcome.

~ GOLDA MEIR

If a door slams shut it means that God is pointing to an open door further on down.

~ ANNA DELANEY PEALE

Supporting myself at an early age was the best training for life I could have possibly received.

~ LEA THOMPSON

If You Play it Safe, You Can Never Win Big

Pleasure is not pleasant unless it cost dear.

~ ANON.

If I win several tournaments in a row, I get so confident I'm in a cloud. A loss gets me eager again.

~ CHRIS EVERT

And remember, expect nothing and life will be velvet.

~ LISA GARDINER

Those lose least who have least to lose.

~ ROSE O'NEIL

True feeling justifies, whatever it may cost.

~ MAY SARTON

Taking One Day at a Time

A Little Progress Every Day Produces Satisfying Results

Home wasn't built in a day.
~ JANE ACE

Happiness is a tide: it carries you only a little way at a time; but you have covered a vast space before you know that you are moving at all.
~ MARY ADAMS

Yard by yard, it's very hard. But inch by inch, it's a cinch.
~ ANON.

I never stop to plan. I take things step-by-step.
~ MARY MCLEOD BETHUNE

Youth is the time of getting, middle age of improving, and old age of spending.
~ ANNE BRADSTREET

You don't just luck into things.... You build step by step, whether it's friendships or opportunities.

~ BARBARA BUSH

If we take care of the moments, the years will take care of themselves.

~ MARIA EDGEWORTH

My parents told me that people will never know how long it takes you to do something. They will only know how well it is done.

~ NANCY HANKS

The only way to find out if you can write is to set aside a certain period every day and try. Save enough money to give yourself six months to be a full-time writer. Work every day and the pages will pile up.

~ JUDITH KRANTZ

There are very few human beings who receive the truth, complete and staggering, by instant illumination. Most of them acquire it fragment by fragment, on a small scale, by successive developments, cellularly, like a laborious mosaic.

~ ANAÏS NIN

Connections are made slowly, sometimes they grow underground.

~ MARGE PIERCY

Instead of thinking about where you are, think about where you want to be. It takes twenty years of hard work to become an overnight success.

~ DIANA RANKIN

The world doesn't come to the clever folks, it comes to the stubborn, obstinate, one-idea-at-a-time people.

~ MARY ROBERTS RINEHART

Human successes, like human failures, are composed of one action at a time and achieved by one person at a time.

~ PATTY H. SAMPSON

It takes time, love, and support to find peace with the restless one.
~ DEIDRE SARAULT

Inspiration does not come like a bolt, nor is it kinetic energy striving, but it comes to us slowly and quietly and all the time.
~ BRENDA UELAND

Quiet streams erode the shore.
~ YIDDISH PROVERB

Keep Moving toward Your Goal

I'm not there yet, but I'm closer than I was yesterday.
~ ANON.

The growth of understanding follows an ascending spiral rather than a straight line.
~ JOANNA FIELD

I look at victory as milestones on a very long highway.
~ JOAN BENOIT SAMUELSON

It's a long old road, but I know I'm gonna find the end.
~ BESSIE SMITH

No first step can be really great; it must of necessity possess more of prophecy than of achievement; nevertheless it is by the first step that a man marks the value, not only of his cause, but of himself.
~ KATHERINE CECIL THURSTON

Everyone Can Make a Difference

Let me tell thee, time is a very precious gift of God; so precious that He only gives it to us moment by moment. He would not have thee waste it.

~ AMELIA BARR

One of the greatest evils of the day among those outside of prison is their sense of futility. Young people say, What is the sense of our small effort? They cannot see that we must lay one brick at a time, take one step at a time; we can be responsible only for the one action of the present moment.

~ DOROTHY DAY

If you don't like the way the world is, you change it. You have an obligation to change it. You just do it one step at a time.

~ MARIAN WRIGHT EDELMAN

We must not, in trying to think about how we can make a big difference, ignore the small daily differences we can make which, over time, add up to big differences that we often cannot foresee.

~ MARION WRIGHT EDELMAN

Step Back to View Your Progress—Or Just to Relax

Leisure for reverie, gay or somber, does much to enrich life.

~ MIRIAM BEARD

I am convinced that there are times in everybody's experience when there is so much to be done, that the only way to do it is to sit down and do nothing.

~ FANNY FERN

One by one the sands are flowing,
One by one the moments fall;
Some are coming, some are going;
Do not strive to grasp them all.

〜 ADELAIDE PROCTOR

I learned … that inspiration does not come like a bolt, nor is it kinetic, energetic, striving, but it comes to us slowly and quietly and all the time, though we must regularly and every day give it a little chance to start flowing, prime it with a little solitude and idleness.

〜 BRENDA UELAND

Don't Worry about Tomorrow

There is hope for all of us. Well, anyway, if you don't die you live through it, day in, day out.

〜 MARY BECKETT

It is only possible to live happily-ever-after on a day-to-day basis.

〜 MARGARET BONNANO

Don't Be Discouraged By Setbacks

Sadness and gladness succeed each other.

〜 ANON.

Regression in grief must be seen and supported as a means toward adaptation and health.

〜 LILY PINCUS

See how time makes all grief decay.

〜 ADELAIDE PROCTOR

Even the Grandest Plan Has Small but Necessary Steps

Every worthwhile accomplishment, big or little, has its stages of drudgery and triumph; a beginning, a struggle, and a victory.
~ ANON.

If we take care of the moments, the years will take care of themselves.
~ MARIA EDGEWORTH

Cultural transformation announces itself in sputtering fits and starts, sparked here and there by minor incidents, warmed by new ideas that may smolder for decades. In many different places, at different times, the kindling is laid for the real conflagration—the one that will consume the old landmarks and alter the landscape forever.
~ MARILYN FERGUSON

It is not the straining for great things that is most effective; it is the doing the little things, the common duties, a little better and better.
~ ELIZABETH STUART PHELPS

Connections are made slowly, sometimes they grow underground.
~ MARGE PIERCY

We can do no great things—only small things with great love.
~ MOTHER TERESA

One only gets to the top rung of the ladder by steadily climbing up one at a time, and suddenly all sorts of powers, all sorts of abilities which you thought never belonged to you—suddenly become within your own possibility and you think, "Well, I'll have a go, too."
~ MARGARET THATCHER

Live in the Moment

Acting can work a peculiar magic on the actor.... It can cure you (at least for the length of a performance) of a whole variety of ailments. Migraine headaches, miserable colds or toothaches will suddenly disappear as you're up there going through your paces.

~ BARBARA HARRIS

Life is a succession of moments. To live each one is to succeed.

~ CORITA KENT

Love the moment and the energy of the moment will spread beyond all boundaries.

~ CORITA KENT

You have to count on living every single day in a way you believe will make you feel good about your life, so that if it were over tomorrow, you'd be content.

~ JANE SEYMOUR

Having Vision

Imagine, And Make Your Dreams Reality

Imagination is the highest kite that can fly.
～ LAUREN BACALL

Make-believe colors the past with innocent distortion, and it swirls ahead of us in a thousand ways—in science, in politics, in every bold intention. It is part of our collective lives, entwining our past and our future ... a particularly rewarding aspect of life itself.
～ SHIRLEY TEMPLE BLACK

By going over your day in imagination before you begin it, you can begin acting successfully at any moment.
～ DOROTHEA BRANDE

Man's mind is not a container to be filled but rather a fire to be kindled.
～ DOROTHEA BRANDE

Imagination took the reins, and Reason, slow-paced, though sure-footed, was unequal to a race with so eccentric and flighty a companion.
～ FANNY BURNEY

We are governed not by armies, but by ideas.

~ MONA CAIRD

That's what being young is all about. You have the courage and the daring to think that you can make a difference.

~ RUBY DEE

What man can imagine he may one day achieve.

~ NANCY HALE

All acts performed in the world begin in the imagination.

~ BARBARA GRIZZUTI HARRISON

Who would ever give up the reality of dreams for relative knowledge?

~ ALICE JAMES

Art is the objectification of feeling.

~ SUZANNE K. LANGER

I believe that each work of art, whether it is a work of great genius, or something very small, comes to the artist and says, "Here I am. Enflesh me. Give birth to me."

~ MADELEINE L'ENGLE

A daydreamer is prepared for most things.

~ JOYCE CAROL OATES

All prosperity begins in the mind and is dependent only upon the full use of our creative imagination.

~ RUTH ROSS

Dreams are the sources of action, the meeting and the end, a resting place among the flight of things.

~ MURIEL RUKEYSER

One of your most powerful inner resources is your own creativity. Be willing to try on something new and play the game full-out.

~ MARCIA WIEDER

If You Have Vision, You Will Always Have Hope

Some of my best friends are illusions. Been sustaining me for years.
~ SHEILA BALLANTYNE

Those interested in perpetuating present conditions are always in
tears about the marvelous past that is about to disappear, without
having so much as a smile for the young future.
~ SIMONE DE BEAUVOIR

Inside myself is a place where I live alone and that's where you
renew your springs that never dry up.
~ PEARL S. BUCK

If I had influence with the good fairy who is supposed to preside
over the christening of all children I should ask that her gift to each
child in the world be a sense of wonder so indestructible that it
would last throughout life, as an unfailing antidote against the
boredom and disenchantments of later years, the sterile
preoccupation with things that are artificial, the alienation from the
sources of our strength.
~ RACHEL CARSON

If we have not achieved our early dreams, we must either find new
ones or see what we can salvage from the old. If we have
accomplished what we set out to do in our youth, we need not weep
like Alexander the Great that we have no more worlds to conquer.
~ ROSALYNN CARTER

Within your heart, keep one still, secret spot where dreams may go.
~ LOUISE DRISCOLL

No vision and you perish;
No ideal, and you're lost;
Your heart must ever cherish
Some faith at any cost.
Some hope, some dream to cling to,
Some rainbow in the sky,
Some melody to sing to,
Some service that is high.

　　　　　～ HARRIET DU AUTERMONT

With our progress we have destroyed our only weapon against
tedium: that rare weakness we call imagination.

　　　　　～ ORIANA FALLACI

When we can't dream any longer, we die.

　　　　　～ EMMA GOLDMAN

A healthful hunger for a great idea is the beauty and blessedness of life.

　　　　　～ JEAN INGELOW

Never turn down a job because you think it's too small; you never
know where it may lead.

　　　　　～ JULIA MORGAN

The song that we hear with our ears is only the song that is sung in
our hearts.

　　　　　～ OUIDA

Planning Gives Substance to Your Vision

To look backward for a while is to refresh the eye, to restore it, and
to render it more fit for its prime function of looking forward.

　　　　　～ MARGARET FAIRLESS BARBER

A problem clearly stated is a problem half solved.

　　　　　～ DOROTHEA BRANDE

The insight to see possible new paths, the courage to try them, the judgment to measure results—these are the qualities of a leader.

∿ MARY PARKER FOLLETT

The best impromptu speeches are the ones written well in advance.

∿ RUTH GORDON

Every day give yourself a good mental shampoo.

∿ SARA JORDON

Sometimes a person has to go back, really back—to have a sense, an understanding of all that's gone to make them—before they can go forward.

∿ PAULE MARSHALL

The engineering is secondary to the vision.

∿ CYNTHIA OZICK

Keep an Open Mind and Let Ideas Flow Freely

What a surprise to find you could shift the contents of your head like rearranging furniture in a room.

∿ LISA ALTHER

Four be the things I am wisest to know: idleness, sorrow, a friend, and a foe.

∿ ANON.

Little girls are cute and small only to adults. To one another they are not cute. They are life-sized.

∿ MARGARET ATWOOD

You can always trust information given you by people who are crazy; they have an access to truth not available through regular channels.

∿ SHEILA BALLANTYNE

There are no little events in life, those we think of no consequence may be full of fate, and it is at our own risk if we neglect the acquaintances and opportunities that seem to be casually offered, and of small importance.

~ AMELIA BARR

Where there is an open mind, there will always be a frontier.

~ DOROTHEA BRANDE

I've dreamt in my life dreams that have stayed with me ever after, and changed my ideas: they've gone through and through me, like wine through water, and altered the color of my mind.

~ EMILY BRONTË

Opportunities are often things you haven't noticed the first time around.

~ CATHERINE DENEUVE

Some people go through a forest and see no firewood.

~ ENGLISH PROVERB

A closed mind is a dying mind.

~ EDNA FERBER

Creativeness often consists of merely turning up what is already there. Did you know that right and left shoes were thought up only a little more than a century ago?

~ BERNICE FITZ-GIBBON

Conflict is resolved not through compromise, but through invention.

~ MARY PARKER FOLLETT

Creative minds have always been known to survive any kind of bad training.

~ ANNA FREUD

Off-the-rack solutions, like bargain basement dresses, never fit anymore.

~ FRANCOISE GIROUD

514

The most beautiful thing is inevitability of events, and the most ugly thing is trying to resist inevitability.

~ KATHERINE HATHAWAY

I have tried to be as eclectic as I possibly can with my professional life, and so far it's been pretty fun.

~ HOLLY HUNTER

Anything, everything can be learned if you can just get yourself in a little patch of real ground, real nature, real woods, real anything … and just sit still and watch.

~ LAUREN HUTTON

The trouble with most people is they think there's only one right way to do anything.

~ VELDA JOHNSTON

That's the way things become clear. All of a sudden. And then you realize how obvious they've been all along.

~ MADELEINE L'ENGLE

Underground issues from one relationship or context invariably fuel our fires in another.

~ HARRIET LERNER

As the traveler who has once been from home is wiser than he who has never left his own doorstep, so a knowledge of one other culture should sharpen our ability to scrutinize more steadily, to appreciate lovingly, our own.

~ MARGARET MEAD

Her mind traveled crooked streets and aimless goat paths, arriving sometimes at profundity, other times at the revelations of a three-year-old.

~ TONI MORRISON

A great novel is a kind of conversion experience. We come away from it changed.

~ KATHERINE PATERSON

We have thought that because children are young they are silly. We have forgotten the blind stirrings, the reaching outward of our own youth.
～ MABEL LOUISE ROBINSON

Every day is a messenger of God.
～ RUSSIAN PROVERB

Great imaginations are apt to work from hints and suggestions and a single moment of emotion is sometimes sufficient to create a masterpiece.
～ MARGARET SACKVILLE

It is seldom in life that one knows that a coming event is to be of crucial importance.
～ ANYA SETON

Parents learn a lot from their children about coping with life.
～ MURIEL SPARK

We start out in our lives as little children, full of light and the clearest vision.
～ BRENDA UELAND

A mind enclosed in language is in prison.
～ SIMONE WEIL

Children, like animals, use all their senses to discover the world. Then artists come along and discover it the same way all over again.
～ EUDORA WELTY

In their sympathies, children feel nearer animals than adults. They frolic with animals, caress them, share with them feelings neither has any words for.
～ JESSAMYN WEST

There can be no one best way of organizing a business.
～ JOANNE WOODWARD

No answer is also an answer.
～ YIDDISH PROVERB

Stubbornness is the greatest ill.
～ YIDDISH PROVERB

Your Vision May Impact Others

Real education should educate us out of self into something far
finer; into a selflessness which links us with all humanity.
～ NANCY ASTOR

We look into mirrors, but we only see the effects of our times on
us—not our effects on others.
～ PEARL BAILEY

Your audience gives you everything you need. They tell you. There is
no director who can direct you like an audience.
～ FANNY BRICE

We must not, in trying to think about how we can make a big
difference, ignore the small daily differences we can make which,
over time, add up to big differences that we often cannot foresee.
～ MARIAN WRIGHT EDELMAN

Columbus only discovered that he was in some new place. He didn't
discover America.
～ LOUISE ERDRICH

People who concentrate on giving good service always get more
personal satisfaction as well as better business. How can we get better
service? One way is by trying to see ourselves as others do.
～ PATRICIA FRIPP

A bad cause requires many words.
～ GERMAN PROVERB

When I'm gone, somebody else will take it up and do it. This is how we've lived all these years.

~ CLARA MCBRIDE HALE

It is the function of art to renew our perception. What we are familiar with we cease to see. The writer shakes up the familiar scene, and, as if by magic, we see a new meaning in it.

~ ANAÏS NIN

Only when men are connected to large, universal goals are they really happy—and one result of their happiness is a rush of creative activity.

~ JOYCE CAROL OATES

The artist is the voice of the people.

~ ALICE WALKER

Those with Vision Are Not Limited by Their Physical Being

Some of my best friends are illusions. Been sustaining me for years.

~ SHEILA BALLANTYNE

You can imprison a man, but not an idea. You can exile a man, but not an idea. You can kill a man, but not an idea.

~ BENAZIR BHUTTO

Death is the last enemy: once we've got past that I think everything will be all right.

~ ALICE THOMAS ELLIS

Children seldom have a proper sense of their own tragedy, discounting and keeping hidden the true horrors of their short lives, humbly imagining real calamity to be some prestigious drama of the grown-up world.

~ SHIRLEY HAZZARD

One may have good eyes and yet see nothing.
～ ITALIAN PROVERB

There is no balking genius. Only death can silence it or hinder.
～ ELLA WHEELER WILCOX

Not Everyone Will Agree with Your Vision

No one can figure out your worth but you.
～ PEARL BAILEY

Prejudices, it is well known, are most difficult to eradicate from the heart whose soil has never been loosened or fertilized by education; they grow there, firm as weeds among rocks.
～ CHARLOTTE BRONTË

Creative minds have always been known to survive any kind of bad training.
～ ANNA FREUD

A bad cause requires many words.
～ GERMAN PROVERB

Art is not for the cultivated taste. It is to cultivate taste.
～ NIKKI GIOVANNI

Most of the basic truths of life sound absurd at first hearing.
～ ELIZABETH GOUDGE

Art is a wicked thing. It is what we are.
～ GEORGIA O'KEEFE

The Ability to Have Vision Is a Great Gift

Genius is the talent for seeing things straight. It is seeing things in a straight line without any bend or break or aberration of sight, seeing them as they are, without any warping of vision. Flawless mental sight! That is genius.

～ MAUDE ADAMS

I've dreamt in my life dreams that have stayed with me ever after, and changed my ideas: they've gone through and through me, like wine through water, and altered the color of my mind.

～ EMILY BRONTË

Ordinary people believe only in the possible. Extraordinary people visualize not what is possible or probable, but rather what is impossible. And by visualizing the impossible, they begin to see it as possible.

～ CHERIE CARTER-SCOTT

It's our dreams that keep us going, that separate us from the beasts. I wouldn't even want to live if I thought it was all just eating and sleeping and taking off my clothes.

～ MARY CHASE

The idea was fragrant with possibilities.

～ JEAN FERRIS

By learning to contact, listen to, and act on our intuition, we can directly connect to the higher power of the universe and allow it to become our guiding force.

～ SHAKTI GAWAIN

Children see things very well sometimes—and idealists even better.

～ LORRAINE HANSBURY

Freedom is always and exclusively freedom for the one who thinks differently.

～ ROSA LUXEMBURG

The person who can combine frames of reference and draw connections between ostensibly unrelated points of view is likely to be the one who makes the creative breakthrough.

～ DENISE SHEKERJIAN

Art is the signature of civilizations.

～ BEVERLY SILLS

Inspiration is the richest nation I know, the most powerful on earth. Sexual energy Freud calls it; the capital of desire I call it; it pays for both mental and physical expenditure.

～ SYLVIA ASHTON WARNER

There is no balking genius. Only death can silence it or hinder.

～ ELLA WHEELER WILCOX

Act On Your Ideas and See Them Through

It takes people a long time to learn the difference between talent and genius, especially ambitious young men and women.

～ LOUISA MAY ALCOTT

The man who goes fishing gets something more than the fish he catches.

～ MARY ASTOR

Envisioning the end is enough to put the means in motion.

～ DOROTHEA BRANDE

An Arabian proverb says there are four sorts of men:
He who knows not and knows not he knows not: he is a fool—shun him.
He who knows not and knows he knows not: he is simple—teach him.
He who knows and knows not he knows: he is asleep—wake him.
He who knows and knows he knows: he is wise—follow him.

～ LADY ISABEL BURTON

The painter ... does not fit the paints to the world. He most certainly does not fit the world to himself. He fits himself to the paint. The self is the servant who bears the paintbox and its inherited contents.

~ ANNIE DILLARD

The insight to see possible new paths, the courage to try them, the judgment to measure results—these are the qualities of a leader.

~ MARY PARKER FOLLETT

Beware of people carrying ideas. Beware of ideas carrying people.

~ BARBARA GRIZZUTI HARRISON

For a long time it seemed to me that real life was about to begin, but there was always some obstacle in the way. Something had to be got through first, some unfinished business; time still to be served, a debt to be paid. Then life would begin. At last it dawned on me that these obstacles were my life.

~ BETTE HOWLAND

The engineering is secondary to the vision.

~ CYNTHIA OZICK

Beware of the danger signals that flag problems: silence, secretiveness, or sudden outburst.

~ ELEANOR H. PORTER

It May Take Courage to Realize Your Dreams

What you are afraid to do is a clear indicator of the next thing you need to do.

~ ANON.

The insight to see possible new paths, the courage to try them, the judgment to measure results—these are the qualities of a leader.

~ MARY PARKER FOLLETT

Courage is not afraid to weep, and she is not afraid to pray, even when she is not sure who she is praying to.

> ∼ J. RUTH GENDLER

Fear has a large shadow, but he himself is small.

> ∼ J. RUTH GENDLER

It is only by following your deepest instinct that you can lead a rich life, and if you let your fear of consequence prevent you from following your deepest instinct, then your life will be safe, expedient, and thin.

> ∼ KATHERINE HATHAWAY

Commit Fully to Your Vision and Its Success

The woman who sees both sides of an issue is very likely on a fence or up a tree.

> ∼ ANON.

I feel that one must deliberate then act, must scan every life choice with rational thinking but then base the decision on whether one's heart will be in it.

> ∼ JEAN SHINODA BOLEN

We do not believe until we want a thing and feel that we shall die if it is not granted to us, and then we kneel and believe.

> ∼ FRANCES HODGSON BURNETT

There is no such thing as expecting too much.

> ∼ SUSAN CHEEVER

Writing a novel without being asked seems a bit like having a baby when you have nowhere to live.

> ∼ LUCY ELLMAN

They were so strong in their beliefs that there came a time when it hardly mattered what exactly those beliefs were; they all fused into a single stubbornness.

〜 LOUISE ERDRICH

We always attract into our lives whatever we think about most, believe in most strongly, expect on the deepest level, and imagine most vividly.

〜 SHAKTI GAWAIN

It seems safe to say that significant discovery, really creative thinking, does not occur with regard to problems about which the thinker is lukewarm.

〜 MARY HENLE

For a long time it seemed to me that real life was about to begin, but there was always some obstacle in the way. Something had to be got through first, some unfinished business; time still to be served, a debt to be paid. Then life would begin. At last it dawned on me that these obstacles were my life.

〜 BETTE HOWLAND

All bonafide revolutions are of necessity revolutions of the spirit.

〜 SONIA JOHNSON

Unfortunately, sometimes people don't hear you until you scream.

〜 STEPHANIE POWERS

The beautiful feeling after writing a poem is on the whole better even than after sex, and that's saying a lot.

〜 ANNE SEXTON

I always thought that if I was popular I must be doing something wrong.

〜 SUZANNE VEGA

Search for the Truth within Your Vision

Illusion is the dust the devil throws in the eyes of the foolish.
~ MINNA ANTRIM

There's a period of life when we swallow a knowledge of ourselves
and it becomes either good or sour inside.
~ PEARL BAILEY

You never find yourself until you face the truth.
~ PEARL BAILEY

To see a shadow and think it is a tree—that is a pity; but to see a tree
and to think it a shadow can be fatal.
~ PHYLLIS BOTTOME

Prejudices, it is well known, are most difficult to eradicate from the
heart whose soil has never been loosened or fertilized by education;
they grow there, firm as weeds among rocks.
~ CHARLOTTE BRONTË

Truth is simply whatever you can bring yourself to believe.
~ ALICE CHILDRESS

I write entirely to find out what I'm thinking, what I'm looking at,
what Ii see and what it means, what I want, and what I fear.
~ JOAN DIDION

There's folks 'ud stand on their heads and then say the fault was i'
their boots.
~ GEORGE ELIOT

There is only one large circle that we march in, around and around,
each of us with our own little picture—in front of us—our own
little mirage that we think is the future.
~ LORRAINE HANSBURY

Whenever at an accusation blind rage burns up within us, the reason is that some arrow has pierced the joints of our harness. Behind our shining armour of righteous indignation lurks a convicted and only half-repentant sinner ... [and] we may be almost sure some sharp and bitter grain of truth lurks within it, and the wound is best probed.

　∾ JANE HARRISON

Now that I'm here, where am I?

　∾ JANIS JOPLIN

I do not want the peace which passeth understanding, I want the understanding which bringeth peace.

　∾ HELEN KELLER

Think of a fine painter attempting to capture an inner vision, beginning with one corner of the canvas, painting what he thinks should be there, not quite pulling it off, covering it over with white paint, and trying again, each time finding out what his painting isn't, until he finally finds out what it is. And when you finally do find out what one corner of your vision is, you're off and running.

　∾ ANNE LAMOTT

People with bad consciences always fear the judgment of children.

　∾ MARY MCCARTHY

Truth has divine properties, and the ability to see it is a gift that's given, not acquired.

　∾ KATHERINE NEVILLE

The truth does not change according to our ability to stomach it emotionally.

　∾ FLANNERY O'CONNOR

A false vision was better than none.

　∾ MARTHA OSTENSO

Truth is the pearl without price.... Those who have the truth would not be packaging it and selling it, so anyone who is selling it, really does not possess it.

～ PEACE PILGRIM

Sometimes it takes years to really grasp what has happened to your life.

～ WILMA RUDOLPH

I had to grow up and learn to listen for the unspoken as well as the spoken—and to know a truth.

～ EUDORA WELTY

It is in our idleness, in our dreams, that the submerged truth sometimes comes to the top.

～ VIRGINIA WOOLF

$\mathcal{I}$ndex of Names

Bachmann, Ingeborg 27
Bacon, Martha 178
Baez, Joan 67, 83, 144, 366, 392, 397, 429
Bailey, Pearl 13, 15, 17, 60, 103, 111, 128, 141, 149, 236, 282, 408, 442, 482, 517, 519, 524, 525
Baillie, Joanna 17, 42, 84, 149, 180, 184, 222, 366, 410, 431, 470
Baker, Anita 71, 131, 150, 188
Baker, Dorothy 455
Baker, Ella 9, 179, 238
Baker, Josephine 147
Baker, Mary 269, 479
Bakker, Tammy Faye 182
Baldwin, Christina 31, 63, 102, 127, 161, 204, 239, 436, 480
Baldwin, Faith 232, 239, 452, 483
Baldwin, Monica 17, 42, 154
Ball, Lucille 20, 124, 141, 234, 244, 400, 409
Ballantyne, Sheila 249, 256, 477, 511, 513, 518
Bambara, Toni Cade 22, 127, 214, 289, 300, 390
Bamber, Helen 133, 479
Ban Breathnach, Sarah 42, 252
Bancroft, Ann 70
Bankhead, Tallulah 24, 150, 157, 209, 235, 271, 382, 399, 440
Banning, Margaret Culkin 86, 234, 321
Barber, Margaret Fairless 109, 443, 512
Barcus, Nancy 290

Bardot, Brigitte 17, 24, 121, 172, 185
Barnes, Djuna 429, 492
Barnes, Sondra Anice 381
Barney, Natalie Clifford 257, 260, 486, 496
Barnhouse, Dr. Ruth Tiffany 121
Barr, Amelia 15, 169, 220, 230, 231, 244, 311, 385, 392, 404, 446, 484, 505, 514
Barrett Browning, Elizabeth 17, 121, 136, 225, 494
Barrett, Colleen C. 251, 414
Barrett, Ethel 26, 154
Barrett, Rona 124, 339
Barrows, Sydney Biddle 39, 233
Barry, Lynda 446
Barrymore, Ethel 36, 86, 106, 154, 357, 427
Barthel, Mildred 15, 212
Barton, Clara 128, 153, 205, 231, 256, 303, 304
Bashkirtseff, Marie 26, 162, 297, 306, 356, 439
Basinger, Kim 307
Basset, Lucinda 11, 222
Bateson, Mary 312, 317, 343, 365, 460
Battani, Judge Marianne O. 321
Battelle, Phyllis 6, 493, 498
Baugh, Laura 200
Baum, Vicki 24, 35, 195, 315, 447
Baxter, Anne 238
Beal, Louise 323
Beard, Mary Ritter 312, 317
Beard, Miriam 238, 505

L

U

V

W

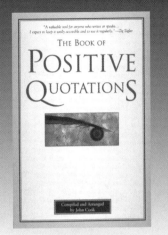